CONFLICTS AND WARS

Previous Publications

Economic Sanctions: Examining Their Philosophy and Efficacy, with J. Forrer, H. Teegen, and J. Yang. New York: 2003.

Case Studies of Economic Sanctions: The Chinese, Cuban, and Iranian Experiences, with J. Forrer, H. Teegen, and J. Yang. New York: 2003.

The Middle East Oil Exporters: What Happened to Economic Development? Foreword by Robert M. Solow. Cheltenham, UK: 2006, and Northampton, US: 2007.

Globalization and Islamic Finance: Convergence, Prospects, and Challenges, with Z. Iqbal and A. Mirakhor. Singapore: 2009.

The Stability of Islamic Finance: Creating a Resilient Financial Environment for a Secure Future, Foreword by Sir Andrew Crockett, with Z. Iqbal, N. Krichene, and A. Mirakhor. Singapore: 2010.

Islam and the Path to Human and Economic Development, Foreword by Ali Allawi, with Abbas Mirakhor. New York: 2010.

Risk Sharing in Finance: The Islamic Finance Alternative, with Zamir Iqbal, Noureddine Krichene, and Abbas Mirakhor. Singapore: 2011.

Conflicts and Wars

Their Fallout and Prevention

Hossein Askari

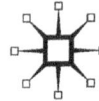

First published in 2012 by
PALGRAVE MACMILLAN®
in the United States—a division of St. Martin's Press LLC,
175 Fifth Avenue, New York, NY 10010.

Where this book is distributed in the UK, Europe and the rest of the world,
this is by Palgrave Macmillan, a division of Macmillan Publishers Limited,
registered in England, company number 785998, of Houndmills,
Basingstoke, Hampshire RG21 6XS.

Palgrave Macmillan is the global academic imprint of the above companies
and has companies and representatives throughout the world.

Palgrave® and Macmillan® are registered trademarks in the United States,
the United Kingdom, Europe and other countries.

ISBN: 978–1–137–02094–9

Library of Congress Cataloging-in-Publication Data

Askari, Hossein.
    Conflicts and wars : their fallout and prevention / Hossein Askari.
        p. cm.
    Includes bibliographical references.
    ISBN 978–1–137–02094–9 (alk. paper)
        1. War—Economic aspects. 2. War, Cost of. 3. War—Environmental
    aspects. 4. War—Prevention. 5. War—Termination. 6. Iran-Iraq War,
    1980–1988. 7. Persian Gulf War, 1991. 8. Iraq War, 2003– I. Title.

JZ6401.A75 2012
303.6′6—dc23   2011052914

A catalogue record of the book is available from the British Library.

Design by Newgen Imaging Systems (P) Ltd., Chennai, India.

First edition: July 2012

To the men, women, and children whose lives have been ended or compromised by conflict and war

Contents

Tables

Figures

Foreword

In *Conflicts and Wars: Their Fallout and Prevention*, Hossein Askari provides fresh insight and a novel approach to reducing intrastate and interstate conflicts and wars. War and its consequences have been mankind's greatest failure since the dawn of time. His analysis and proposal will be invaluable to the peacemakers who have all too often been overwhelmed by the forces on the other side.

Professor Askari begins by surveying the burden of military expenditures and of conflicts and wars. Their dollar expenditures, which are close to 15 percent of global GNP, exceed the cost of our financial crisis, of global warming, and what would be required for worldwide poverty reduction. He examines the nature of modern conflicts and wars, which are increasingly intrastate and regional and overwhelmingly the offspring of earlier disputes. He looks into the recent conflicts in the Persian Gulf—the Iran-Iraq War and the two Gulf Wars—to extract how modern-day conflicts are bred in a region that has been a major importer of arms. He assesses the methodologies for measuring the fallout of conflicts and calculates their cost in the Persian Gulf. This sets the stage for Professor Askari to provide his road map for the prevention of conflicts. He bases his approach on three interrelated propositions: aggressors do not pay the full price of their aggression; governments will do nothing to change this state of affairs on their own; and, as a result, the process of reducing conflicts must originate in the private sector.

Ronald Reagan suggested: "History teaches that war begins when governments believe the price of aggression is cheap." In other words, there is market failure in conflicts and wars—aggressors do not pay for the fallout of their aggression and may at times even profit from it. To prevent conflicts and wars the market must force all aggressors to pay a price that approaches, or exceeds, the full cost of their misdeeds. But governments will not reconstitute a market where aggressors are forced to pay for their aggressions. The most powerful governments, whose cooperation is essential, are under the illusion that they benefit from selling arms and from using their power to shape the world. They espouse peace but in reality use aggression to gain advantage over their adversaries. In the words of Thomas Jefferson, "Governments constantly choose between telling lies and fighting wars, with the end result always being the same. One will always lead to the other." Professor Askari argues that the structure of the United Nations—and, specifically, the composition of the Security Council—prevents it from achieving peace. Thus, prevention of conflicts must originate in the private sector with a coordinated approach of NGOs. Although NGOs have their own limitations, once they achieve some measure of success in raising the cost of aggression, weaker governments will join their effort and, in time, the powerful will be forced to embrace the idea of a world without conflicts as the best road forward for humankind.

Professor Askari proposes a framework to make the price of aggression its full cost—so that pain is borne by all the aggressors: be they leaders, their supporters, countries, or companies. He acknowledges that for his proposal to succeed, a number of initiatives must be adopted simultaneously—including forced mediation, mandatory reparations, restricted arms exports, uniform prosecution of all aggressors at the International Criminal Court, and extensive global exposure of all aggression. Hossein Askari is passionate about putting an end to conflicts, but he is also keenly aware of the landmines along the way. His proposal will require the support and resources of a significant foundation. Even then, it will take time and initial success to persuade weaker countries to embrace this framework as the best approach to bringing peace to their region of the world.

This provocative book is concise, focused, and well-timed. The world is in need of resources and cannot afford the cost of continued military expenditures, much less the cost of prolonged regional conflicts. The message of *Conflicts and Wars: Their Fallout and Prevention* is clear: conflicts and wars are more costly than we imagine. We must find a path to reduce and prevent them. The ways of the past have not succeeded. In 2012, the inability of the United Nations Security Council to put an end to intrastate bloodshed is all too evident, as is the record level of arms exports to favored dictators around the world. We need a new approach to prevent conflicts. Professor Askari provides us with a new and imaginative road map.

This book is essential reading for everyone who labors in the pursuit of peace. That especially includes policy makers and politicians who espouse peace while supplying and supporting aggressors around the globe.

GEORGE A. AKERLOF
Nobel Laureate in Economics, 2001
Koshland Professor of Economics, University of
California at Berkeley

Preface

Our world faces a number of simultaneous and interrelated challenges that defy easy solution—global warming, poverty, hunger, aging populations, escalating medical expenses and shrinking retirement benefits, severe national budgetary and debt constraints, accompanied by costly military expenditures, conflicts, and wars. The high level of debt has become a major constraint to almost any major economic initiative in a number of advanced countries, and it could be reasonably argued that some societies are even faced with challenges that are existential.

In addition to the all-important moral reasons, the global economy can no longer support high levels of military expenditures and especially the fallout from conflicts and wars. Although the United Nations was established as the institution to achieve global peace, it has failed because of its flawed structure and manipulation by its most powerful members in pursuit of their selfish interests. Conflicts and wars rage around the world because the price paid by leaders and governments for their acts of aggression is low, and sometimes even negative, a point made by President Reagan when he said: "History teaches that war begins when governments believe the price of aggression is cheap." We cannot rely on governments to raise the price of aggression to end wars. In the words of President Jefferson: "Governments constantly choose between telling lies and fighting wars, with the end result always being the same. One will always lead to the other." It is time for an initiative to achieve what governments and the United Nations have not. The global citizenry must be mobilized into action, action that is today made easier in the age of the Internet, social media, smart phones, and tablets.

This is a book that explains the intolerable burden of conflicts, the principal reason that spawns them—the low price of aggression—and why governments will not end them. The many dimensions of conflicts and wars are examined. Recent conflicts in the Persian Gulf are discussed to illustrate the reasons for acts of aggression. We propose a framework, to be initiated in the private sector, to raise the price of aggression to its full cost in order to reduce and, in time, end conflicts and wars.

Acknowledgments

I am indebted to three of my former students at the George Washington University—Anwar Aridi, Mojdeh Khorasani, and Amirhossein Najafi—for their dedicated assistance with this book. They deserve much credit for early drafts of three chapters and to Mojdeh for the indexing. The advice of an anonymous referee is greatly appreciated. I am truly grateful to Professor George Akerlof for contributing the Foreword to this book. He is among the most admired and respected economists of his generation and for me it is an honor to have this association. I also thank Robert Bendetson, Robert Looney, and Mac Maharaj for endorsing this book. The comments of my dear friend Keith Elliott have been helpful and encouraging. I am grateful to my editor Farideh Koohi-Kamali at Palgrave Macmillan and her team that worked on this book, Sarah Nathan, Katie Haigler, and Deepa John. Most importantly, my wife Anna has supported and encouraged me throughout this endeavor.

Chapter 1

Introduction and Overview

The title of this book may be sufficient to classify me as a lunatic, naïve college professor with little better to do than to put idle dreams on paper. While my lunacy and naivety may be open to debate, the insinuation that dreams have no practical use is false. Dreams provide the energy to break free from the chains of the past and to bring change. Dreams have even provided the fuel for global initiatives. Who would have thought that Global Zero—the movement to end nuclear warheads—would have achieved so much success in a short span of five years or so? Its success may have been in part sparked by the now famous article in the *WSJ* in January of 2007 by the "four horsemen of the apocalypse," Henry Kissinger, Sam Nunn, Bill Perry, and George Shultz. These men had been firm backers of nuclear deterrence, but they then changed tack to argue that nuclear weapons could no longer be considered a deterrence but had instead become the greatest risk of a global war. The dream of Bruce Blair and Matt Brown to launch Global Zero coupled with the warning of the four senior statesmen has helped reduce the number of nuclear warheads held by Russia and the United States to a level unimaginable only five years ago in 2006. Yes, dreams, hard work, and a little bit of luck can go a long way in bringing changes that might once have been considered unimaginable.

If the world can reduce nuclear warheads, why not conflicts and wars? The decision to engage in conflict or to go to war is typically, but not always, taken by a group of people, whether a monarch, a prime minister, a president, or a dictator and his or her advisors, and sometimes in democracies with the approval of a national legislature. "Educated leaders," who should be more thoughtful and concerned for society, invariably initiate most wars. Wars are invariably premeditated and so afford time for resolution, occur frequently in full view of mankind, and could be known to millions if reported by the media. In the age of instant communication and social media, it should be easier to instigate and take action to thwart conflicts and wars. Thus, it would appear that conflicts and wars could be more readily prevented than common crimes, which are typically the work of one person and are often hidden from sight.

While conflicts and wars are far fewer in number than common criminal acts, failure to resolve them exacts a much heavier psychological, social, and economic toll on mankind, and has implications for generations well into the distant future. Conflicts and wars are becoming more and more lethal and costly. Some are continued in overt, and covert, belligerence for years after the "formal" conflict has ended, and many erupt yet again in the form of renewed conflicts far into the future. The world can ill afford to go on paying for acts of aggression, the surest testimonies to human folly. We must use our limited resources more rationally than to fight each other, which does little to advance the welfare of humankind.

Today, our planet is faced with a number of simultaneous and inter-related challenges—global warming, poverty, hunger, aging populations, higher and higher medical expenditures and retirement benefits, severe national budgetary and debt constraints, costly conflicts and wars, and heavy military expenditures—that defy easy solutions. It could be reasonably argued that some societies are even faced with existential challenges.

Most scientists the world over acknowledge that we cannot continue to abuse our planet and its resources in ways that will ultimately destroy us all. Some justify this practice in the name of economic necessity, arguing that it is economically too costly and impractical to reduce environmental degradation decisively and quickly. The planet may be on a path to destruction unless we begin to respect the environment and radically change our economic priorities, policies, and practices to incorporate the basic needs and interests of future generations. Sir Nicholas Stern, in his widely reported study for former United Kingdom prime minister Tony Blair, claimed that climate change represented the biggest market failure in history (because those who cause environmental degradation do not pay the full price for the damage that they cause), requiring an investment of about 1 percent of the global economic output (global GDP) for a number of years as well as other associated measures to reduce the global carbon footprint in order to avoid disaster down the line. The world could be losing 5 percent (and potentially as much as 20 percent) of global economic output or gross domestic product (GDP) each and every year forever, endangering hundreds of millions of lives. More recently, Sir Nicholas has upped his required investment estimate to 1 to 2 percent of global output (Rotman). While his report has been criticized on many of its details, the general and broad message appears to be still widely accepted, namely, we must start to address environmental issues sooner as opposed to later, if we are to mitigate disaster for future generations.

Around the world, the disadvantaged suffer with little hope. The real income of a majority of the population in the United States, as well as in other so-called rich countries, has been stagnant for about 30 years. In the United States, arguably still the richest country in the world, 44 million live below the official poverty line ($21,954 for a family of four) in 2011, with about the same number relying on food stamps to put food on the table; but with the cost of the food stamp program doubling from 2008 to 2011 (to about $65 billion) because of the financial meltdown, there are plans in 2011 in the US Congress to cut back on this essential assistance. Malnutrition around the world is on the rise with food prices soaring to record levels. Over a billion humans go to bed hungry every night, and the number of those classified as living below the poverty line of $1 per day is on the rise. The availability of basic health care is deficient the world over and not just in poor countries.

All the while, rich countries profess that they can do very little to relieve financial pressures at home, much less contribute to lowering need at the international level. They correctly claim to have looming economic difficulties of their own. Their populations are aging rapidly, with the certainty that there will be fewer and fewer people working to support those in retirement and that the bill for health care and long-term care will continue to rise. The growing bill for social expenditures, especially for retirement—namely, pension and medical services—is putting severe, and ever growing, pressures on budgets at a time when rich countries face unprecedented budgetary constraints with historically high levels of national debt and budget deficits, all accompanied by high rates of unemployment and sluggish economic growth with little expectation of a dramatic turnaround any time soon. All of these developments have severely reduced everyone's policy flexibility to handle crises.

While a well-positioned few around the world may be getting richer, future generations will be poorer if we continue down the current path. Besides degrading the environment and depleting resources at record rates, such as oil and various metals, governments around the world, especially those of the rich countries, have been accumulating mountainous levels of debt. They have borrowed to pay today's bills, including those for wars, while postponing the burden of repayment further and further down the road. The unprecedented levels of debt have bound a number of so-called rich countries, including the United States, the United Kingdom, France, and Japan, in a straightjacket with little room for maneuver. Others, such as Greece, Ireland, and Portugal, are dangerously close to financial default, while still others, such as Spain and Italy, are in a state of financial limbo.

From recent academic research (Reinhart and Rogoff), it would appear that when the ratio of national debt to GDP reaches roughly 90 percent, things go from bad to worse. In the summer of 2011, Greece had a national debt to economic output ratio of 160 percent. The ratio exceeded 90 percent for a number of other "rich" countries, and for the United States the net public debt (excluding the debt held by the Social Security Trust) was around 65 percent in 2011 and the gross ratio (which includes the debt held by Social Security) was close to 100 percent, with both climbing to levels not seen in over 60 years. In the summer of 2011, after much political wrangling in Washington, Standard and Poor's (S&P) downgraded US debt by one notch for the first time in history. While we could reasonably dismiss this financial downgrade as an indictment of the political wrangling in Washington, things could turn out to be even worse than what these figures suggest today. Interest rate levels have a significant impact on the size of the budget deficit and the national debt. In the aftermath (and somewhat even before) of the financial crisis of 2008, interest rates have been at historically low levels in a number of advanced countries. When interest rates go up to their "normal" trend line, as they will, the deficit and debt issues in the United States and in most other advanced countries will become even more pressing. If interest rates in the United States were to go up to their normal levels, the extra interest rate expense would be around $4.9 trillion over the coming decade (Lindsey). This is a large number relative to the size of the US national debt and the spending cuts proposed by the White House or even by the Republican leadership.

These are not simply problems facing the present generation in the United States; they have legs that go far into the future and are global.

On the face of it, all of these issues could be solved if there were unlimited economic resources, a miraculous pool of funds that would allow us to invest in the restoration of our environment, provide retirement benefits and medical care for the growing number of retired citizens, pay for the medical expenses of those who do not have coverage, feed the poor and hungry around the world, afford more income to those whose incomes have stagnated for years, and yes, even take a big bite out of the national debt to reduce it to a level that restores budgetary flexibility and does not compromise the interest of future generations. This miraculous pool of funds actually exists before our very eyes, but we either refuse to recognize it or we believe that it cannot be touched.

The pool of funds before our very eyes are the resources that would become globally available, and the vast increase in global economic output that would follow, if we could only put an end to conflicts and wars and significantly reduce military expenditures.

Such an achievement would not only release resources to address most economic woes of every country but would also reduce human misery in other ways as nothing else could. Vast numbers of people would not be killed or seriously injured each and every year; millions would not be left without hands, legs, and other body parts; untold numbers of children would not be rendered orphans; and our medical services, already stretched thin by the needs of an ageing global population, would not also be required to provide treatment to veterans and civilians injured in conflicts for decades after the official end of the conflict. In addition, ending conflicts and wars would directly benefit the environment. Generals, admirals, soldiers, and sailors can hardly be concerned with environmental degradation while risking their lives fighting and bombing their adversaries into submission; the use of aircraft, planes, ships, and other military vehicles wastes fuel and pollutes the planet, not to mention the damage caused by raging hostilities.

Although Sir Nicholas Stern was right to focus global attention on protecting the environment, he was, without a doubt, *wrong* when he called climate change the biggest market failure of all time. The biggest market failure of all time is the market failure in acts of aggression. Aggressors do not face the true (full) price, or cost, of their aggression. While President Reagan said that the price for aggression was cheap, we would add that the price may at times be so low as to be negative—not only do aggressors not pay, they may at times even benefit from their aggression—initiating armed conflict, sowing the seeds of conflict, selling arms that are used in conflicts, robbing the general citizenry, and the like.

Just consider the resources that would become available if we could end conflicts and wars. World leaders talk of budgetary constraints while annual global military expenditures in 2007, as estimated by the Stockholm International Peace Research Institute (SIPRI), exceeded $1.2 trillion, which is equivalent to over 2.5 percent of global economic output. More recently, we estimate annual global military expenditures in 2009 as exceeding $1.3 trillion, or nearly 2.7 percent of global economic output. But this is only the tip of the iceberg, because much more can be achieved by eliminating conflicts and wars.

Estimates of the negative effect of conflicts and wars on national economies range from 1 to 10 percent depending on the country. In a comprehensive study, Crain and Crain investigated the economic effects of terror events in 147 countries—more than 11,000 terror events—from 1968 to 2002. Their analysis suggests that in 2002 world economic output would have been $3.6 trillion higher in the absence of terror—or almost 11 percent of global output in that year. As for the economic consequences of civil wars and intrastate violence, a study by the United Nations Development

Program (UNDP) suggests that the cost of civil wars prior to 1990 was between 2.2 and 3.3 percent of GDP per country per conflict, and it was 10 percent after 1990. A Small Arm Survey Review, a specific study on the cost of lost productivity due to criminal violence, estimates the annual cost of lost productivity at 0.14 percent of global economic output. It also suggests that armed conflicts decrease the growth rate of national economies by at least 2 percent per year.

Additionally, a few studies have been focused solely on nonwar, nonterror costs of violence. For example, in its 2002 report, the World Health Organization (WHO) summarizes the expenditures on health services as ranging from 0.3 to 5 percent of GDP in six Latin American countries. Another report by the WHO in 2004 on the economic dimensions of interpersonal violence claims that the health care costs of such violence for the United States is as high as 3.3 percent of GDP. In another study, Cook and Ludwig estimate the cost of gun-related crime in the United States at about 1 percent of US GDP. Heinemann and Verner estimate the cost of crime and violence in Latin America and the Caribbean at 14.2 percent of GDP.

The estimated costs of conflicts and wars and military expenditures would conservatively appear to far exceed 10 percent of global economic output and dwarf, yes dwarf, the estimated loss of less than 1.3 percent in global economic output in 2009 from the financial crisis of 2008 (IMF, 2010), the most severe economic crisis for the world since the Great Depression of the 1930s. The estimates for the toll of wars, although already high, invariably exclude the medical treatment of those injured in wars, an extremely costly element that lingers for many years after a conflict has ended.

We should, however, acknowledge that the impact on national economic output, or GDP, of a dollar of military expenditures and a dollar in war-related damage are not the same. If we were to reduce global military expenditures to zero and replace them with nonmilitary spending, global economic output would not be higher, but those resources could be used for addressing global warming, medical care, poverty, and the like to increase human welfare. In the case of damage from war or the cost of war, these actually reduce the capacity in non-conflict-related sectors to produce goods and services. Still, the sum of these numbers—military expenditures and the damage from conflicts and wars—gives us a rough idea of how much these amounts could contribute to addressing other pressing global issues. From these low ballpark figures it would appear that the benefits of ending conflicts could go a long way to solving most, if not all, of our pressing global problems.

There are, however, better estimates of the impact of aggression on the global economy. While military expenditures and the cost of conflicts and wars provide a window on the burden of conflict and war on global economic output, this accounting does not provide a comprehensive picture of what could be added to global economic output if violence were replaced by peace. If military expenditures were reduced, the result would not be an increase in global economic output but we could produce goods and services that would be useful for society instead of military goods. But we also need an estimate of how much could be added to global output if the destruction of conflicts and wars were to end. Jürgen Brauer and John Tepper Marlin (2009a) calculated the impact on global economic output of replacing all violence (internal and external conflict) by peace. While classifying their results as an order of the magnitude number and not definitive, they do stress that their estimate is still a conservative, or a lower bound, estimate; and their estimate is roughly in line with other estimates that we have cited above for conflicts, wars, and military expenditures. They estimate that the total effect of peace on global economic output in 2007 would have been $7.2 trillion or 13.4 percent of global economic output in that year, with $2.4 trillion (or 4.4 percent of global GDP) representing the reallocation of resources from violence to peace activities (what the authors refer to as static effect) and $4.8 trillion (or 9 percent of global GDP) in net gain in global economic output (referred to as dynamic effect) due to previously unharnessed "economic resources being released." It is worth repeating the fact that this gain dwarfs the estimated loss in global economic output of less than 1.3 percent in 2009 from the financial crisis of 2008 (IMF, 2010) and that this economic gain from ending conflicts would be available for each and every year into the future.

This truth, namely, that ending conflicts and wars could solve many of the financial constraints faced by the world, is inescapable. Thus, in addition to the moral arguments for ending conflicts and wars, we must recognize the compelling economic reasons. This is why we have to reduce, and in time end, all conflicts and wars.

A global peace dividend, if peace were tenable, could solve most of our global economic problems, representing a total of 13.4 percent of global economic output in 2007 (again, with one-third of this in substitution of nonmilitary output and two-thirds in additions to global economic output). Even half of this peace dividend would go a long way to relieving financial pressures around the world. Brauer and Marlin summarize their broad findings by stating:

> We estimate that violence, or the credible threat thereof, led the world to forgo about 9% of GWP [Gross World Product] that year. A major finding...is that the economic effects of the ongoing world violence crisis are much more severe than the effects of periodic world economic

crises…Worldwide recessions occurred in the mid-1970s, early 1980s, early 1990s, and late 2000s. Even if our 9% cost of violence estimate for 2007 overestimates the unknown annual cost of worldwide violence by two or three times, this cost still would easily outrank the economic crises, in part because economic crises occur only sporadically whereas the violence crisis is continuous. (2009b, 126)

We don't even have to eliminate conflict and war. Imagine the rewards if we could just achieve a significant reduction in conflicts and wars, with the hope of eliminating them in the more distant future.

The estimated benefits of peace are global and cannot be expected to accrue proportionately (relative to their national economic outputs), much less equally in absolute size of benefit, for countries and groups. Countries that today are at peace and have low military expenditures, such as Japan, would reap relatively less from peace than countries that are in a state of turmoil, such as Zimbabwe, with a 3 percent dynamic peace dividend for Japan and a peace dividend of more than 100 percent for Zimbabwe! Depending on the structure of different economies, the gains differ also by sector (for example, agriculture and industry) across countries also.

The world could spend 1 percent of global economic output (about $500 billion) to restore the environment as originally estimated by Sir Nicholas Stern and still have more than 12 times that, or trillions of dollars, to tackle other pressing needs. This would allow the world to feed the over 1 billion people who go hungry, lift out of poverty ($1.25/day) the roughly 1.5 billion people living with such limitations, and still have funds left over to address global health issues and to reduce the level of national debt to zero for most countries around the world in less than a decade.[1] How can we resist such possibilities?

While peace could solve many, if not most, of the economic and financial problems the world faces today, leaders pay only lip service to peace as they promote their perceived short-term interests and, knowingly or unknowingly, sow the seeds of conflict and lay the foundations for even bigger conflicts (and the resulting financial crises) in the future. One day, countries sell or even "donate" arms to clients, and then the next day they try to mediate for peace or go to war against the very same client. The major countries, those with veto power at the UN Security Council (UNSC), espouse peace and yet they veto the very measures needed to bring about peace. The world is crying for an end to conflicts and wars, if for no other reason than that we can no longer simultaneously pay for wars and for a country's or a region's reconstruction, as in Iraq or Afghanistan, and at the same time hope to pay for the needed education, health care, and nutrition of a growing population while reducing national debt to sufficiently low levels to achieve budgetary flexibility and preserve the interests and the rights of future generations. Something has to give. We have no other choice but to dream and act to end conflicts and wars in a generation or two!

Why have we achieved so little in abating conflicts and wars since the dawn of time and over recent centuries? For a start, some would argue that mankind is instinctively aggressive. Conflicts are not limited to different religious groups, races, and nations; conflicts are inherent even in families and among friends. To end conflicts would be tantamount to remaking mankind. On a more practical, and less philosophical, level, conflicts and wars continue because there is little effective deterrent. As we stated above, the biggest market failure of all time is conflict and war.

Again, the late US president Ronald Reagan said the same thing perhaps best in his usual hard-to-duplicate manner: "History teaches that war begins when governments believe the price of aggression is cheap." Let's briefly explore this profound statement, the foundation of our proposal in this book to reduce conflicts and wars. What is the price paid by leaders (and countries) who are aggressors and fuel conflict? And let's not forget that in most countries it is the leader, be he a dictator, prime minister, president, or general, who invariably initiates aggression. Do leaders or those in power pay for this aggression, or do the broad citizenry and their descendants pay? Do they face an appropriate price (a price that represents the full cost of their aggression) for their aggression or is there indeed market failure, with the price of aggression being too cheap or even negative at least for the leaders?

Does a leader face severe punishment if he abuses his own people and discriminates against a group in his country, be it a minority, a majority, or a particular religious group, thus sowing the seeds for conflict? What if he uses torture and imprisonment as tools of governance? What if he fails to deliver social and economic progress and destroys the lives of millions of innocent human beings? Shouldn't there be responsibility in such massive crimes that affect millions, as there is when an individual commits a criminal act affecting one person? What if a leader, his family, and cronies rob the citizenry of their wealth? Does such a leader forfeit his ill-gotten gains (as would a robber)? Does such a leader stand trial for his crimes? Does he receive his just punishment or do his backers (global powers) protect him and even reward him as long as he does their bidding? The answer to all of these questions is, it depends.

If a country is a global power, then nothing, or almost nothing, happens. The country's leadership never pays a price that represents the full fallout of the aggression. In cases where a global power considers a country to be strategically important and where the leader of the country does the global power's bidding, then the leader of that country may be untouchable and get all the support that he needs to stay in power. Just consider the Arab Spring of 2011: Mubarak in Egypt and Gadhafi in Libya received little outside support, but the Al-Sauds in Saudi Arabia and the Al-Khalifas in Bahrain were not even seriously criticized by the United States and the rest of the West. Bashar Al-Assad in Syria initially received little criticism, with one global leader even calling him a "reformer!" Only when his mass slaughter of his own citizenry ran into the thousands did heads of Western countries and some Arab leaders begin to come out on the side of human rights and peace. Once a dictator secures strong external backing, his options are clear: he can rob his country, deposit the wealth in a number of banks in friendly countries, brutally crush all dissent, and, yes, have an escape route ready. He pays almost nothing; more correctly, he pays a negative price for his criminal acts, which, in turn, plant the seeds of conflict, reducing global economic output and increasing human misery for current and future generations.

What price do a country and its leader pay when negotiations are shunned, global warnings are ignored, and hostilities are initiated against another country? What happens if people are killed, injured, tortured, and imprisoned, and if towns, cities, factories, infrastructure, and homes are destroyed? What if hostilities rage for years and generations are scarred, with malnutrition and inadequate health care, and with much of the citizenry robbed of a decent education? Are there accurate and representative calculations of the costs of repression? Are commensurate reparations actually paid by aggressors? Are the leaders of aggressive countries brought to justice for the economic and financial cost of their crimes? Again, it depends. Iraq invaded Iran and an eight-year brutal war ensued. Iraq was declared the aggressor by the United Nations in 1988 (UNSC Resolution 598), roughly eight years after the conflict started and during the last days of the then secretary-general's term in office.[2] But no reparations were even assessed, much less paid, by Iraq. To its credit, the regime in Tehran publicly forgave Iraq after the fall of Saddam Hussein, blaming him and absolving Iraqis of responsibility for reparations. Such an act of unilateral and unforced forgiveness is rare and may of course be reversed in the future if relations deteriorate.

There was no attempt by the international community to indict Saddam Hussein and to punish him after he invaded Iran. Just imagine how much conflict might have been avoided if Saddam Hussein had been brought to justice and punished years ago! Yes, Iraqis and Iranians (and Kurds) paid a heavy price, but Saddam Hussein was not held responsible for initiating the conflict and Ayatollah Khomeini was not accountable for not accepting earlier offers of ceasefire. The basic reason for this duplicitous treatment was that Iraq was supported by most of the outside world, and none of the global powers wanted to indict Saddam Hussein who was doing their bidding against the mullahs in Tehran. But when Saddam Hussein invaded Kuwait in 1991, Iraq was declared a pariah; reparations were assessed and are being paid. Still, Saddam Hussein was not indicted, much less arrested or put on trial for his invasion of Kuwait. The price for aggression is thus not consistent, transparent, or proportional to the total cost, or fallout, of the aggression. Everything depends on who the aggressor is.

What kind of message was thus sent to dozens of other tyrants around the world? You can do anything you want as long as you have a strong backer. If Saddam Hussein had paid an appropriate price for his transgressions early on, then he would not have committed even more crimes and, most importantly, other dictators might have taken note and changed their ways. Again, looking at the Arab Spring in 2011, the International Criminal Court quickly indicted Gadhafi for his crimes but was silent when it came to Mubarak, Al-Khalifa, and Al-Assad. It would appear that there is no clear-cut system of justice, and clever tyrants with strong external support are untouchable, escape any and all punishment, and even benefit from their aggression! Aggression will not be reduced, much less ended, in a world where its price is not the same for everyone.

Some people talk of "just" or "moral" wars, forgetting the fact that even so-called just or moral wars invariably kill, maim, and bring about human misery, as do all wars. The pursuit of justice invariably brings more deaths, more misery, more hatred, more claims for revenge, and more future conflict. There is, in essence, a simple choice—pursue justice or forgive. The pursuit of justice or the prevention of further injustice by means of war, although an option, is not our preferred option. Our preferred option (presented in chapter 6) is a transparent and uniformly applied system to raise the price of aggression to its market level, to the full cost of its fallout, and thus, in time, to end all conflicts and wars. Once such a system is firmly in place, we believe that all potential aggressors (leaders and countries) will be much less likely to adopt aggressive acts; but if they do, the pain they face (in the form of external and internal pressures) will more readily end their aggression than would armed intervention to force a change.[3] The pursuit of justice is a never-ending labyrinth of heartaches and pain, while forgiveness and reconciliation result in a break from the past and afford at least the chance of happiness within a generation and a lifetime. Forgiveness and reconciliation are the supreme recognition that all of humankind is interconnected. We are one on this earth, we share the earth, and our actions, good and bad, affect those around us and all those around the world, with implications for all future generations.

After their crimes and acts of aggression, some leaders (their families and their cronies) are allowed to keep the wealth that they have illegally accumulated, while the accounts of others are frozen. Some leaders are given a free passage to live in luxury in another country, while others are indicted, arrested, tried, and sentenced. Again, there is little consistency. Generally, leaders of most countries perceive that there is a low price to pay for their abusive policies. They are arguably even encouraged to abuse their people and to steal their nation's wealth and share it with prominent individuals and lobbyists who carry influence in the powerful countries around the world. And as they do so, leaders continue to be accorded global respect as long as they wield power and are useful to their powerful foreign backers. They are basically free to do as they wish as long as they support the interests of an important global power(s), especially one(s) with veto power in the UNSC.

There seem to be numerous markets for aggression, depending on who the aggressor is but not on the nature of the crime. The market for aggression is clearly segmented, with a low or negative price in one market and a significant but opaque price in another market. Potential aggressors are given very mixed signals as to the price of their aggression.

While the fate of tyrants in developing countries may depend on their superpower backing, what is the fate of the superpowers backing them? What if the leader of a global power supports a tyrant in another country in the name of political expediency? Is there a price to be paid by the global power? Is there any deterrent in place? Isn't the supporter of a tyrant as guilty as is the tyrant? Is there any global justice? Well, depending on who the leader is and which country we are talking about, nothing at all may happen. Has any leader or country been penalized for supporting Saddam Hussein? No. Has any US, Russian, Chinese, British, or French leader been indicted by the International Criminal Court and brought to justice? No, and it should be noted that only Britain and France are even members of the ICC.

It would appear that President Reagan was correct: the price of aggression is low. The price of tyranny may be very low too, both for the tyrant and for the global power that supports the tyrant. That price may even be close to zero or negative for a leader who has external support, is not answerable to an electorate, and is supported by a global power with a veto in the UNSC. At least in a democracy, a leader and his or her party may be voted out of office, putting an end to his aggression (although not its fallout), but not so in a dictatorship. Yes, his country may suffer some degree of pain, depending on the specifics of the case. The citizenry could suffer a great deal or not at all. The country may pay some or no reparations. Depending on the form of national governance, the citizenry's only two options may be to suffer or to rise up and overthrow their ruler. As for the ruler, he may not suffer at all and may even benefit.

Are leaders given the incentive to think through the details of what their actions may lead to? Do they understand, much less worry about, the consequences of their aggression for their country, for themselves, and for their adversaries? Do leaders and citizens consider how their aggressive actions today may sow the seeds of bigger hostilities in the future? It would appear that autocratic leaders give very little attention to the suffering and deprivation of their people when it comes to aggression because the world does not hold them accountable. In dictatorial regimes, it is invariably one man's decision that determines whether there is peace or war; and tyrants are unlikely to weigh the costs and benefits of war and peace. The instrument of governance for a dictator is fear, the price paid by the citizenry is of little import, and the dictator sees himself as above the law, with no price to pay in a conflict or war. To deter conflicts and wars, tyrants should be constantly reminded of the consequences of their actions and of the high price to be paid. These tyrants should be named and shamed. But there is no mechanism for the determination of consequences and prices for acts of aggression.

While the low price that leaders pay for their aggression may be the principal cause for internal and external conflicts and wars, what are the underlying reasons and related factors that make the price of conflict low and thus fuel conflicts around the world? The structure of the United Nations and the pursuit of selfish interests by world powers, the inconsistent and ineffective system of international justice as applied to rulers and leaders, the arms industry, special interest groups, lobbyists, and the global media all play a part, although admittedly with very differing degrees of impact, in keeping the market for aggression segmented, and thus promote conflict and war.

The United Nations was envisaged as the preeminent international organization designed to combat aggression and crimes against humanity and to bring about global peace. Yet, powerful countries use conflicts to achieve their own political and economic ends, namely, to sell arms, to dominate world politics, to undermine their adversaries, and to gain strategic advantage whenever they can. The UNSC is organized in a way that makes it largely ineffective when it comes to halting acts of aggression quickly, or to preempt them in the first place by imposing a heavy price. The five major powers after World War II—the United States, Russia, China, the United Kingdom, and France—were accorded a veto over the council's decisions. As a result, any of these five countries can support a tyrant, sell him arms, and be totally complicit in his crimes, and can at the same time veto any UN action that would even criticize their puppet dictator, much less help remove him from office. Such a structure has been justified because some of the major powers would not support the creation of a United Nations with a Security Council unless they enjoyed a veto. And now other important emerging countries—such as Brazil and India—understandably want their own permanent council status. These new powers are lobbying to replace France and the United Kingdom, but realistically France and the United Kingdom will not be replaced and instead the number of permanent UNSC members is likely to be expanded, with more veto power being held in the future.

The powerful countries use their veto at the UNSC without shame to further their perceived national, not human, interests, be it to start a conflict, to fuel it, or to stall its ending. Rarely does this body stand up and deter conflicts and wars. The United Nation's structure and the national interests of the powerful preclude most action to save humanity. In some cases the intervention of other countries, whether to take sides or to limit a war, can be counterproductive and can even widen a conflict. But an appropriately empowered, strong international body could, in theory, deter conflicts by increasing the price of aggression—through international pressure in the form of predetermined sanctions and international agreements, and through peaceful intervention to keep the warring parties apart, among others. For peace to have a chance, the United Nations needs to be reorganized. The permanent five must be persuaded that a structural change eliminating their single country veto power, although perceived as costly in the short run, serves their and everyone's long-term interests.

For a brief period from 1953 to 1961, there was a glimmer of hope that the United Nations might realize its goal of global peace. UN Secretary-General Dag Hammarskjöld, possibly the greatest statesman of his time, energized the United Nations and worked tirelessly to promote peace and deter conflict. He acted independently of the major powers. He protected the interests of the weaker nations. Realizing that he had to mobilize the world community to achieve peace, he traveled the world himself to thwart conflicts and facilitate reconciliation. He established the UN armed peace-keeping mission. In July 1960, with his support, the Security Council adopted UNSC Resolution 132, which established the United Nations Operation in the Congo (ONUC). Unfortunately, with the passage of time, UN forces became involved in the fighting that had divided the country. His involvement in the Congo and more accurately his opposition to Lumumba brought on the wrath of the Soviet Union. This episode proved to be a highly controversial episode both in UN history and in his tenure as secretary-general.

While all leaders, especially those from the advanced economies, espouse peace, justice, and freedom, their actions invariably belie their noble words. The powerful countries seem to pursue their perceived short-term selfish interests and seem to care little if their policies increase conflicts and wars around the world. Leaders from both the East and West continue to lobby on the international scene for their arms industries. They encourage the sale of lethal weaponry to their client states, no matter how tyrannical the leader or undemocratic the country. Lobbyists press the interests of the global arms industry in a number of ways. They argue that a strong innovative arms industry and large military expenditures are essential for national security. They also reason that an arms industry and international arms exports give a country international leverage; and if one country does not sell arms to a tyrant, another country will. The major exporters of arms invariably look the other way if the arms they supply are used to suppress peaceful protestors or to incite acts of aggression against neighboring countries. It is only when NGOs expose such abusive human rights policies that international sales of arms are suspended. The arms industry is also supported because it is a significant provider of jobs in some countries. Germany, the third largest exporter of arms in the world, espouses more ethically based arms exports, such as weighing an importing country's human rights record, assessing whether the country may use the arms in a conflict, and not prioritizing its own need for job creation. But even Germany was considering the sale of tanks to Saudi Arabia in 2011 after that country's bloody intervention in Bahrain, depriving the majority of Bahrainis of their human rights, and Sweden had signed a secret agreement to build an advanced arms industry in Saudi Arabia.

While there is some validity to most of the arguments promoting a strong arms industry and arms exports, countries must begin to balance their short- and long-term interests better. Does the sale of a few billion dollars in arms today make up for the potential cost of a future war where those same arms might be used against the arms-exporting country? Would arms be so readily exported if there were a price to pay if ever the exported arms were used in conflicts and wars? Could goods other than arms be produced, resulting in other jobs and exports? How will an exporter of arms be perceived when a tyrant uses those arms against his own people, and what is the ultimate cost of such an event to the arms-exporting country? Realizing that no country would unilaterally forsake all arms exports, is it not sensible to begin a movement for all countries to restrict and simultaneously reduce lethal arms exports?

Isn't this state of affairs very much reminiscent of persuading countries to reduce their barriers to international trade after World War II? We knew for centuries that free trade would benefit the world, but no country would unilaterally reduce trade barriers because of the impact on jobs and on the country's balance of payments unless others did the same. Also, after

World War II most countries, principally the United States, would not accept an international trade supervisory organization that impinged on its national sovereignty. As a result, trade liberalization was achieved in a number of small confidence-building steps. The first step was an organization, namely, the General Agreement on Tariffs and Trade (GATT), under whose auspices barriers to trade could be reduced in steps and by mutual agreement. This organization, whose coverage included only goods (not services), had no enforcement power. With the passage of time and a number of tariff rounds that reduced trade barriers significantly, confidence gradually increased and the benefits of the global trading system became clear. In 1995 GATT was replaced by the World Trade Organization (WTO), an organization that had much wider trade coverage (including services and investment) as well as enforcement powers (something that the world could not agree to after World War II) and was thus more effective.

Similarly, is it not reminiscent of the hurdles that the world faced to begin the process of reducing the size of US and Russian nuclear arsenals simultaneously, with verification and on a step-by-step basis to build confidence? Is it not time to call every country's bluff when they claim that they export arms only because others do and would gladly restrict arms exports if the mandate to do so were globally accepted? How about a General Agreement to Reduce Arms Trade (GARAT), to be followed by a World Anti-Arms Organization (WAAO)?

It would appear that a number of measures could truly reduce conflicts and their fallout. Namely, the structure of the United Nations should be reorganized to deter aggression. Direct belligerent parties to conflicts, as well as the powerful countries that support them and the companies who supply them, should be confronted with the full price of their actions. The system of international justice, whereby all leaders are held accountable for their acts of aggression against countries and groups, should be applied on a consistent basis to all leaders and governments. The world should adopt an agreement to control and reduce the global arms trade and in turn, to reduce military expenditures.

How can conflicts be reduced or, even better, eliminated? On one level, the answer is simple. Raise the price of aggression for leaders (governments) and for countries that initiate aggression as well as for those who support aggressors. But to achieve this end we suggest some simple guidelines. Before anything else, a number of initiatives have to be adopted simultaneously because most acts of aggression and their fallout or price are indirectly supported and affected by many diverse factors, and we must tackle them all at the same time if we are to have a chance for success: (i) all potential and actual conflicts should be mediated (or mediation facilitated), regardless of whether the conflicting parties are countries or groups, and the party that refuses to negotiate must be automatically declared the aggressor; (ii) the full costs of all conflicts and reparations should be calculated on a transparent basis and their payment must be enforced; (iii) leaders must know that they will be held accountable for their crimes against humanity, whether in their own country or in other countries; (iv) leaders must realize that wealth illegally acquired by them, their families, and their cronies will be expropriated and returned to the legitimate government of their country; (v) leaders, would-be leaders, and dissidents must be confronted with the reality that no one accused of crimes against humanity will be given a free passage to a life of luxury in foreign lands; (vi) a global effort to reduce the arms trade (with the eventual goal of reducing military expenditures simultaneously in all countries) must be launched; (vii) the United Nations, including the UNSC, must be structurally changed to eliminate the single country veto that essentially affords a free pass to five countries to do as they wish; (viii) the powerful countries must be placed on notice that they will be held responsible for inciting and fueling aggression around the world; (ix) transparent efforts to promote democratic reforms in all countries must be initiated so that leaders understand that aggression, corruption, and other failures will translate into defeat at the polls and possible legal action; and (x) regional economic projects should be promoted with the expectation that such efforts would deter regional conflicts and wars.

The above list of ten initiatives looks like a dream! How can a world unable even to eliminate hunger begin to contemplate such a list of initiatives designed to increase the price of aggression and thus end conflicts and wars? How can a world where countries cannot decide whether to increase taxes or reduce expenditures adopt such initiatives? The answer is simple. We have little choice, if we want to save humanity.

Can countries be persuaded to take the lead in adopting and enforcing the antiaggression initiatives listed above, or will the process have to be initially sparked by nongovernmental organizations (NGOs)? What is the best course of action, a governmental or private sector initiative?

Realistically, no credible government or international organization will take the lead to increase the price that aggressors pay for aggression. No single country has the legal right to enforce such an initiative. If for no other reason, this is not a politically realistic position to take, especially as it will not be initially supported by the majority of countries and especially by none of the powerful countries. There are risks. There are too many variables that affect the price of aggression, and no country controls all of them. No serious government will want to risk looking like a naïve university professor! And governments invariably take on difficult agendas only when they have no other choice. That is not the case when it comes to conflicts and wars today. At the same time, if a government were to lead the initiative, it would damage the unbiased and unaffiliated focus of this proposal, because governments invariably have agendas and are generally not trusted by any party to a conflict. NGOs have a much better chance of being accepted by all, or at least by more parties. To be an effective intermediary or facilitator in conflict resolution, an entity must have developed trust and credibility with the parties to a conflict. While this process takes time, government officials come and go with some frequency, and officials will not take on the time-consuming role of a facilitator/intermediary, especially if it is to play a role in initiatives that afford little guarantee of success. NGOs, on the other hand, can maintain such a role for as long as needed.

Thus the place to start such a broad initiative, to garner global support, to reduce the risk of failure for governments and other official organizations, and to build confidence for success, on a step-by-step basis, is in the private sector, with nongovernment organizations, or NGOs, later to be replaced by an effective international organization.

What have probably had the biggest impact on affecting a change in attitudes toward environmental degradation are a number of high-profile private sector efforts, such as the movie "An Inconvenient Truth" and the work of a number of dedicated NGOs. These, and their associated publicities, have raised global awareness and backed world leaders into a corner to acknowledge global warming and to take action. On the practical level, a number of approaches to reduce carbon footprints have been forthcoming. While there has been at least some recognition, albeit slow and painful, of the necessity of reversing the degradation of our environment, there has been little or no progress in reducing conflicts and wars and their attendant economic, environmental, and human costs throughout the centuries. When it comes to ending conflicts and wars and achieving global peace, we have only made half-hearted attempts with the League of Nations and with the United Nations. It is as if wars and conflicts were built into the human DNA. World leaders and world institutions, principally the United Nations, espouse their commitment to peace in our time, yet they adopt policies and practices that do the opposite. If leaders will not act, then we, the citizens of this world, must do so. There is no choice but to develop a privatized solution for ending conflicts and wars. We must acknowledge that the success, management, and governance of NGOs, and in particular that of a number of high-profile NGOs, have been seriously questioned and criticized, which we discuss in some detail in chapter 6. While we are aware of these, we believe that our initiative can be managed in a way to avoid most of these shortcomings.

Specifically, our proposed approach is to simultaneously establish and develop a number of NGOs under a broad umbrella with the goal of increasing the price of aggression to its full fallout for all parties to aggression. Some of our proposed initiatives could be incorporated into existing NGOs whose main mission is in line with the proposed initiative. For instance, a setting for active mediation already exists in the form of the Oslo Forum Network of Mediators. This forum was started nine years ago and is sponsored by the Norwegian Ministry of Foreign Affairs and the Centre for Humanitarian Dialogue (based in Geneva).[4] But our proposed NGOs would be active in a number of other areas that affect conflict and wars, namely, assessing and calculating damages and reparations resulting from conflicts and wars (based on a well-publicized methodology) on an ongoing basis for all potential and actual conflicts; publicizing the names of countries and groups who have been named as aggressors, the reparations that countries and groups to conflict have been assessed and must pay, and global boycotts against countries and groups that have been assessed reparations but have not paid; encouraging democratic reforms around the world by naming abusive rulers, monitoring their abusive activities (especially those in areas of basic human rights and corruption and theft of national wealth that rob their countries), exposing the support of foreign powers (including ongoing details) for such tyrants, and advertising these globally to isolate these rulers and to shame their foreign backers; monitoring and exposing the international arms trade, the companies and countries who export arms, the end uses of lethal weapons, the human and economic harm they inflict, and the activities of the powerful countries that incite and fuel conflicts around the world; and finally, developing and promoting regional economic projects and cooperation to increase the pain of regional hostilities. NGOs armed with modern technologies could be highly effective in naming and shaming aggressors and their supporters into changing their policies.

We need a moral compass on the international level to eradicate conflicts and wars from the human experience. Adam Smith, the professor of moral philosophy, provides us the foundation to move forward in his two monumental contributions to Western thought—"sympathy" and "a sense of justice." Sympathy for the plight of others is at the heart of moral judgment. Without a sense of justice, nothing permanent can be built. As Nicholas Phillipson says in his biography of Smith (238): "The *Wealth of Nations*, like the *Theory of Moral Sentiments* and the lectures on which it drew, was a call to his contemporaries to take moral, political and intellectual control of their lives and of those for whom they were responsible." In this vein, we must acknowledge that we are all responsible for the fate of those who suffer from the horrors of wars and conflicts, from malnutrition and inadequate health care, and from the denial of basic human rights, and we are also responsible for the environment and for the state of the world that we pass on to future generations. The world is not for us to destroy but to preserve, improve, and pass on to those who follow in our footsteps. This is the morally required stewardship.

It is in this spirit that we propose this initiative to reduce, hopefully, in time, to end, all conflicts and wars, and to restore hope and humanity to those who have so little. In many ways, our proposal is to create a privatized United Nations—a United Nations NGO, which would be effective and would be entrusted with the mission and all the means to achieve global peace. With the passage of time, it is hoped that the demonstrated success of this United Nations NGO and its affiliated NGOs would inspire the world community to give birth to international institutions that embrace the same goals and support these efforts. The global citizenry must reignite the dream of global peace, a peace that is eventually managed by an effective United Nations. We should recognize the simple fact that we must do this also for ourselves, as we can no longer afford to go down the well-worn path that humanity has traveled since the dawn of time.

This may be the optimal time for this endeavor because of a number of simultaneous global pressures—the worst financial and economic crisis in over 70 years, unprecedented public budgetary deficits and levels of public (and private) debt in a number of advanced countries, record food prices with over 20 percent of the world going hungry each and every night, rising numbers of people around the world in a state of poverty, aging populations requiring increasing retirement and medical benefits, global warming that poses serious problems for future generations, all accompanied by a number of ongoing conflicts and wars around the world that make little sense. There is also a unique opportunity for statesmanship at a time when China is on the rise and the United States and Western Europe are in stagnation or possibly in decline. It is tempting for the United States to think that it has the upper hand in its weaponry and military preparedness and has no need to make any concessions to China. And it is equally tempting for China to believe that with its increasing economic importance it can make the United States cower. But the United States and China should come to their senses and see the future for what it is, namely, an arms race between China and the United States, which neither side can afford. Both nations must now show true vision and statesmanship and negotiate a massive reduction and, in time, an end to military expenditures. Once a new arms race begins, even more resources will be wasted; with ever more lethal weapons on the horizon, special interest groups will have more at stake, conflicts will beget new conflicts, and it will become increasingly difficult to develop trust. The quest for military superiority will eclipse everything else.

Our book is organized as follows. In chapter 2, we present a brief history of wars and a collage of some of the wars and conflicts since 1945. What have the characteristics of these more recent wars and conflicts been? What have the economic cost and the human casualties been? What can we learn about the initiation of conflicts and wars? In chapter 3, we report the different ways in which the cost of wars are estimated, discuss the various approaches to arrive at these estimates, and suggest a framework for our proposed NGO to calculate the burden of wars and the appropriate reparations to be paid by aggressors. In chapter 4, we endeavor to draw out in more detail the factors that affect the price of aggression and why conflicts and wars occur when the price of aggression is low; we also include the limitations of the United Nations. To this end, we look at the case of the Persian Gulf over the last 30 or so years to provide some specifics and lend more realism to our discussion. This is a region that has become heavily armed and militarized over the last 40 or so years and that has witnessed three of the most devastating wars of the last 30 years—the Iran-Iraq War, the First Persian Gulf War, and the Iraq War. Why did these conflicts arise? What was done to stop them or to fuel and sustain them? Could they have been stopped? Could peace have been restored earlier? In chapter 5, we use our recommended framework (developed in chapter 3) to calculate the cost, or the price, of these three most recent wars in the Persian Gulf—again, the Iran-Iraq War, the First Persian Gulf War, and the Iraq War. Finally, in chapter 6, we lay out in more detail the proposed organizational structure for our umbrella NGO and its affiliated NGOs. We detail their activities to increase the price of aggression to a level representing its full cost to end conflicts and wars—by devising financial reparations and legal penalties, by publicizing, shaming, and enforcing costs for aggressors in conflicts and for the sellers of arms whose weapons are used in conflicts.

We hope that a foundation, or a group of well-intentioned philanthropists, will adopt our broad proposal as its mission and establish the needed NGOs (collaborating with existing NGOs where appropriate) to support and nurture the global vision of ending conflicts and wars.

It is our hope that, with the passage of time, the successful activities of the proposed NGOs will motivate and inspire governments, initially the weak but later followed by the strong, to join and to create parallel international organizations, and that the world will embrace the effort to formally and permanently end conflicts and wars around the globe so that future generations can inherit a world without war.

Chapter 2

A Glance at Recent Conflicts and Wars

A Brief Accounting of Recent Conflicts and Wars

The early part of the nineteenth century, from 1815 to 1845, was a peaceful period in Europe with unprecedented industrial expansion. In America, there was political tranquility with rapid economic growth up to the outbreak of the American Civil War.[1] World military expenditures were generally low because many imagined that peace would be permanent. By mid-century, however, tensions were increasing and intense rivalry once again developed between England and France. The latter half of the century was marked by a number of conflicts: the Crimean War, the American Civil War, the Austro-Prussian War, the Franco-Prussian War, the Russo-Turkish War, the Boer War, and the Spanish-American War (Zapotoczny). According to the COW (Correlates of War, at the University of Michigan) project,[2] there have been around 490 major conflicts from the beginning of the nineteenth century, with more than 38 million battle-related fatalities; and since 1945 alone, there have been roughly 170 conflicts with nearly 6 million battle-related deaths; while according to SIPRI, since 1988 worldwide military expenditures have accounted for more than $26 trillion (in 2009 constant prices).[3]

Heightened global concern about renewed interstate conflicts after World War I brought about the establishment of the League of Nations, which was later (after World War II) replaced by the United Nations because countries were encouraged to use diplomacy to solve emerging conflicts. Many issues such as self-determination, national sovereignty, and the territorial integrity of countries were not addressed after World War II, resulting in conflicts in the ensuing period of decolonization. The ratification of the United Nations Charter in 1945 recognized the right of self-determination (free choice of one's own acts, especially sovereignty and international political status, without external compulsion) in the framework of international law and diplomacy, but it did not advocate full independence as the best road to self-governance, nor did it include enforcement mechanisms. New states were recognized in such a way that the old administrative boundaries would become international boundaries upon independence, even if they had little relevance for linguistic, ethnic, cultural, tribal, or religious divisions. Over time, national self-determination has challenged the principle of territorial integrity or sovereignty of states because it is the will of peoples that makes a state legitimate. Although there are far more self-identified nations than there are existing states, there is no legal process to redraw national boundaries according to the will of the affected peoples. Thus territorial, resource, and border issues have led to a number of conflicts and independence movements, both between and within states.

After World War II, with the threat of a nuclear war, a bipolar system emerged, pitting the East against the West, and resulted in a number of conflicts and wars. The cold war was the protracted military, geopolitical, ideological, and economic struggle that emerged in the form of a nuclear and conventional arms race, networks of military alliances, economic warfare and trade embargos, propaganda, espionage, and proxy wars, especially those involving superpower support for opposing sides of civil wars. Proxy wars were common between the two nuclear-armed superpowers. These proxy wars included conflicts in Afghanistan, Angola, Korea, Vietnam, the Middle East, and Latin America. The fact that these armed conflicts rarely ended but instead fueled even more subsequent conflicts has rarely been acknowledged. Unfortunately, the structure of the United Nations Security Council (UNSC), affording the power of the veto to five permanent council members, and the selfish policies of the powerful UN members have made it impossible to significantly reduce proxy conflicts around the world involving surrogates of the powerful five.

After the collapse of the Soviet Union, the system that emerged was unipolar, with the United States as the sole superpower. It was hoped that this new paradigm might mean the ending of ideological conflicts through the promotion of the Western ideology of liberal economic and political systems. However, although the East and the West reduced their support of client governments, artificial borders and divisions, coupled with the increasing weakness of governments, led to the rise of internal ethnic and religious conflicts. Consequently, a regional system emerged whereby countries became regional allies to benefit from special regional resources, unique geographical positioning, or collective protective capacity (Glaser). The emergence of new identities, built around new free countries, has promoted regionalization. Regional powers tend to regulate their interests independently, prompting or forcing other countries in the region to group around them or to ally with them. These new regional powers (countries such as India, Turkey, and Nigeria) do not compete for global hegemony, but they are of special interest to superpowers competing for supremacy. Conflicts among regional powers tend to be mostly over resources or territory.

The Changing Trends and Characteristics of Conflicts and Wars

According to Glaser,

> since the 18th Century [a period of only about two hundred years], some 471 wars were fought resulting in about 120 million war-related deaths; over 90% of these deaths occurred in the 20th Century. Of the 250 wars fought in the 20th Century, 194 occurred in the period 1945–1995, 90% of them taking place in developing countries, causing some 45 million war-related deaths; in the period 1990–1995 alone, 70 states were involved in 93 wars in which 5.5 million people died.

Several important characteristics of recent conflicts stand out. First, the overwhelming majority of wars are intrastate conflicts, with classic interstate conflicts accounting for only 15 percent of all conflicts. The share of civilian deaths has been increasing; the average percentage of civilian deaths in World War I was 50 percent, rising to 73 percent for wars in the 1970s, and was estimated at 85 percent in the 1980s. Lacina et al., using revised information on battle-related deaths from 1900 to 2002, demonstrated that the risk of death in battle declined significantly after World War II and again after the end of the cold war.[4] Another important characteristic of recent conflicts is that most were fought in developing countries and regions. Politicians invariably focus on ethnicity, linguistics, and religion, and emphasize the differences between people rather than their similarities. This fuels both interstate and intrastate conflicts, both of which can be a mixture of independence movements or anti-regime movements. In recent years, there has been a significant overlapping of organized crime and insurgencies, with rebels profiting from crime because of the close connection of the arms and drug trades, enabling criminals to use political conflict to cover their activities.

Most recently, the number of armed conflicts has been declining from their peak in the early 1990s. This is in part the result of successful international efforts to negotiate settlements and because of an increase in the number of democratic governments worldwide (Hewitt et al.). However, this trend appears to have come to an end in large part because of instability and failure in poor countries. The rate of recurring conflicts has increased notably since the end of the cold war. The majority of conflicts in the past ten years have been a recurrence of previous conflicts. According to Hewitt et al., of the 39 different conflicts that became active in the past ten years, 31 (or 80 percent) were recurrences of previous conflicts as compared to eight conflicts fought over new issues and interests, a trend with ominous implications for the future. These figures do not include the uprisings, conflicts, and resulting casualties that have been identified with the Arab Spring of 2011.

War Trends: Some Details

Based on the Uppsala Conflict Data Program (UCDP) definition, an armed conflict is defined as "a contested incompatibility that concerns government or territory or both, where the use of armed force between two parties results in at least 25 battle-related deaths in a year." UCDP also categorizes conflicts according to their intensity:

- minor armed conflicts: at least 25 battle-related deaths in a year but fewer than 1,000, and
- war: at least 1,000 battle-related deaths in a year.

Furthermore, UCDP distinguishes between conflicts by type:

- interstate-armed conflict occurs between two or more states,
- internationalized internal armed conflict occurs between the government of a state and internal opposition groups, with intervention from other states with troops, and
- internal armed conflict occurs between the government of a state and internal opposition groups.

In figures 2.1 to 2.8 and tables 2.1 to 2.4 we portray war trends and characteristics in a little more detail.

Number of Conflicts

According to Harbom and Wallensteen, since World War II, there have been 244 armed conflicts in 15 locations worldwide. In figure 2.1, we show the number of conflicts and dyads (pair of warring parties) in the period between 1946 and 2009. The number of armed conflicts increased since World War II, and after peaking in the early 1990s, the trend has been downward. The figure also shows the dyadic trends. In interstate conflicts, the warring parties are governments of states, whereas in intrastate conflicts, one side is the government and the other is a rebel group. A conflict can involve a number of dyads, as the government may be fighting many rebel groups over time. Thus, dyadic information can reveal more about conflicts; for example, the complexities facing efforts at conflict resolution.

Intensity of Conflicts

In figure 2.2, we show wars by their intensity from 1946 to 2009. Most of the conflicts were minor. The share of wars (as opposed to minor conflicts) has been decreasing.

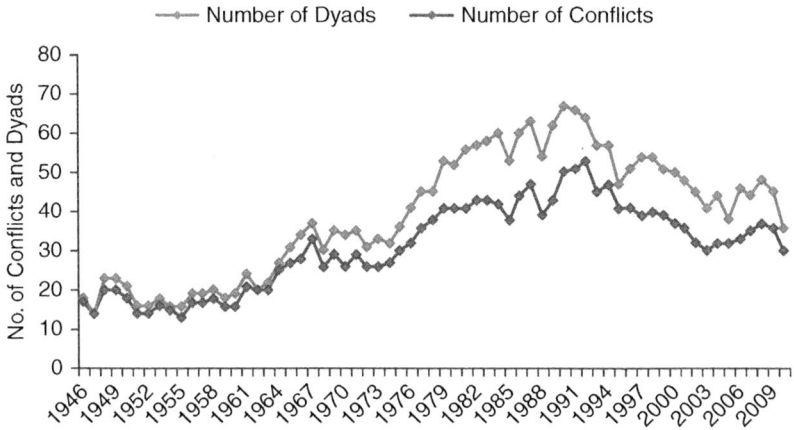

Figure 2.1 Conflicts and Dyads, 1946–2009

Source: Uppsala University " UCDP Database." (2011) Retrieved from: www.ucdp.uu.se/database.

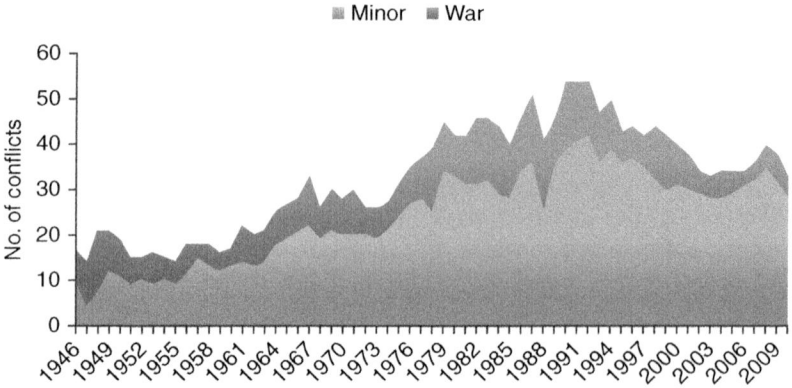

Figure 2.2   Armed Conflicts by Intensity, 1946–2009

Source: Uppsala University " UCDP Database." (2011) Retrieved from: www .ucdp.uu.se/database.

Type of Conflicts

Figure 2.3 shows the number of conflicts by type. Interstate conflicts have been low in number with a declining trend, while intrastate wars have been the dominant form of conflict. No interstate war has been initiated since 2004. The number of internationalized intrastate wars, in which outside countries intervene in a civil war, has been generally low. Also, the number of new conflicts has been low. Thus the increase in the number of conflicts until 1992 was the result of the accumulation of wars that did not end or that recurred. Also, the main reason for the declining trend of wars since 1992 is the successful termination of wars and also the steady, but small, decline in the number of new conflicts (Buhaug et al.).

Conflicts by Region

In figure 2.4, we show that the number of armed conflicts by region has declined significantly in recent years. The peak in European conflicts came in the early 1990s and the peak in American conflicts in the 1980s. In the Middle East, the number of conflicts increased in the 1980s and has been generally constant over time (again, excluding figures for the protests and conflicts that erupted in the spring of 2011). However, there has been an upward trend in the number of conflicts in Asia and Africa. Asian and African conflicts account for a significant portion of the total.

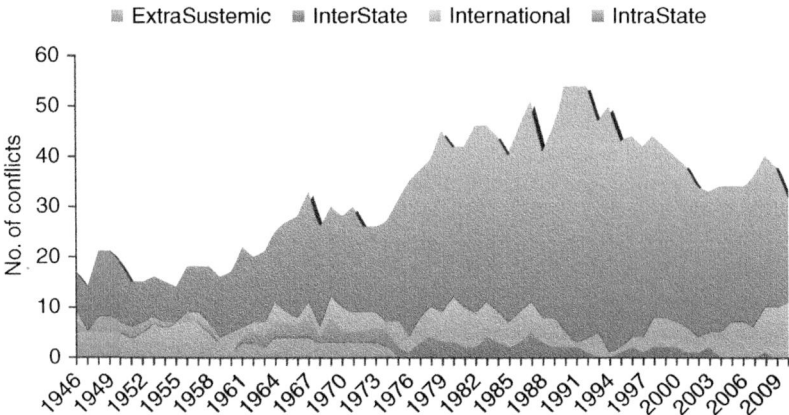

Figure 2.3   Armed Conflicts by Type, 1946–2009

Source: Uppsala University " UCDP Database." (2011) Retrieved from: www. ucdp.uu.se/database.

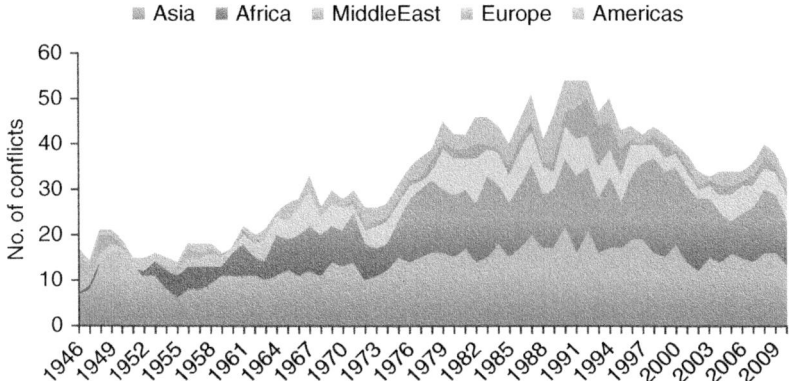

Figure 2.4   Armed Conflicts by Region, 1946–2009

Source: Uppsala University " UCDP Database." (2011) Retrieved from: www. ucdp.uu.se/database.

Some plausible reasons are that these are populous countries with a larger proportion of younger and low-income groups, and some may have low economic growth potential (little hope for a better future) with unstable and oppressive governments.

Casualties of Wars

Figures 2.5 and 2.6 show the trend in casualties in the period between 1960 and 2010. The figures convey the number of annual battle deaths caused by conflicts between warring parties and include military and civilian deaths that are directly due to armed conflicts. Despite the fact that the number of interstate wars is low compared to intrastate wars, interstate wars account for a disproportionately large number of deaths. The general trend of war casualties is decreasing mainly because the number of wars is decreasing. The other reason contributing to the declining trend of war casualties is that despite the increase in the number of intrastate wars, many of them involve developing countries with limited lethal military capabilities (Lacina et al.). Additionally, when the warring party is a developed country, medical advances and protective equipment have become significant in protecting lives and decreasing the number of war-related deaths. According to Buhaug et al., a few conflicts account for the bulk of the casualties. The two world wars caused a large number of deaths and cannot be compared to other wars. In figure 2.5, the Korean War and the Chinese Civil War are the cause of the first peak. The Vietnam War (1965–75) accounted for the second peak, and the third peak came about because of the Iran-Iraq War (1980–88) and the Soviet-Afghanistan War. The civil war in the Democratic Republic of Congo (1996–2001) is the cause of the last peak. If we were to include non-state, namely, ethnic or sectarian, violence in the statistics, we would see an additional peak in 1994 with the Rwandan genocide and, potentially, in the more recent years (Iraq and Afghanistan).

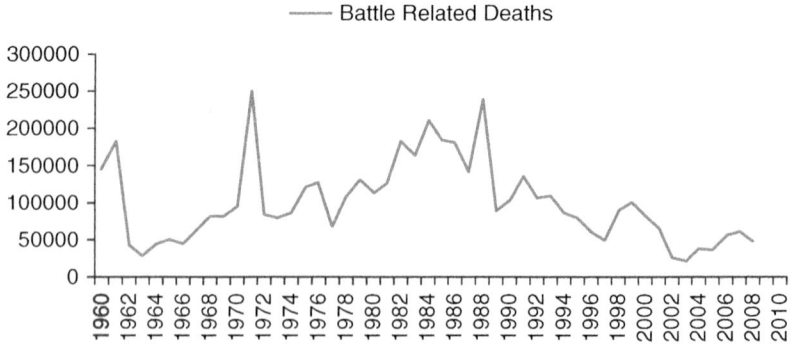

Figure 2.5   Battle Deaths, 1960–2010

Source: World data Bank "World Development Indicators (WDI)." (2011) Retrieved from: http://databank.world.org/ddp/home.do

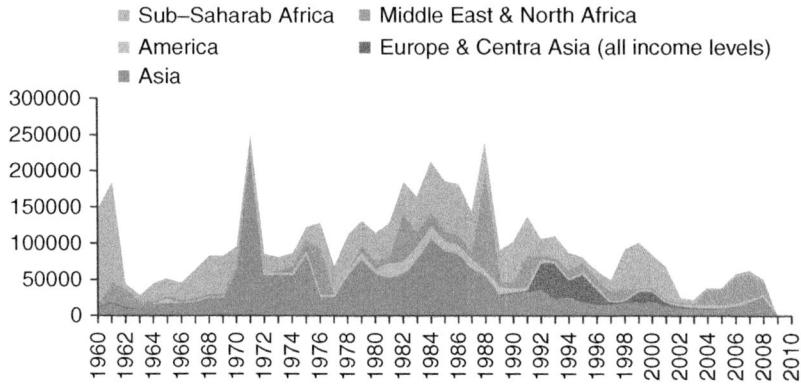

Figure 2.6   Casualties in Armed Conflicts by Region, 1960–2010

Source: World data Bank "World Development Indicators (WDI)." (2011) Retrieved from: http://databank.world.org/ddp/home.do

Military Expenditures

Military expenditures accounted for approximately 2.7 percent of global GDP in 2009. There was a global increase in military expenditures in 2009 over 2008, except in the Middle East. The 2008 global financial and economic crisis did not impact military spending, because many countries increased public spending to provide economic stimulus for their ailing economies, postponing deficit reduction during the crisis. Table 2.1 shows the trend in worldwide military expenditures and compares military expenditures to health and education expenditures as a percentage of GDP.

Figure 2.7 shows the top ten military spenders. They accounted for 75 percent of world military spending, with the United States alone accounting for 43 percent of the world total. In the list of the top ten military spenders, the names of the countries have not changed in the recent years, but their ranking has, with European countries moving down the list.

For countries to have increased military expenditures during the financial crisis, they invariably had to sustain large fiscal deficits, thus small or poor countries that could not finance large fiscal deficits had to cut their military spending. In many developing countries, revenues from depletable natural resources, such as oil, natural gas, and diamonds, play a major role in conflicts. Increased prices and production of natural resources afford authoritarian regimes higher revenues and, as a result, dictators are in a position to increase military expenditures to keep a tight hold on power

Table 2.1   Trend in World Military Expenditures

Year	GDP (current billion US$)	Military Expenditures (current billion US$)	Expenditures (% of GDP)		
			Military	Public Health	Public Education
1988	18,698.48	652.04	3.49		
1989	19,624.36	770.89	3.93		
1990	21,920.79	795.52	3.63		
1991	22,995.57	693.07	3.01		
1992	24,546.40	732.46	2.98		
1993	24,915.08	703.66	2.82		
1994	26,752.11	706.41	2.64		
1995	29,692.89	724.75	2.44	5.47	
1996	30,303.29	718.42	2.37	5.45	
1997	30,222.36	717.05	2.37	5.32	
1998	30,115.11	699.32	2.32	5.36	
1999	31,231.32	707.27	2.26	5.41	4.21
2000	32,240.38	730.66	2.27	5.35	4.05
2001	32,046.35	739.95	2.31	5.58	4.29
2002	33,304.64	804.42	2.42	5.74	4.27
2003	37,465.97	926.67	2.47	5.78	4.41
2004	42,228.98	1,042.20	2.47	5.76	4.37
2005	45,658.32	1,128.83	2.47	5.70	4.43
2006	49,506.29	1,207.37	2.44	5.67	4.53
2007	55,848.90	1,338.77	2.40	5.62	4.38
2008	61,304.54	1,513.70	2.47	5.68	4.45
2009	58,088.28	1,570.72	2.70	6.09	
2010	63,123.89	1,653.14	2.62		

Source: World Bank Database

and also to protect their valuable resources from outside aggression. This upward trend slowed down in 2009 because of the decrease in commodity prices, but it resumed in 2010 along with rising commodity prices. Figure 2.8 shows military expenditures by region.

War Expenditures

Since 9/11, the US Congress has authorized more than $1 trillion for military operations worldwide, especially for Afghanistan and Iraq (Daggett). Table 2.2 shows the cost of major wars throughout US history. It presents figures both in "current dollars," namely, in prices in

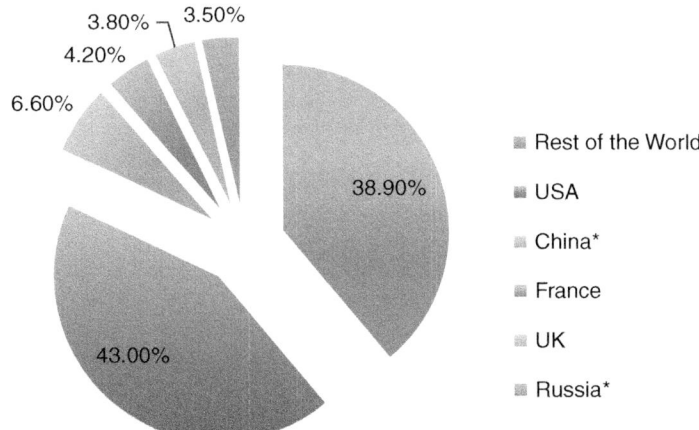

Figure 2.7   World Share of Military Expenditures by Country, 2009
Source: Stockholm International peace

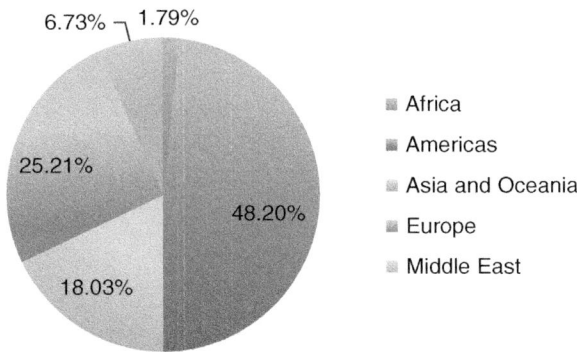

Figure 2.8   World Share of Military Expenditures by Region, 2009
Source: Stockholm International peace

effect at the time of each war, and in inflation-adjusted "2011 constant dollars" to afford more meaningful comparisons. These are the estimated costs of military operations and do not include three important items—the cost of veteran benefits (which continue for years into the future after the conflict has ended), interest paid for borrowing money to finance wars, and financial assistance to allies. The table also provides estimates of the cost of each war as a share of GDP during the peak year

Table 2.2 Military Costs of Major US Wars, 1775–2010

	Years of War Spending		Peak Year of War Spending	Total Military Cost of War in Billions of US$		% GDP in Peak Year of War	
	Beginning year	Ending year		Current Year	Constant 2011	War Cost	Total Defense
American Revolution	1775	1783	NA	0.101	2.407	NA	NA
War of 1812	1812	1815	1813	0.09	1.553	2.20	2.70
Mexican War	1846	1849	1847	0.071	2.376	1.40	1.90
Civil War: Union	1861	1865	1865	3.183	59.631	11.30	11.70
Civil War: Confederacy	1861	1865	NA	1	20.111	NA	NA
Spanish American War	1898	1899	1899	0.283	9.034	1.10	1.50
World War I	1917	1921	1919	20	334	13.60	14.10
World War II	1941	1945	1945	296	4104	35.80	37.50
Korea	1950	1953	1952	30	341	4.20	13.20
Vietnam	1965	1975	1968	111	738	2.30	9.50
Persian Gulf War	1990	1991	1991	61	102	0.30	4.60
Iraq	2003	2010	2008	715	784	1.00%	4.30
Afghanistan/Other "Operation Enduring Freedom"	2001	2010	2010	297	321	0.70	4.90
Total Post-9/11: Iraq/Afghanistan/Other	2001	2010	2008	1046	1147	1.20	4.30

Source: Daggett, S. "Costs of Major US Wars." Congressional Research Service, 2010.

of the conflict and of overall defense spending as a share of GDP in the peak.

In the most comprehensive (including veteran's benefits and interest expense of debt-financed wars) ongoing project (Eisenhower Research Project) on the cost of wars to the United States since 9/11, Lutz, Crawford, and their associates have calculated the cost of the wars in Afghanistan and Iraq. Among their major findings are:[5]

> The U.S. wars in Afghanistan, Iraq, and Pakistan will cost between $3.2 and $4 trillion, including medical care and disability for current and future war veterans. This figure does not include substantial probable future interest on war-related debt. More than 31,000 people in uniform and military contractors have died, including the Iraqi and Afghan security forces and other military forces allied with the United States. By a very conservative estimate, 137,000 civilians have been killed in Iraq and Afghanistan by all parties to these conflicts. The wars have created more than 7.8 million refugees among Iraqis, Afghans, and Pakistanis. Pentagon bills account for half of the budgetary costs incurred and are a fraction of the full economic cost of the wars. Because borrowing has financed the war almost entirely, $185 billion in interest has already been paid on war spending, and another $1 trillion could accrue in interest alone through 2020. Federal obligations to care for past and future veterans of these wars will likely total between $600 and $950 billion. This number is not included in most analyses of the costs of war and will not peak until mid-century.

In order to afford some perspective on these estimated costs, we should note that $4–5 trillion in budget deficit reduction over a decade was the supposed goal of the failed negotiations between Democrats and Republicans in the United States leading up to the debt ceiling agreement of early August 2011.

Active Wars in 2010

In table 2.3 we present the list of active wars in 2010: conflicts that produce a significant number of violent deaths (fatality figures include both civilian and military deaths) defined as in excess of 1,000 per year (such as the Afghan Civil War); conflicts that were initiated a number of years ago and have produced significant deaths over time (see the last column) but today can be classified as minor conflicts with less than 1,000 deaths per year (such as the conflict in Korea); and conflicts that have not resulted in a significant number of deaths over time and are today minor conflicts (such as the conflict in Senegal).

Table 2.3   Active Wars with Casualties

Start Year	Conflict	Location	Cumulative Fatalities (since the onset of the war)
Major Conflicts (>1,000 deaths per year)			
1967	Naxalite-Maoist insurgency	India	10,500+
1978	Afghan Civil war	Afghanistan	600,000–2,000,000
1991	Somali Civil War	Somalia	300,000–400,000
2003	War in Iraq	Iraq	100,746–110,043
2004	War in North-West Pakistan	Pakistan	30,452
2004	Shi'ite Insurgency in Yemen	Yemen	12,833–16,439
2006	Mexican Drug War	Mexico	36,226+
2009	Sudanese Nomadic conflicts	Sudan	2,000–2,500
2011	Libyan Civil War	Libya	10,000+
Minor Conflicts (<1,000 deaths per year)			
1948	Korean conflict	North Korea, South Korea	~900,000
1948	Internal conflict in Burma	Burma	40,000–121,000
1948	Israeli–Palestinian conflict	Israel, Palestinian	14,500+
1964	Colombian Armed conflict	Colombia	50,000–200,000
1964	Insurgency in Northeast India	India	25,000–40,000
1969	Insurgency in the Philippines	Philippines	75,000–120,000
1978	Turkey–Kurdistan Workers' Party conflict	Turkey, Iraq	30,000–100,000
1987	Lord's Resistance Army insurgency	Uganda, Sudan, DR Congo, Central African Rep	12,000–46,000
1989	Insurgency in Jammu and Kashmir	India	27,000–68,000
1990	Casamance conflict	Senegal	~1,000
2002	Insurgency in the Maghreb	Algeria, Mali, Mauritania, Morocco	~6,000+
2004	Conflict in the Niger Delta	Nigeria	4,000–5,000
2004	Baluchistan conflict	Iran, Pakistan	2,500+
2004	Iran–Party for a Free Life in Kurdistan conflict	Iran	150–300

Continued

Table 2.3   Continued

Start Year	Conflict	Location	Cumulative Fatalities (since the onset of the war)
2004	South Thailand insurgency	Thailand	~4,100
2005	Fourth Civil War of Chad	Chad	1,140+
2008	Cambodian–Thai border standoff	Cambodia, Thailand	40–200+
2009	Insurgency in the North Caucasus	Russia	1,110+
2009	South Yemen insurgency	Yemen	180+
2010	Yemeni Al-Qaeda crackdown	Yemen	570+

Source: Harbom, L. and P. Wallensteen. "Armed Conflicts, 1946–2009." *Journal of Peace Research* vol. 47, no. 4 (2010): 501–509.

The Relationship between Defense, Education, and Health Expenditures

Defense expenditures can be both the cause and the outcome of wars and can have a significant impact on economic growth. If the effect of military expenditures on economic growth were positive, it would suggest that an increase in military expenditures boosts economic activity. This might conceivably be true in a country where increased military expenditures are heavily associated with significant research and development, education, and infrastructure enhancement, all of which are positive inputs for economic growth. On the other hand, if the relationship between military expenditures and economic growth is negative, it suggests that increased military expenditures hinder economic growth by taking resources from productive activities such as education and health (Obreja Brasoveanu).

There have been numerous studies focusing on the relationship between military, education, and health expenditures; Hirnissa et al. present a comprehensive literature review of these relationships with a number of conclusions from the studies that follow. Yildrim and Sezgin claim that decisions on military expenditures are taken independent of education and health expenditures, but there is a trade-off between military and welfare expenditures. The trade-off is positive between military and education expenditures and negative between military and health expenditures. The study suggests that increasing defense expenditures reduces resources available for health, implying that defense has priority in the budgeting process because of external and internal security considerations. In contrast to this, a positive correlation of defense and education expenditures would suggest that defense expenditures do not crowd out education spending. Caputo suggests that the assumption of an explicit trade-off between military and welfare expenditures should be reconsidered because even if there is a trade-off between military and health expenditures, it may not be significant.

Dabelko and McCormick examine the opportunity cost of military expenditures for health and education spending and conclude that: (1) the opportunity cost of military expenditures for health and education spending is small; (2) the level of economic development has little or no impact on the opportunity cost; and (3) personalist regimes have a higher opportunity cost of military expenditures than centrist and polyarchic regimes.[6] Scheetz examines central administration functional expenditures for four Latin American countries (Argentina, Chile, Paraguay, and Peru) over a 20-year period (1969–1987). He concludes that defense expenditures are greater than all public sector expenditures combined in Latin American countries. In addition, defense expenditures are growing faster than those for health and education. He also argues that military regimes tend to spend more on defense than do civilian regimes. However, unlike Dabelko and McCormick, he concludes that the relationship of defense expenditures to the level of economic development is negative. Apostolakis also studies the impact of military expenditures on welfare expenditures in Latin America from 1953 to 1987 and concludes that military expenditures hinder the allocation of funds for raising welfare.

Knight, Loayza, and Villanueva investigate the effect of a reduction in military expenditures on economic growth. They claim that a substantial long-run "peace dividend"—in the form of higher output capacity that would differ widely across regions—may result from lower military expenditures that were achieved in most regions during the late 1980s. Additionally they simulate the long-run gains in output capacity that could result from large military spending cuts associated with generalized peace. They assume that the military spending ratio in each region declines steadily over a ten-year period from the regional average level that prevailed during the period between 1986 and 1990 to just fewer than 2 percent of GDP. Based on a 50-year simulation, they conclude that output capacity levels in Eastern Europe and the Middle East would have been respectively 50 percent and 46 percent higher if these permanent reductions in military spending ratios had occurred. In the developing countries of Asia and North Africa, the long-run gain would be 30 percent to 40 percent, and in sub-Saharan Africa, over 10 percent. For industrial countries, output capacity per capita would eventually be higher by 20 percent. These represent significantly higher levels of productive capacity.

Building on the work by Knight, Loayza, and Villanueva, the impact of the cost of wars could be estimated in a simplistic manner, essentially assuming that war costs are equivalent to military expenditures in their impact, which we realize they are not (table 2.4). The estimation assumptions are as follows:

- The total cost of wars is equal to military expenditures and war-related expenditures.
- There is a linear relationship between GDP increase and war-related costs.

Table 2.4   Estimate of the Increase in GDP by Eliminating War-Related Costs

	GDP (1972–1985) (billions of 2005 dollars)	Military Spending Cut (% GDP)	War Spending Cut (% GDP)	Total War and Military Spending Cut (billions of 2005 dollars)
Industrial Countries	16,356.136	2.03	2.03	664.059
Asia	3,218.052	4.41	4.41	283.832
Eastern Europe	119.223	9.81	9.81	23.392
Middle East	546.000	8.40	8.40	91.728
North Africa	115.614	6.19	6.19	14.313
Sub Saharan Africa	355.044	1.18	1.18	8.379

	GDP (1972–1985) (billions, in 2005 dollars)	Increase in GDP (% GDP)	Increase in GDP (billions, in 2005 dollars)
Industrial Countries	16,356.136	39.60	6,477.030
Asia	3,218.052	65.40	2,104.606
Eastern Europe	119.223	99.40	118.508
Middle East	546.000	92.40	504.504
North Africa	115.614	79.20	91.566
Sub-Saharan Africa	355.044	26.20	93.022

Source: Knight, M., N. Loayaza, and D. Villanueava. "Military Spending Cuts and Economic Growth." Staff Papers, *International Monetary Fund* vol. 43, no. 1 (1996): 1–37, and author's estimates.

Based on what are disputable assumptions (that military expenditures and war-related costs have the same impact), an aggregate decrease of $1,086 billion in war-related expenditures would increase aggregate GDP by $9,389 billion for selected regions.

The negative effect of military expenditures on economic growth may be less pronounced for developed countries, because the portion of their military budget that goes to the military industrial complex may lead to breakthrough inventions and high technology equipment and infrastructure. However, developing countries import their military equipment, so for them there are few or no GDP growth effects or technical progress to offset military spending (Collier).

Does the type of conflict affect the magnitude of the economic burden?

The current trend of wars indicates that civil wars are the most common type of war and that they last longer than other wars. Collier et al. show that recent civil wars have lasted almost three times longer than civil wars prior to 1980. Moreover, the cost of these wars is considerable. During civil wars, growth rates of GDP decreased by an average of 2 percent. These losses can continue after the war, because investors feel less confident about investing in a country that they perceive to be more risky or to have an unstable environment. The other main reason is that investors expect civil wars to reoccur, an important and alarming trend. Bigombe et al. estimate that there is a 50 percent risk of war reoccurrence during the first five years after a civil war. Moreover, whole regions can be affected by civil wars, with fighting spilling over to neighboring countries and reducing regional growth (Murdoch and Sandler). This reduction might be caused by the increased perception of risk and uncertainty in the region or by the reduction of regional demand resulting from the decline in income in the affected countries.

In sum, there are numerous studies confirming that military spending has a significant opportunity cost for health and education spending. Moreover, military expenditures impede economic growth by crowding out the resources from productive sectors, especially in developing countries. Wars damage productive capacity and thus reduce economic output. Civil wars may have a longer lasting impact and a higher probability of recurrence than interstate wars with spillover effects into a region. A conservative estimate of the impact of aggression (military expenditures and the fallout of wars) was presented in chapter 1. Jürgen Brauer and John Tepper Marlin (2009a) estimated that the total effect of peace on global economic output in 2007 would have been $7.2 trillion or 13.4 percent of global economic output in that year, with $2.4 trillion representing the reallocation of resources from violence to peace activities (what the authors refer to as static effect) and $4.8 trillion in net gain in global economic output (referred to as dynamic effect) due to previously unharnessed "economic resources being released." We reiterate their conservative estimate here because we believe that it is of the utmost importance to repeat this number so that politicians, the military, arms manufacturers, lobbyists, and the global citizenry begin to acknowledge the necessity for the reduction and end of all conflicts and wars. Just consider the benefits of increasing available resources by roughly 15 percent if we could only eliminate conflicts and wars! The only way to do that is to try and try until we succeed.

Broad Policies to Prevent Conflicts and Wars

Wars can be catastrophic, deadly, and expensive, and they have significant negative effects on the welfare of societies and the economic growth of countries. Moreover, the human toll of wars has been terrible throughout the course of recorded history. Broad policies have been suggested for avoiding conflicts and wars. These policies can be classified by type of conflict.

Policies to Avoid Interstate Conflicts

The prevention of interstate wars has been a major focus of international relations. For example, the 1815 Congress of Vienna put into effect a number of measures for this, such as mutual consultations, the establishment of neutral states and demilitarized zones, and the peaceful settlement of conflicts. Moreover, the African union, the European Union, the United Nations, and other regional organizations were founded with the major goal of preventing conflict through interstate interaction and cooperation. According to Ganiyu (30–37), these efforts can be summarized as follows:

- Deterrence of aggressor states: deterrence can be achieved by the formation of an alliance or it can be a unilateral step and can prevent deadly conflicts by threatening to pose unacceptable costs on states that initiate them. The creation of NATO, the US-Japan Security Treaty for nuclear deterrence, and the US-Korea alliance are all examples of this type of prevention.
- Arms control: arms control can make war less likely, the preparation for war more expensive, and the war itself less destructive. For

example, the US-Soviet cold war arms control agreement was designed to reduce the likelihood of war and to establish measures to make it harder for parties to prepare for war. Moreover, SALT (Strategic Arms Limitation Talks), START (Strategic Arms Reduction Talks), the NPT (Nuclear Non-Proliferation Treaty), the NFZ (establishing nuclear-free zones), and the CFE (Treaty on Conventional Armed Forces in Europe) are all example of agreements to eliminate or reduce conventional weapons in Europe and in other regions.

- Development of an open international economy: economic inter-dependence and open trading systems encourage peaceful relations between states and promote prosperity and even democracy, thereby reducing the potential for conflict. Such economic initiatives include the creation of the IMF, the World Bank, the European Union, the GATT, and, more recently, the WTO.
- Strengthening of international institutions promoting norms and cooperative security relations: international norms of peace and coop-eration can help prevent conflict by creating a sense of accountability to the norms. Such institutions include the United Nations, where the rules for membership are clearly outlined in the UN Charter and Universal Declaration of Human Rights, as well as regional organiza-tions such as ASEAN and the OSCE.

A reason for the decline in interstate wars could be the significant effort devoted to preventive action and capacity building. Examples of conflicts and crises that have been handled or resolved before eruption since the end of the cold war include the Cuban missile crisis, the border conflicts between China and Kyrgyzstan, and the Nigeria-Cameroun land dispute. However, these efforts are few and far between, and the effectiveness of these measures, including those of the United Nations, is debatable.

In sum, a successful conflict prevention policy requires an accurate interpretation of the root causes of conflict and an understanding of the conflicting issues. The United Nations has enormous unfulfilled potential but has not lived up to expectations. Conflicting interests of member states and structural inadequacies in the United Nations make it an ineffective vehicle to respond to growing tensions and emerging conflicts. On the other hand, the international community will be able to continue contrib-uting to conflict-prevention efforts if states maintain their support and political will. States should utilize the mandate and the preventive tools available from the United Nations. States must also improve their social, political, and economic infrastructures and should encourage neighboring countries to do the same.

Policies to Avoid Intrastate Conflicts:

As intrastate conflicts have in recent years become the dominant form of conflict, it may be appropriate to ask what the principle factors are that led to civil wars. Hegre and Sambanis (514–522) identified the following factors as contributing to intrastate conflicts:

- Demographic factors: countries with higher populations have more armed conflicts but fewer casualties per capita; countries with a larger proportion of their population between 15 and 24 years of age have a higher risk for conflict.
- Economic factors: a large number of internal conflicts occur in low-income or low-economic growth countries. One possible reason might be the inability of countries to provide satisfactory basic living conditions or hope for a better future. Similarly, countries with high natural resource dependence for national income have a high risk of internal conflicts. These may arise because of corruption and associated rent-seeking activities, but strong political institutions can decrease the risk of conflict.
- Political factors: political instability and inconsistent political institutions (institutions that are neither democratic nor authoritarian) give rise to internal conflicts. Inconsistent political institutions are more ineffective in controlling insurgencies as compared to authoritarian regimes. Moreover, semi-democratic institutions are attractive for nationalistic and sectarian movements and can cause conflicts by encouraging institutional change.
- Regional factors: countries in nondemocratic regions are more prone to conflicts. Rebels and insurgents are often dependent on help from outside their country. Rival and nondemocratic neighboring countries are more likely to provide support to rebel groups. In contrast, democratic and stable neighborhoods improve regional stability and peace.
- Affiliation and identity factors: countries with sizeable minority ethnic populations have a higher risk of internal conflicts. This factor is stronger when the minority group resides in the periphery of the country.

According to Buhaug et al. (1–11), the current (recent) trends of these factors are as follows:

- Demographic trends: the increase in the number of conflicts through the early 1990s can be explained by the increase in the world population and in the number of independent countries.

- Economic trends: the rate of regional economic growth affects the number of conflicts in a region. Latin America has had moderate economic growth and has also had a considerable decrease in the number of conflicts. The rapid economic growth in East Asia was accompanied by a huge decrease in the number of conflicts in this area. However, economic growth in the Middle East has not been linked to a reduction in the number of conflicts in the region. One possible explanation might be their heavy reliance on revenues from the depletion of natural resources. In sub-Saharan Africa there has been low economic growth and the number of conflicts has not been significantly affected.
- Political trends: a number of countries are democratizing. Stable and consistent democracies decrease the risk of internal conflicts. However, the transition to democracy is highly conflict prone.

To stabilize the downward trend of conflicts, based on the factors influencing conflicts and their trends, Buhaug et al. (1–11) propose a policy set to decrease the risk of inciting internal conflicts.

Policy Recommendations to Decrease the Risk of Inciting Internal Conflicts

- Improve economic growth as a long-term strategy for reducing the risk of conflict.
- Promote free trade along with transparent and fair revenue distribution in low- and middle-income countries.
- Focus on regional development strategies to help build a democratized region.
- Promote greater democracy and better human rights in low- and middle-income countries.
- Encourage constraints on the administration of nondemocratic countries through mechanisms to ensure budgetary transparency, auditing bodies, independent media, and private organizations.

Policy Recommendations to End Ongoing Armed Conflicts

- Promote UN and other peacekeeping operations.
- Support long-term guarantees of rapid intervention, which motivate countries to reduce military spending (for example, the UK guarantee in Sierra Leone).

- Promote post-conflict aid with defined limits on military spending to restrict and limit aid spillover into military spending.
- Promote the role of the International Criminal Court to criminalize crimes during war.
- Promote international regimes such as the Kimberley Process[7] to regulate trade in contraband resources used to finance war.

In general, promoting better social, political, and economic conditions decreases the likelihood of conflicts. Support for free trade and democracy can lead to higher economic growth and can improve the quality of life, which will subsequently decrease the probability of conflicts and wars. World Bank sponsorship of international development in middle- and low-income countries or International Monetary Fund stabilization of the global economic environment can indirectly improve the trend of conflicts. The United Nations, with its stated missions to facilitate cooperation in international law, international security, economic development, social progress, human rights, and world peace should play an overarching role in preventing conflicts and wars. However, the United Nation's structure, the shortsighted policies of its most important members, and its operational shortcomings have prevented it from reaching its potential.

The Impact of the UN Structure on Conflicts

As we have said a number of times before, the structure of the United Nations is not the most conducive for eliminating conflicts and wars. One of the main organs of the United Nations is the UNSC, which is responsible for the maintenance of international peace and security. Its authority includes peacekeeping operations, military action, and the establishment of international sanctions. The UNSC has 15 members, with five permanent members (China, France, Russia, the United Kingdom, and the United States) and ten elected members, with two-year terms, that are not permanent. There is disagreement about UN governance and its operations, especially peacekeeping. The five permanent members of the UNSC, all nuclear powers, use the United Nations in part to address their own strategic interests. An example of this would be how some members protected oil-rich countries such as Kuwait in 1991 and Libya in 2011 while ignoring the plight of resource-scarce countries.

Ironically, the five permanent members of the UNSC are five of the top ten largest arms-exporting countries in the world (Shah). Moreover, a

powerful country can ignore the UN Charter with essentially no consequences, the US invasion of Iraq in 2003 being a recent example. Another
example is the Darfur crisis, where Arab Janjaweed militias, supported by
the Sudanese government, have committed repeated acts of ethnic cleans-
ing and genocide against civilians. Three hundred thousand civilians have
been killed, yet the United Nations has continuously failed to act against
these ongoing human rights abuses. The United Nations also failed to
address the massive human rights violations in Bahrain and Syria during
the Arab Spring of 2011.

An important criticism of the UNSC involves the veto of its five permanent members. A "no" vote by any one of the permanent UNSC members
is enough to strike down any given proposal. Permanent members often
use this veto power to strike down operations that are contrary to their
individual perceived national interests. For example, during the period
from 1982 to 2007, the United States vetoed 32 UNSC resolutions that
criticized Israel (Mearsheimer and Walt, 2007b).

There is also evidence of corruption in the UN structure. Kuziemko
and Werker showed that a member's US aid increases by 59 percent and its
UN aid by 8 percent when it rotates onto the council. This effect increases
during key diplomatic events as votes become more valuable, and the tim-
ing of the effect closely tracks a country's election to, and exit from, the
council. This suggests that some rotating members trade their votes for
political or financial favors during the two years in which they are in the
sun and enjoy a boost to their diplomatic importance.

To our mind, the UN structure and operations are seriously flawed,
making it a poor international forum for conflict prevention. However, it
is important to note that while the United Nations could be at the fore-
front of conflict prevention if it were governed differently, it is currently
not. There is a lack of clear authority, self-dependence, and leadership by
the United Nations. Sometimes a regional organization expects the United
Nations to act based on its broader powers, while the United Nations, on
the other hand, expects the regional organization to intervene first because
of its proximity to the conflict. This causes a lack of coordination when
dealing with conflict prevention. Hence, in the opinion of some, conflict
prevention is successful only through joint efforts of the international
community, states, and regional organizations to implement theories and
policies (Ganiyu).

States and regional organizations have not and will not rise up to the
challenge because governments tie their hands. Thus it is time for the private sector (NGOs) to assume this critical responsibility and to take the
lead, as we will elaborate in chapter 6.

Summary

The major characteristics and trends of recent conflicts and wars have been:

1. Intrastate conflicts and wars have become much more numerous and prominent than those that are interstate. The popular concept of war, involving two or more countries, is not as prevalent today as it was a century ago and earlier.
2. The current trend of wars indicates that civil wars are the most common type of war and last longer than other wars, with recent civil wars lasting almost three times longer than civil wars prior to 1980.
3. The cost of civil wars is high, with GDP growth rates decreasing by an average of 2 percent.
4. Most conflicts occur in undemocratic, low-income, and low-growth countries and regions.
5. The vast majority (roughly 80 percent) of recent and ongoing conflicts are the result of conflict reoccurrence. The fact that the majority of conflicts beget new conflicts is an important consideration for facilitating conflict mediation before conflicts turn into armed struggles.
6. The ratio of civilian deaths to direct combat-related deaths has been increasing dramatically in recent conflicts.
7. The ratio of serious injuries to fatalities has been increasing significantly, especially where advanced economies (as a result of better equipment and better medical care) are parties to a conflict.
8. Wars and military expenditures have a significant effect on global economic welfare.
9. There are a number of helpful policies to discourage or impede the outbreak of conflicts and wars and also to end them. It would appear that there is insufficient political will, especially in the United States, China, and Russia, to develop a comprehensive initiative to reduce conflicts, wars, and military expenditures. An important reason for this is that these powers believe they receive a net benefit from their military strength, even though it is supported at tremendous economic cost to them.
10. While the United Nations was conceived as the global guardian of peace, its structure has not been supportive of its mission. It may have been handicapped by design.

11. The elimination, even a significant reduction, of conflicts and wars would increase global economic output and free up considerable resources for use in other desperately needed areas.

12. In an era of tight economic resources and budgets, putting an end to conflicts and wars may be the best hope for an economic turn-around to address a number of pressing, and even existential, global economic and social problems.

Chapter 3

Estimating the Price of
Conflicts and Wars

The toll of conflicts and wars can be reduced if the price of aggression is raised for leaders and countries—those who are direct parties to conflict as well as those who incite and fuel conflict—to a level that represents the full fallout of their aggression on all those who are affected. But what is the burden of aggression? How should it be estimated when assessing the cost of aggression and subsequent reparations?

For a variety of reasons, estimating the price or the real fallout of aggression is more difficult than it might at first appear. There is no universally accepted framework for calculating the cost of a conflict or war. Most conflicts and wars have no standard beginning, middle, or end. At one extreme, some even argue that wars could generate results that are on balance positive, because they bring about new technologies resulting in gains in production efficiency, while others are adamant that the outcome of all wars is negative. What are the fallouts of conflicts and wars and how should their calculation be framed? Even if costs and burdens are accurately assessed to every party's satisfaction, there is only a price to aggression if the guilty parties pay or are forced to pay. In this chapter, we look at how to assess the cost of conflicts and wars and in chapter 5 we use this framework to estimate the cost of three recent wars in the Persian Gulf.

When assessing the cost of war, one would ideally like to come up with one figure, but given that costs are incurred at different times, we have to bring future costs to the present by discounting them and then adding them to costs already incurred. As a result, we need the costs already incurred and the discounted cost of future fallouts—losses in production of goods and services, the cost of replacing damaged infrastructure and other destroyed structures, including historic buildings and museums, the cost of replacing damaged machinery and equipment, the economic cost associated with human fatalities and injuries, the cost of replacing destroyed military equipment, other government war-related expenditures that are above the normal day-to-day cost to maintain its military, the cost of environmental degradation (including historic and natural sites), and the associated cost of future policies (such as higher military expenditures) and wars that are a direct or indirect consequence of the war.

All of this is no easy task, but what if it is the government's borrowing that finances war-related expenses? Is the long-term impact of rising public debt irrelevant because the cost (no matter how it is financed) has already been included? Some would suggest that it is prudent to isolate the human toll in casualties and in seriously injured as a distinctly separate category of war-related cost and include only the cost of additional medical treatment and social payments due to the conflict or war, now and in the future. Even in a straightforward definition such as this, estimating many of these individual costs is difficult and would be subject to debate. What is the appropriate cost of a human life or of permanent disabilities? How should environmental destruction be assessed, especially if one is talking about a natural treasure such as a beach or a forest? Over what time period should losses be amortized? What is the appropriate discount rate for bringing future costs to today's dollars?

Conflicts have pervasive effects on people's lives and on societal structure. The intangible effects of war are hard to isolate and, in turn, estimate. The resulting cost of social instability from a civil war and the cost of the psychological damage to people involved in a war are almost impossible to quantify. The effects on human health, welfare, happiness, education, environment, and future generations are also difficult to identify and quantify. Such costs are usually categorized under indirect or intangible costs of conflict. Although indirect costs may be as pervasive and detrimental as direct costs, they are usually omitted from numerical estimates and only mentioned in a paragraph to avoid methodological criticism.

Different answers to these and other questions would result in vastly different estimates for the fallout, or price, of conflicts and wars. We need a standard framework that is transparent for leaders and countries to get a reasonably accurate idea of the price of their actions, a price that is invariably paid by others.

Wars usually involve more than the direct aggressors. When assessing the cost of a war, one has to choose the geographical limits of assessment. Defining the countries affected directly or indirectly may be difficult. In addition, there is a cost on the global level, for instance, how does one define and estimate the impact of a war on the price of oil and other commodities?

Usually, news about a conflict disappears from the headlines after the shooting stops (or, if its geographic location is of little interest, even as the shooting continues), but the consequences of war may be apparent and real for those affected for many years thereafter. Wars have an immediate impact on economic growth during the postwar period. The characteristics of a war, the countries themselves, their prewar status and their postwar policies in part determine the economic outcomes of a war. Estimating postwar costs is usually more complicated than calculating the direct cost of the war during the years of hostilities. One could even make the case that the postwar cost of World War I was World War II because of the size of the reparations that were assessed on Germany and the adopted trade measures. The cost of any conflict or war, even after its end has been declared, should be continually updated. There is extensive literature on estimating the cost of wars, with some focusing on restricted components of cost and others incorporating a broader set of elements. Some have dealt with civil wars; others have focused on international or global wars.

We examine this literature, identifying classical studies in addition to contemporary estimates, to get an idea of the varied costs involved. We first outline the methodologies used to estimate the costs and outcomes of conflicts, namely, civil wars, global wars, and interstate wars as well as postwar costs, we then present what is our preferred methodology or framework. This discussion should, in turn, lend further support to the belief that conflicts and wars impose a high cost on the global economy, but a cost that is *not* paid by those who initiate, fuel, and sustain them.

Civil Wars

Civil wars differ from global or interstate wars in their origin, conduct, and consequences. Besides the "normal" factors that affect the cost of all wars, the cost of civil wars also depends on the functionality of existing state institutions and on whether foreign countries or groups support one or more of the fighting parties. The macroeconomic costs of civil wars are usually higher than those of interstate wars. Civil wars damage the social and cultural networks that are at the foundation of society and undermine the institutions that support society and the economy, while interstate wars normally spare some of these elements or affect them more marginally. Other factors, such as the duration, intensity, and geographic location of a war, also affect the overall cost. The longer a country stays in a state of war, the greater the cost, although the remaining institutions and affected populations learn to adapt with time. The larger the geographic area of the conflict and the closer it is to the capital or major production centers, the more severe the impact. Due to these intrinsic characteristics, civil wars have different consequences in terms of costs, requiring a different method of measurement (DiAddario). We briefly examine studies on four civil wars in different countries and eras.

The American Civil War

Goldin and Lewis reexamined the cost of the American Civil War after a number of earlier studies. Rather than following the method of adding total military expenditures to the destruction of physical capital, Goldin and Lewis adopted another approach to estimate the cost of the American Civil War for both the Union and the Confederacy. Their estimates were of two types: direct and indirect costs. Direct costs included the summation of all related expenditures and losses, namely, all Union and Confederate war expenditures and the human and physical capital destroyed in military actions. Since these estimates were considered incomplete, they estimated additional indirect costs. Indirect costs were estimated on the assumption that a particular economic consumption stream would have existed in the absence of war. They calculated the indirect cost of the war as the difference between the estimated consumption stream and the actual stream. The attributes they used to calculate the direct costs were applied separately and then aggregated to provide the total direct cost of the Civil War (see table 3.1). Since the destruction of physical capital was concentrated in the South, it was included only in direct costs for the South. They estimated these costs as the difference between the discounted and deflated value of physical capital (excluding slaves) at the end of the war and their value before the war started.

In essence, Goldin and Lewis estimated the indirect cost of the Civil War by creating a hypothetical scenario wherein the North and South did not fight a war during the period between 1861 and 1865. In the absence of war, they supposed that the economy would have grown at the average of its prewar rate (1839–1859). Thus the indirect cost of the war is the discounted difference between the consumption streams of the hypothetical (if there had been no war) and the actual (with the war). It is important to note that they assumed that consumption, not income, was the relevant measure of the cost of a war, arguing that war may not affect measured income but it could dramatically affect consumption. The indirect cost estimates also included the effects of the emancipation of slaves and

Table 3.1 Direct Cost of the American Civil War

	Cost Variable	Description
1	Expenditures by the federal government	Includes costs incurred during the war and demobilization periods minus a hypothetical cost of maintaining defense in the absence of war.
2	Expenditures by state and local governments	Similar to the calculation of federal government expenditures, with the addition of bounties paid to attract quota-filling soldiers.
3	Additional cost due to the draft	The 1863 draft and amount paid to drafted soldiers.
4	Human capital loss: (a) killed (b) wounded	(a) The monetary loss from these casualties was estimated as the present value of the foregone income that these men would have earned. (b) The estimated cost of the wounded was the difference between their actual and hypothetical earnings.
5	Subtract the risk premium in soldiers' wage bills	The cost of the monetary compensation for the risk of death and injury were already included in the soldiers' wage bills.
	Total Direct cost	The summation of (1–4) items minus (5).

Source: Table compiled from Goldin, C. and F. D. Lewis. "The economic cost of the American Civil War: Estimates and implications." *The Journal of Economic History* vol. 35, no. 2 (1975): 299–326.

reconstruction. These calculations excluded the forgone consumption of those who were killed during the war. They extended the lives of those who were killed to include their hypothetical consumption as an indirect cost of the war.

Goldin and Lewis adopted two ways for calculating the indirect costs for the US population. First, they calculated the indirect costs for the "native" population that was living in the United States in 1861 and for their descendants. This excluded the war's impact on those who immigrated to the United States after 1861. Second, they also calculated the indirect costs of the war for all persons living in the United States including those who immigrated during the war. Thus, the total indirect costs represent all net consumption by the US population of either "natives" or "all residents" that was forgone due to the Civil War. Finally, they aggregated direct and indirect costs to the North and the South to present the total cost of the American Civil War. They conclude that there is "no evidence that the Civil War benefited either the North or the whole US even in a gross way" (Goldin and Lewis, 322). They showed that the cost of the war was "wide-ranging and persistent" to an extent that the direct costs constituted only 42 percent of the total costs for the entire nation.

Nicaragua 1980–1987

The cost of the civil war in Nicaragua was estimated by the United Nations' Instituto Latinoamericano de Planificacion Economico y Social (ILPES) to be used by the International Court of Justice in a case against the United States for its role in the war (International Court of Justice, 1988). In order to estimate the resulting loss in GDP, the ILPES used the so-called two-gap method, with the two gaps being the foreign exchange and savings gaps. The ILPES estimated that GDP losses were 26 percent of the cumulative GDP between 1980 and 1987, with a peak of 41 percent in 1986. The "two-gap" analysis assumed that the Nicaraguan economy had two effective constraints: an aggregate demand restriction (savings) and an import capacity restriction (foreign exchange). The physical destruction in an exporting country and the disruption of its trade channels cause a major reduction in foreign exchange earnings with an impact on general output (International Court of Justice, 1988, Annex IV.3). The method generated two multipliers: a foreign exchange multiplier and a savings multiplier constraint for the two gaps. The categories that ILPES used to estimate GDP losses are summarized in table 3.2.

DiAddario criticized the method used by ILPES to estimate GDP losses. After assessing the two-gap model used by ILPES, he provides an alternative approach that detects structural breaks in economic behavior during the conflict to provide an alternative estimate of the losses. He considered two possible methods for estimating the cost of the conflict as reflected in GDP. The first method was to calculate the difference between the estimated GDP assuming there was no war and the actual (with war) observed GDP. The calculation of the estimated level of GDP in the absence of war was done using pre-conflict data and assuming that there was no change in economic conditions or policies. The second method to estimate the loss in GDP was based on an analysis of how economies function during wars. DiAddario adopted this method, known as "behavioral analysis." Through this approach, the elements that were specific to the conflict were singled out and the ways in which they affect production were investigated. The ILPES approach assumed that most behavioral relationships do not change during a conflict. Specifically, the import function and the consumption function should have changed under conflict conditions,

Table 3.2 Estimate of Nicaragua's GDP Losses, 1980–1987

	Category	Description
1	Material damage and production losses	(a) Cost of material damage to capital stock from direct military attacks estimated at current dollar market value.
		(b) Loss of production of export goods and domestic consumption goods due to military attacks.
2	Losses from the US trade embargo (imposed in 1985)	Loss in net foreign exchange earnings due to the embargo.
		Cost of shifting the trade from the United States to Europe: price differential between the United States and Europe, increased transport and insurance costs, increased expenses of trade representatives and of meeting the requirements of an alternative market (packing, labeling, etc.).
3	Reduced GDP arising from material damage and production losses	Calculated by applying the ILPES multipliers to the direct losses.
4	Reduced GDP arising from losses due to the US trade embargo	The foreign exchange multiplier and the saving constraint multiplier were applied to the amount of foreign exchange earnings estimated to be lost in order to obtain the overall indirect loss of GDP.
	Total GDP loss	Summation of categories (1–4).

Source: Table compiled from International Court of Justice, Annex III, IV, V. "Activities in and Against Nicaragua: Memorial on Compensation." Retrieved from http://www.icj-cij.org/docket/files/70/9621.pdf.

but such changes were ignored by the ILPES approach. The consumption function would be affected both by uncertainty and the shortage of consumer goods. Similarly, the import function would also be affected by increased demand for losses in domestic production and the availability of foreign aid.

DiAddario considered structural breaks that significantly altered the underlying economic relationships, the effects of the revolution before the war (1978–79) and during the war (1981–88), and assumed that the propensity to consume and the propensity to import changed significantly over the period between 1970 and 1991. Based on DiAddario's approach, the overall loss was about three quarters of the level estimated by ILPES (19 percent compared to 26 percent of GDP estimated by ILPES). As an implication, foreign exchange losses had much less of an impact on GDP than that assumed by the ILPES approach.

Sri Lanka Civil War 1983–2009

Arunatilake et al. assessed the economic costs of the ethnic conflict in Sri Lanka beginning in 1983. They classified the economic costs of the conflict into two categories: direct and indirect costs. Direct costs include costs currently or immediately related to the conflict, such as the destruction and damage to capital assets and labor, extra military expenditures incurred by all fighting parties, and the cost of caring for refugees. The cost of damage or destruction to capital was defined as "the sum of the discounted net present value of the stream of capital services that would have been generated by them" (1,486). The government's war-related military expenditures were identified as the difference between actual military expenditures during the war and the normal level of expenditures the government would have had in the absence of war. The direct cost of the Liberation Tigers of Tamil Eelam (LTTE) to the Sri Lankan economy was defined as the amount of funds spent by the government on the war that could otherwise have been spent on consumption or investment. The direct and indirect costs calculated by Arunatilake et al. are summarized in table 3.3. Using a

Table 3.3   Direct and Indirect Costs of the Sri Lanka Civil War

	Category	Description
Direct Costs		
1	Direct military expenditures of: (a) Government (b) LTTE	(a) The difference between actual military expenditures during the war and the normal level of expenditures in the absence of the war. (b) The amount of funds spent on the war that could have been spent on consumption or investment (estimated at 10% of the military expenditures incurred by the government).
2	Government expenditures on relief services	Providing shelter and relief for refugees, resettlement, repair, and reconstruction compensation.
3	Cost of lost infrastructure (capital asset and land)	Value of the lost capital services that could have been generated.

Continued

Table 3.3 Continued

	Category	Description
Indirect Costs		
1	Lost income due to forgone investment	War adversely affected the level of output and efficiency of investments, hence lowering the long-term growth rate. The authors estimate the loss in growth by calculating the difference between an estimated growth rate and the actual rate. To calculate the counterfactual growth rate the authors compare the Sri Lankan model with the experience of similar countries rather than with past trends in Sri Lanka itself. The authors also calculate the value of lost output due to higher military expenditures and the effects of military expenditures on GDP. The cost of higher military expenditures also includes the growth forgone due to the crowding out of investment both by domestic and foreign investors and its impact on the efficiency of investment.
2	Lost income from reduced tourist arrivals	The authors calculate the difference between the counterfactual amount of gross earnings that a similar country with similar attractions and facilities could earn and the actual earnings in Sri Lanka during the war.
3	Lost earnings due to foregone foreign investment	To estimate the counterfactual size of investment flows, the authors assumed that under normal conditions the foreign direct investment flows to the country would have been similar to figures during times of peace.
4	Lost income due to lost human capital from dead or injured persons	The authors assume that the cost to the economy from the lost lives is the foregone output due to the reduced labor force and that the economy lost the productive capacity of only half of its wounded.
5	Output foregone due to displacement of people	Based on the number of displaced families, the authors discount the productivity of just one income earner per family, with the aggregate value of the lost incomes attributed to the cost of displacement.
6	Output foregone in the Northern Province in 1996	Due to the government's "Operation Riviresa."

Source: Table compiled from Arunatilake, N., S. Jayasuriya, and S. Kelegama. "The Economic Cost of the War in Sri Lanka." *World Development* vol. 29, no. 9 (2001): 1483–1500.

Table 3.4 Cost of the Nepal Civil War

	Category	Description
1	Growth in real GDP	GDP growth fell from 5.1% per annum in the prewar period (average for the seven years before the war, 1987/88 through 1994/95) to 3.8% in the war period (average of the seven-year war period 1995/96 through 2001/02). Industries with foreign participation shut down and production of carpet and garments fell significantly.
2	Growth in real agricultural GDP	Growth remained stagnant at 3.2%.
3	Growth in real nonagricultural GDP	Growth in real nonagricultural GDP fell from 6.6% before the war to 3.9% during the war.
4	Real per capita income	Declined from $232 in 1991 to $162 in 2001.
5	Export and import growth	Export growth fell from 26% before the war to 16% and import growth fell from 24% to 8%. Imports of machinery and equipment fell due to the postponement of public and private projects. Imports also fell due to the collapse of tourism.
6	Tourism	Tourism growth declined from 5% to 1%.
7	Remittances	Remittances grew from 2% of GDP in the mid 1990s to over 5% of GDP by 2001/02.
8	Foreign exchange	Foreign exchange earnings fell from 4% of GDP to 2% of GDP due to lost earnings from tourism and other exports.
9	Social services	Investment in social services fell from 2.7% of GDP to 1.8% of GDP, contributing to a net loss in welfare.
10	Development expenditures	Development expenditures fell from 12% to 9% of GDP, although current expenditures rose from 7% to 10% of GDP during the war period.
11	Public and private sector capital formation	Public sector capital formation did not exceeded 8% of GDP since the 1990s.
12	Domestic savings	Domestic savings fell from 15% of GDP in the late 1990s to 12% by 2002/03.
13	Foreign aid	Foreign aid fell from 6% of GDP in the mid 1990s to 3% by 2001/02.

Source: Table compiled from Sharma, K. "Economic Policy and Civil War in Nepal." Working Paper, *WIDER conference* (2004). Retrieved from http://website1.wider.unu.edu/conference/conference-2004-1/conference%202004-1-papers/Sharma-1905.pdf.

conservative 5 percent interest rate, the estimated accumulated total cost up to 1996 was 168.5 percent of the 1996 GDP. These calculations do not include reduced health quality and labor productivity, breakdown of law and order, emigration of skilled labor, disruption in the education system, reduced efficiency in investments, or infrastructural bottlenecks.

Nepal Civil War 1995–2006

Sharma presented the economic and social effects in Nepal focusing on the economic policy failure that led to the country's civil war. Sharma (1) considered that "the failure to redistribute the gains from economic growth was the net cause of the civil war that erupted in Nepal in 1995." The war resulted in the loss of more than 10,000 lives and massive damage to infrastructure and institutions. It also resulted in a drop in national output and earnings from exports and tourism. Sharma approached the consequences of the civil war by providing estimates of losses in output (GDP) and foreign exchange earnings in addition to losses from declining social services (see table 3.4). Sharma did not provide an aggregate cost for the civil war. He did not assign dollar values to the reduction in GDP and its future growth. A study conducted by the World Bank in 2005 assessed the impact of the conflict on the state and on the people of Nepal, including associated human rights, freedom of information, and civil society implications (Pyakuryal and Uprety).

Global and Interstate Wars

Global and interstate wars are conflicts between states for land, resources, ideologies, domination, religion, and other similar issues. Global wars involve a larger number of direct aggressors than do interstate wars, and interstate wars are invariably fought in a wider geographic area. Most importantly, and as a general rule, the consequences and losses of global wars are more severe than those of interstate wars. The two global wars discussed here are World War I and World War II. Interstate wars are smaller-scale wars, although they might include more than two aggressors. The interstate wars covered in this section are the Vietnam War and the Korean War. Costs of global and interstate wars depend on several variables such as the duration of the war, the proximity of where fighting is taking place to a hostile country, the absolute and the relative military

strength of the warring parties, and the results of the war, namely, victory
or defeat.

World War I

Seligman's study on World War I had focused only on the direct money
costs to the warring countries. His definition of direct money costs or
governmental expenditures on the war include "not only the actual outlays for military and naval purposes but also the whole range of expenditures incurred in industrial life to prepare the wherewithal for the
army and navy; and they also comprise the sums devoted to the maintenance of the families and soldiers" (741). These direct money costs also
include the compensation paid to citizens for war damages, pensions
to wounded soldiers and dependents of the dead, reconstruction costs,
higher prices, and loss on foreign exchange transactions due to depreciated currencies.

Seligman defined the average daily expenditures for the purposes of war
for each of the participating countries, distinguishing between expenditures in the war and expenditures for the war, by deducting from the actual
wartime expenditure the amount of ordinary or peacetime expenditures.
Peacetime expenditures are hard to estimate because they tend to grow
from year to year, and expenditures prior to the war might include preparations for the impending war. Because of the impracticality of making these
detailed corrections, Seligman deducted the amount of the expenditures in
the last year of peace from the expenditures in time of war. He estimated
war expenditures for most of the belligerent countries and made adjustments for double counting by deducting items such as the loans granted
by the United States, Great Britain, France, and Germany to their allies.
He also added the expenditures related to the war expected by the end of
1920. After these adjustments, the real money cost of the war is estimated
at $215 billion.

Seligman discussed the steps taken by different countries to meet
their outlays. He distinguished the differences in war-financing policies
adopted by different countries and the circumstances that influenced
their choices. He found that all countries relied on public loans, but
that Great Britain and the United States raised a greater share by taxation than did other countries. Seligman delved further into calculating
the amount of money raised by taxation compared to loans. He calculated the proceeds of the additional taxes raised during the war and not
the total yield of all taxes. Only slightly more than one-sixth of Great
Britain's war expenditures were in fact derived from war taxes. France,

because it was invaded and occupied and thus had difficulty imposing any new taxes, was not able to cover any part of its war expenditures by war taxes. Similarly, Russia did not rely on revenue from war taxation. War taxes raised by Italy were only sufficient to pay the interest on the war loans. Only DM5 billion of the DM204 billion in Germany's war expenditures were derived from sources other than loans. In the United States, less than one-fourth, or 23.3 percent, of war expenditures were paid from war taxes. Seligman pointed out that in almost all of the continental countries equal additional revenues were raised from indirect taxation as from direct taxation.

Seligman calculated the total indebtedness of the various aggressors after the war and found that Germany had the largest debt of all countries. The net debt of the world attributable to the war was calculated by subtracting total prewar debt from the debt at the close of the war, a sum amounting to $196 billion. Comparing the total amount of loans to the total cost of the war ($210 billion) clearly indicates the fact that almost the entire cost of the war was financed by loans. The $14–15 billion raised by taxes were mostly attributed to the efforts of Great Britain and the United States. Seligman concluded by stating: "It remains true, therefore, that the war was conducted almost entirely on credit" (770).

Clark's book, *The Costs of World War to the American People*, was based on the multiplier principle in anticipation of Keynesian economics (Fiorito). In his book, Clark considered "the cost of the war primarily as social aggregates of goods and services," which "are not postponed as a result of war borrowing" (Clark, 79). He believed that the social costs included the goods and services bought and spent by the government in time of war using borrowed money. He also added the cost of collecting war taxes and the fiscal administration of the war taxes and loans through the period of the war. Clark categorized the cost of the war into (1) costs of additional economic effort to provide surplus supplies or private capital invested for war purposes, and (2) goods and services taken out of the channels of normal private use. The elements that Clark considered to be costs of the war are summarized in table 3.5, but he did not provide an aggregate or a total cost for World War I.

World War II and the Korean War

The Ohanian study was focused on the economic effects of war finance. Ohanian evaluated the macroeconomic effects of different policies used to finance World War II and the Korean War. He used these two wars because of their striking differences. US war expenses were primarily

Table 3.5 Cost of World War I

	Category	Description
1	Government expenditures	Expenditures for war-related goods and services (federal, state, and local).
2	Loans and interests	Loans to the US allies and interest on US government borrowing (domestic vs. foreign loans).
3	Fiscal administration	The cost of fiscal administration that increased due to loans and that were spread over a longer period of time after the war ended.
4	Postwar fiscal items	Charges for debt, veteran care, and government compensations to citizens, with cash and services.
5	Taxes and inflation	The effects of increased taxes and inflation on total production.
6	Effect on industrial production	Effects on different industries during and after the war.
7	Extra consumption of natural materials	The extra consumption of coal and oil for war purposes.
8	Loss of life and health	Loss of income to the disabled and to the dependents of the dead, services involved in administering relief, hospitalization, vocational rehabilitation, etc.
9	Postwar military and naval expenses	Increase in military expenditures even after the end of the war.
10	Cost to the railroads	The financial costs of the congestion of terminals and of the strain on railroads due to the war, including government takeover and the reduction in efficiency.
11	Distribution of wealth	Effects of the war on the distribution of wealth between different industries and social classes.
12	Displacement of manpower	The extra effort spent to replace workforce taken from the industry into war service.
13	Immigration restriction and prohibition	Restrictions imposed because of war.
14	Intangible effects	Effects of labor, liberalism, social progress, crime waves, and excesses in lawlessness.

Source: Table compiled from Clark, J. M. *The Costs of the World Wars to the American People.* New York: Augustus M. Kelley Publishers, 1931.

financed by debt in World War II. This policy resulted in high inflation, which reached 9.6 percent during the war. A similar pattern of government financing policies was adapted during the Revolutionary War, the War of 1812, the Civil War, World War I, and, to some extent, during the Vietnam War. However, Korean War expenditures were financed almost exclusively by higher capital and labor taxes, which resulted in low inflation even by peacetime standards. World War II was financed 41 percent by direct taxes and 59 percent by debt. The Korean War was financed 100 percent by direct taxes. The average capital tax rate during the Korean War was 62 percent and the average labor tax rate was 20 percent compared to 60 percent and 18 percent, respectively, during World War II.

Ohanian used a general equilibrium model with capital and labor income taxation to analyze the welfare costs associated with these different policies and studied their effect on variables such as output and capital stock. He applied a counterfactual experiment to explore the implications of World War II financing using policies such as those used during the Korean War. He concluded that using the Korean War balanced-budget policy during World War II would have resulted in much lower economic output and thus in lower welfare. A permanent and significant increase in consumption would have been required to compensate households under the Korean War policy for World War II. The cost was high and it reflected the sharp increase in labor and capital income taxation associated with a policy that maximizes contemporary tax revenue from labor and capital income. Macroeconomic variables such as labor input and output fell considerably and capital stock dropped. The significant decline in capital stock would have resulted in permanent reductions in leisure and consumption after the war. On the other hand, the use of the World War II financing policy during the Korean War would have resulted in modest welfare gains relative to the policy that was eventually used. Ohanian found that the relative cost of the Korean War would have been reduced by about 30 percent if a World War II financing approach had been adopted. He calculated the additional amount of consumption that would have had to be given to households such that their level of satisfaction was constant under a specific policy compared to the baseline policy. This calculation indicated that a 3 percent increase in consumption would have been required to compensate households if the Korean War financing model had been adopted during the World War II. Ohanian emphasized the changes in output and in labor supply that occurred during the two wars and found that these showed sharp increases in World War II, while more modest increases were observed during the Korean War. He associated this increase during World War II to the adopted debt financing policy. Ohanian's results contradict the general Keynesian approach to war financing emphasizing the benefits of higher taxes compared to higher borrowing.

Vietnam War

Although there have been several estimates for the Vietnam War, only a few have accounted for the complete war. Campagna offered such a complete coverage of war costs based on a methodology that included four major components:

- the actual budgetary costs of the war,
- the future budgetary costs related to the war,
- other undetected economic costs of the war, and
- indirect costs attributed to the war.

The final cost of the war was calculated by aggregating all values assigned to these variables. Table 3.6 summarizes the elements included in actual budgetary cost.

In the future budgetary cost category, Campagna included costs that did not stop with the war's official end. He concluded that expenditures associated with veterans after the war were significantly higher than the direct costs of the war. In addition, he argued that if the benefits of veterans' dependents were included, the costs of the war "may extend to as much as 100 years after the war was concluded" (99). He also added the interest expense to the future budgetary costs. Under the economic costs category, he calculated the cost of the military draft and the lost output of those dead and injured. The items included in Campagna's future and economic costs are listed in table 3.7.

In the other costs category, Campagna added losses in foreign trade. He believed that net exports would have been much higher in the absence of the war. His estimates account for merchandise trade, net investment income, net travel balances, and other services. Campagna discussed indirect costs, but he did not include them in his final calculation for the total cost of the war. He concluded that the diversion of resources from the private to the defense sector during the war had harmful effects on the nation's productive capacity. He also included the effects of the war on the defense establishment through deferred military investments; the Department of Defense was forced to downsize its weapons research, development, and testing and construction programs because of the war.

Table 3.6 Budgetary Cost of the Vietnam War

	Category	Description
1	The Office of Management and Budget (OMB) and Department of Defense (DOD) official numbers	These estimates included only material purchased for the Vietnam War excluding items used from existing stocks.
2	Adjustments to DOD numbers	Necessary because the DOD did not include the full personnel costs and because of the understatement of the full costs during the period from 1965 to 1967. The DOD did not make any estimates for the full costs of the personnel in Southeast Asia in the early years of the war. Campagna adjusted the cost of personnel by assuming that for every member of the armed forces in combat there were 1.5 or 2 times that number required for support.
3	Direct personnel costs prior to 1965	Costs not calculated by the DOD.
4	US military aid	Military aid to France and Emperor Bao Dai from 1950 to 1954, Laos and Thailand from 1950 to 1966, Cambodia from 1950 to 1976, and South Vietnam from 1953 to 1965. The author includes those costs based on the assumption that the aid was "motivated by the need to retain control or influence over the other nations contiguous to the conflict" (97).
5	US economic aid	Economic aid to Indochina and South Vietnam 1950–1976.
6	Support for the Free World Military Assistance Forces	Including South Korea, the Philippines, and Thailand from 1965 to 1969.
7	Related CIA expenditures	This item was mentioned but without any estimates since the information was confidential for the funds used by the CIA to "secure cooperation, to finance operations before they were legitimized, and to buy compliance of officials to adhere to U.S. goals" (98).

Source: Table compiled from Campagna, A. S. *Economic Consequences of the Vietnam War*. New York: Praeger, 1991.

Table 3.7   Future and Economic Costs of the Vietnam War

Category	Description
Future Costs	
1 Costs associated with veterans	Campagna used calculations made by Clayton (1970) to estimate the costs associated with war veterans. Clayton estimated veteran benefits to be 101% of the original budgetary cost of WWII and 184% for the Korean war. Campagna applied an average of 142% of the budgetary costs to estimate the future costs of the veteran benefits.
2 Interest costs	Campagna also used Clayton's estimates of interest rate costs: that the costs of interest expense over time would amount to 20% of the total budgetary costs.
Economic Costs	
3 Cost of the draft	The conscription tax applied to those who were drafted or those who volunteered under the threat of induction.
4 Loss of output of the dead or injured	The author multiplied the average annual earning of males aged 20 years and older by the number of people killed (57,777) and by 40 years to get the total earning loss. He did not make estimates for the earnings loss of the disabled or hospitalized.

Source: Table compiled from Campagna, A. S. *Economic Consequences of the Vietnam War*. New York: Praeger, 1991.

Campagna adopted the approach of Robert Stevens in attributing the recession of 1970 through 1972, higher inflation, and the loss of international trade to the war. The cost of the recession was calculated as the difference between actual and potential (in the absence of war) Gross National Product in the recession years of 1970 through 1972. The burden of higher inflation was also added as an indirect cost of the war. Adopting a 2 percent rate as the normal yearly rate of inflation, Stevens multiplied the actual inflation rate in excess of 2 percent in each year by GNP to arrive at an estimate of the cost of higher inflation. Finally, the effects of the dollar devaluations in 1971 and 1973 on international trade, especially on imports, were estimated and added to the indirect costs of the war.

In his final aggregation, Campagna added the direct budgetary costs to future economic and foreign trade costs, resulting in a figure of $515 billion. Adding the indirect costs of deferred military investment, recession, inflation, and loss in international trade to this figure would result in a figure of $900 billion as the total cost of the Vietnam War for the United States alone.

Postwar Costs

The consequences and fallouts of wars never end with armistice, or the official end of wars. Besides the possibility of inciting future conflicts, wars have consequences on economic growth, on physical infrastructure such as power distribution, health, and education, on societal and cultural behavior, and even on literature and art, and these consequences span decades after the last shot has been fired. Valuable research on post-conflict costs has been undertaken to quantify and analyze some of the main components of these consequences. We cover some of this literature with a focus on post-conflict economic growth.

Productivity Effects

Dickinson analyzed the impact of World War I on postwar industrial productivity in the United States. He challenged the prosperity argument for war by examining the effects of World War I on economic growth. He compared postwar production to that of the pre-World War I period. He determined the rate of growth in physical volume of production and other measures of economic activity during the prewar period. He then extrapolated these prewar trends in growth rates into the postwar period to determine whether the rates of growth were maintained at their prewar pace. He chose the years between 1899 and 1913 as the prewar period. Dickinson's findings contradicted the conventional wisdom prevailing at the time by showing that World War I had a negative impact on the US economy (Raemdonck and Diehl). After extrapolating the prewar rates of growth into the two postwar decades, he concluded that only in the best years of the 1920s did the average index of production reach this trend line. He believed that the deficit in production in the postwar period was an after-cost effect of World War I. As a result, Dickinson calculated the post-World War I cost to the American people as almost four times the volume of goods produced in 1929.

Impact on Economic Growth

Van Raemdonck and Diehl covered the literature focusing on postwar economic growth. They classified the major investigations into two, according to their theoretical perspectives on postwar economic growth:

I. Research indicating that wars had positive effects on economic growth:

Argument 1: War resulted in improved efficiency and protection of industry largely because of the protective efforts of a more powerful government. Greater government control over the economy had positive effects. The control and protection of industry by the government continued after the end of the war leading to higher efficiency.

Argument 2: War resulted in technological improvement. Governments expand during war and energize research and development efforts to develop better weaponry. These efforts continued after the end of the war and had positive spillover effects.

Argument 3: War enhanced production efficiency. Plants and industrial equipment destroyed by the war are usually replaced by more advanced and efficient infrastructure.

Argument 4: War prompted exploration for new sources of raw materials.

Argument 5: War resulted in the development of better transportation and communication facilities that yielded benefit after the end of the war.

Argument 6: War led to advances in human capital, including managerial and organizational skills.

II. Research indicating that wars had negative effects on economic growth:

Argument 1: War led to government control over the economy during the war. Greater government control over the economy had negative economic consequences. This greater control often extended into the post-war period.

Argument 2: War caused an immediate and significant decline in economic output, especially in states that lost the war.

Argument 3: War resulted in a dramatic drift in governments' allocation of resources from civilian and development to the military.

Argument 4: War ended with big debt burdens that compromised capital investments.

The authors then looked at the literature covering the two world wars. They found that most authors agreed on the detrimental effects of trade interruption during World War I and the consequent need to make institutional and financial arrangements to ensure economic recovery. As for World War II, they found that there was some consensus among scholars on the economic recovery after the war. They point to three major findings: (1) the planning and reorganization of the international financial system by the allies and the efforts toward European integration led to the free trade of goods and services and to rapid economic expansion; (2) government economic planning and restructuring organized and enhanced domestic economic growth and recovery; and (3) the absence of demand for reparations after World War II (as compared to World War I) helped energize the recovery process. But there was less agreement on the contribution of the European Recovery Plan (ERP), or what is commonly referred to as the Marshall Plan, to economic growth in Europe. The authors concluded that postwar economic growth is dependent on three factors: the characteristic of the war, the characteristics of the countries involved, and postwar economic policies.

Educational Costs of War

Ichino and Winter-Ebmer studied the resulting loss of human capital suffered by school-age children as a result of war. Wars interrupt educational achievement for school-age children. Several factors contribute to this loss in education. During wars, physical access to schools might become compromised because of security reasons, bombings, fighting, army requisitions, and transportation difficulties. Death or injury of a family member might put a financial burden on the family structure, depriving school-age children of the ability to continue their education even after the end of the war. Consequently, children might have to take the place of their lost or impaired family member and become breadwinners by starting to work earlier.

The authors provide evidence of economic losses associated with the impact of war on education by comparing two countries whose civilian populations were severely affected by World War II (Austria and Germany) with two countries that did not directly enter the conflict (Sweden and Switzerland). They found that Austrians and Germans who were ten years old during or immediately after the war went to school for a significantly shorter period of time than similar-aged children in Sweden and Switzerland, and in turn concluded that the disruption of the educational process caused by the war was the most likely explanation. They then assessed the impact of war by calculating the average loss in earnings suffered by the children who received less education. They found that

Austrian and German children whose education was compromised also experienced a loss in labor income that was evident 40 years after the end of the war. On the other hand, Swedish and Swiss children born in the 1930s whose education was unaffected did not experience a loss in income 40 years later. Consequently, the war not only affected the education of children but also their future earnings. This was estimated to have caused a reduction in earnings of 0.8 percent of GDP in Germany and Austria.

Welfare Costs of Conflicts

Hess calculated a lower limit estimate for the welfare costs of war by assessing forgone consumption. He attempted to "price" the effect that war had on economic growth and on consumption volatility. To find this price, he calculated how much individuals would be willing to give up in exchange for living in a peaceful world. Hess compared the expected welfare of each country staying on its actual path of consumption to the counterfactual path of consumption if there had been no war. By equating the two consumption paths he was able to "price" the amount an individual would be willing to give up on an annual basis to be on the peaceful path. Hess (5) tried to answer the question, "What is the direct economic welfare loss from conflict?" The calculation reveals the absolute minimum that people would pay in order to enjoy the economic benefits of peace. Hess estimated the historical effects of conflict on the path of consumption and provided estimates of the change in per capita consumption growth rate and its fluctuation in cases of transition from the current conflict path to a peaceful path for 147 countries. He studied both internal and external conflicts. He divided internal conflicts into ethnic conflicts, genocides, revolutions, and regime changes. External conflicts were further classified based on their impact (big or small) and their geographical location (home or away). Hess adopted the permanent income hypothesis (PIH) to develop a baseline specification for a country's per capita consumption growth and how the conflict might affect it. Among the 147 countries for which consumption data existed, he estimated the effect of conflict on real per capita consumption growth. Similarly, he estimated the effects of eliminating different types of conflict on the variance of mean-adjusted consumption growth to calculate the impact of conflict on economic volatility.

Hess concluded that the world could benefit greatly from eliminating conflicts. He stated that "A world consumer who lives in a country that has experienced conflict over the time period considered...would willingly give up approximately 9 percent of his annual level of consumption as a onetime payment in order to live in a world of perpetual peace" (Hess,

2003, 18). He assigned an actual dollar value to the lower-bound estimate of the cost of war by multiplying each country's calculated cost of conflict by their actual per capita and total consumption. He found that the countries whose citizens would be willing to pay the most to avoid conflict are Iraq, Iran, Qatar, Algeria, and Syria. The total world cost of conflicts in 1985 dollars and for the level of population in 1985 was estimated at $399.12 billion. This, of course, represents a clear and gross underestimate of the cost of conflict because individuals are not aware of the total destruction and damage of war or of its future costs, not only in the form of future conflicts but also in payments to veterans, to those injured by war, and the full impact thereof on economic growth.

A Summary of the Literature and Our Preferred Framework

It would be useful to have a standard framework and methodology to calculate the cost of all wars and conflicts. Would this methodology reflect an accurate cost of each and every war? This seems highly unlikely. But estimates of the cost of wars are still important if conflicts and wars are to be discouraged. It is better to have rough estimates than nothing at all; as John Maynard Keynes famously said, "It is better to be vaguely right than being precisely wrong." The framework and methodology should also assess the consequences of conflicts and wars on the region and on neighboring countries.

Broadly, there are two distinct and broad approaches to assessing the cost of conflicts and wars. First, estimated foregone GDP is used to represent the cost of wars. This approach may result in an underestimation of the cost because it does not include the destruction of certain assets (for example, historic site or general environmental degradation) that cannot be rebuilt and that may not directly contribute to GDP (if, for example, a tourist site was not open to tourists). This approach of looking at foregone GDP to represent the cost of wars may also not fully account for the cost of human fatalities and injuries, because unemployment, for example, would mean that human fatalities would not show up in lost GDP. The second approach is to estimate the cost of all assets that were destroyed, including human fatalities and injuries (the human toll could also be assessed as a separate category). This approach may also result in underestimation because it does not include all lost economic output; the replacement cost of a machine, for example, does not reflect a true picture of economic fallout.

We prefer a third framework or approach, one that combines both of these approaches but is careful to avoid double counting. We should stress that no matter how carefully the calculation is done, it may be difficult to avoid a small degree of double counting. Additionally, even this more "comprehensive" approach must include a discounted value for the post-conflict costs. It should encompass foregone economic output and costs of future wars that might result from the conflict or its unjust settlement. In the following section, we describe in more detail a comprehensive framework for estimating the global cost of wars.

Calculating the Global Cost of War—the Suggested Framework

So far we have discussed various approaches to costing different types of military conflicts. Here we hope to summarize a comprehensive framework to estimate the global cost of wars. By global cost we mean not only the macroeconomic and budgetary costs inflicted on direct belligerents, but also costs incurred by neighboring countries in the region and even farther afield, including budgetary and macroeconomic damage.

One could reasonably argue that if an armed conflict arises between any two countries in a region or between two countries in regions that are far apart, it would impact numerous neighboring countries. Furthermore, that conflict, if long lasting and sufficiently serious, could have some significant economic and political consequences for the rest of the world. For example, the major armed conflicts in the Persian Gulf—namely, the Iran-Iraq War and the two Persian Gulf Wars—have had a profound impact on energy markets and on the local environment and ecosystem.

As already discussed, focusing on the military or budgetary costs of wars neglects what is invariably a major cost of wars, namely, lost economic output. There are also numerous hard-to-quantify costs, such as environmental costs. In our preferred framework, we try to include the most destructive repercussion of wars, namely, macroeconomic costs or the costs to national economies. Table 3.8 contains most, if not all, budgetary and macroeconomic costs to direct belligerents.

In order to develop a comprehensive approach, we categorize the global cost of wars under three groupings: (i) cost to direct belligerents, (ii) cost to neighboring countries, and (iii) cost to the rest of the world. For each grouping (what we could loosely refer to as geographical groupings, especially ii and iii), we consider both budgetary and macroeconomic costs. We must emphasize that classifying the cost of wars in three groups by no means suggests that cost incurred by each group is independent of

Table 3.8 Global Cost of War—Cost to Direct Belligerents

Budgetary Costs	1. Direct war spending (including all combat and support operation costs).
	2. Total cost of veterans' medical care (including all types of medical benefits, disability pay, and treatment costs).
	3. Budgetary cost of fatalities (e.g., government payment to the families of soldiers).
	4. Government expenditures on relief (for refugees and resettlement).
	5. Budgetary cost of reconstruction.
	6. Higher postwar defense spending—as a result of war.
	7. Loan burden and interest payments on war-related debt.
	8. Cost of war reparations.
Macroeconomic Costs	1. Lost economic output (due to forgone domestic and foreign investment, lost oil revenues, higher energy prices,[1] reduced tourist arrivals, destruction of capital and infrastructure, fatalities and disabilities, brain drain, refugees, lower productivity, higher inflation, cost of alternative import/export routes, and economic sanctions and trade embargos).
	2. Accelerated depreciation of military hardware.
	3. Costs associated with diverted government expenditures (because of higher spending on defense instead of productive expenditures such as education, health care, etc.).
	4. Environmental costs (due to military operations and oil spills).

Note: [1]Mainly for energy-importing economies.

the others. For example, if a resource-exporting economy is engaged in a military conflict, the likely higher cost of imports for the rest of the world (due to higher resource prices) is in turn translated to economic benefits for other resource-exporting countries. On the other hand, heightened appetite for more military expenditures in a region because of a conflict—despite having a detrimental long-term effect on the economy of countries in that region—is an opportunity for the world's top arms exporters to boost their defense industries. We should acknowledge that we cannot simply sum up all the costs incurred by all geographical areas—direct belligerents, the neighbors, and the rest of the world—and present the bottom line of the calculation as the global cost of a particular war; such a practice may be exposed to significant double counting.[1] The main purpose for this classification is to investigate the direct and indirect costs of war from three specific perspectives. Thus, we need specific, careful adjustments to our regional cost calculations to arrive at the global cost of wars. Moreover, for moral considerations we should also recognize that the suffering and misery of one nation or region resulting from bad policies and defective decision making cannot, and should not, be cancelled out by the economic benefits of other nations from the same inappropriate policies.

In what follows, we discuss in a little more detail our proposed framework for estimating the global cost of wars. We should also mention that there is another category of war-related costs—items at least equally as important as the other two categories that are even more difficult to estimate and to quantify—that will at least be listed. In chapter 5, we use this framework to estimate the global cost of the Iran-Iraq War, the 1991 Persian Gulf War (the occupation of Kuwait), and the 2003 Persian Gulf War (the invasion of Iraq, also referred to as the Iraq War).

Cost to Direct Belligerents

One could reasonably argue that the direct belligerents to a conflict or war can normally be expected to suffer more than other countries. Direct belligerents incur a number of costs not incurred by other countries, including resources spent on mobilizing troops and acquiring military hardware (including planes, warships, artillery, and air defense systems), the destruction of infrastructure, and invariably a significant reduction in national output due to casualties, injuries, the destruction of factories and industrial areas, and lower investment in productive activities. Direct belligerents not only incur the direct costs of war, chiefly in the form of budgetary costs, but also have to deal with the horrific consequences of war after the cessation of hostilities. The macroeconomic side effects of war, almost totally ignored by policy makers, leaders, and politicians at the onset of the war, are not as straightforward as are budgetary costs. They are profound, long lasting, and detrimental to long-term economic growth, national welfare, and citizens' quality of life. Here, we first itemize all budgetary costs a typical belligerent would incur during the course of a conflict and then turn to macroeconomic costs.

Budgetary costs: The combat and construction components cost are normally reflected on a government's budget and are usually subject to parliamentary approval. But estimating the budgetary cost of war is not as straightforward as it might at first appear.

The first cost item is the direct spending on combat and support operations. As war preparations begin, the first cost is the cost of mobilization. Each party to a dispute has to reorganize its armed forces, hire new personnel, call reserves to duty, and so on. Although initially these costs may be low, the continuing cost of keeping active forces operational, effective, and efficient could quickly spiral upward and paralyze a national economy, especially when the war lasts for months or years. The cost of replacing destroyed, damaged, worn, or out-of-use military hardware and facilities, of buying new jet fighters, warships, and radar facilities, of replenishing missiles and arsenals, of transporting hardware and personnel, and, more importantly, of keeping military personnel operational for an extended period is crippling for almost any country. At the end of war, of course, countries practically reverse what they did at the start of conflict. Demobilization costs consist of all costs required to turn an armed force from wartime to peacetime status. In sum, this cost category includes all mobilization and demobilization costs plus all the military costs of war.

Some of the most significant cost items of war continue well after the war ends, such as the cost of medical care for veterans. In addition to the significant impact of casualties and disabilities on national economic output and the quality of life—which will be discussed in detail later—there are also budgetary implications. In addition to the compensatory payments to the families of fallen military personnel, the most burdensome category of these costs is invariably long-term compensatory payments to the injured and the cost of their long-term medical treatment.

Unfortunately, the devastating consequences of war are not limited to the military. The damage invariably extends to civilians and civilian life. A direct impact on civilians is their displacement and migration to safer locations within the belligerent country, to neighboring countries, or even to countries outside of the region.[2] The cost of resettling refugees in a country embroiled in war invariably falls on the government, because governments are generally responsible for transporting refugees to safer areas, building new residential areas, and providing new infrastructure and support. These costs could easily skyrocket if a war lasts long enough to persuade displaced populations not to go back to their homeland and instead simply abandon their original homes. Here we need to emphasize that the consequences of population displacement is significant, deleterious, and long lasting, and cannot be simply reflected in a country's lost economic output during the course of the war.

One thing that governments usually ignore completely, or downplay when they are about to engage in a military conflict, is the cost of reconstructing cities and infrastructure. When a war continues for some time, civil and industrial areas, roads, transportation systems, and infrastructure become targets. The consequence is devastated infrastructure, industries, and civil areas. Postwar, a significant increase in military budgets is not as apparent as other categories of war-related costs. It can be reasonably expected that after a war the sense of security in a society as a whole, and specifically among politicians, collapses, resulting in the adoption of more conservative and aggressive policies. The first consequence of this changed political atmosphere and sense of insecurity is significantly higher-than-normal military budgets and investments in defense industries. Of course, this is not solely the case for direct belligerents. The sense of insecurity and lack of peace in a region affects not only policies adopted in countries involved in a conflict but also motivates neighbors and even countries far away from the area of conflict to increase their defense expenditures. One way to detect this incremental increase in defense budgets is to track the trend of military expenditures before, during, and after a conflict and see whether an unusual trend emerges after a war.

Military conflict rapidly exacerbates a government's financial footing. While this might not be as readily apparent for global powers that are rich, have mature economies, and are sufficiently advanced and flexible to absorb the economic shock of military conflicts, the government sources of income in most developing economies are insufficient to finance a costly war. However, the 2008 financial crisis has laid bare the budgetary constraints of even the United States in meeting its domestic needs while simultaneously fighting two costly foreign wars. In the early stage of war, developing countries usually draw resources from other sectors of the economy to finance their war effort, but after domestic resources are depleted, governments inevitably turn to foreign sources for loans.[3]

A final cost item—in budgetary cost to direct belligerents—is war reparation. A word of caution is in order. When we include war reparation in our calculation, it is important to be careful how reparations are accounted for and what the figures mean. If the assessed war damage was $100 and the aggressor paid reparations of $100, adding up the damage and the payment of war reparations would result in $200 as the cost of the war. This is clearly incorrect. From a country standpoint, the receipt of reparations cancels some (or all) of the ravages of war; for the aggressor, the payment of reparations is an addition to its war-related costs. But from a global perspective, the payment and receipt of reparations is a simple transfer and does not affect the global cost of a conflict. If war reparations are forthcoming, they should be carefully reflected in the country-by-country and global cost calculations. Thus far, we have covered and discussed most important items of budgetary cost to the direct belligerents. In the next section, we focus on the broader category of war-related costs, namely macroeconomic costs.

Macroeconomic costs: As Stiglitz and Bilmes (2008) suggest, macroeconomic costs are totally different from budgetary costs. First, macroeconomic costs are borne by the national economy, while budgetary costs are borne by governments; second, the prices paid by governments do not reflect the full market value of war losses; and finally, macroeconomic costs reflect the long-term impact of war on economic growth while budgetary costs are only limited to costs born by governments. For example, the lost economic output (opportunity costs) due to sending troops—otherwise in duty as civilian servants—to war zones, or the healthcare costs borne by soldiers and their families are examples of costs borne by national economies as a whole.

Lost economic output is a very broad term for what is invariably a devastating effect of war on the national economy of a direct belligerent. There are many channels through which a military conflict affects an economy. War per se is a state of abnormality. Almost all normal economic settings virtually become abnormal during war. The most likely consequence of this shift is a drop in total economic output, especially in developing countries where the national economy is not large and sufficiently flexible to easily absorb the macroeconomic shock of war.

Destruction of infrastructure and capital is one of the main results of national economic decay during and after a war. Besides the budgetary costs of damaged and ruined infrastructure, there exists a significantly higher macroeconomic cost in the form of opportunity cost of diminished or damaged capital and infrastructure. Thus, an economy not only pays the cost of reconstruction but also suffers from the lost economic opportunity of utilizing these physical and capital resources. The destruction of power and transportation systems and physical damage to factories and the industrial sector in general hurt both quantity of output and productivity, resulting in lower output during and after a war.

Apart from the extensive cost of damage to infrastructure and capital, there is another significant cost incurred by belligerents in the form of lost economic output because of fatalities, injured workers, and a displaced population—refugees and the related brain drain. For example, all belligerents in the three major Persian Gulf wars, including the United States, incurred huge opportunity costs. Moreover, even if a country doesn't lose its productive labor force in a conflict and even if workers do not migrate to other countries, there is still another lost opportunity cost, namely, in addition to the budgetary cost of military recruits, there is a macroeconomic cost as labor is shifted from productive civilian occupations, public and private, to military service. As already shown in a number of studies (Stiglitz and Bilmes; Wallsten and Kosec), the human resource-related cost of wars—fatalities, injuries, refugees, and opportunity cost of military recruits—has a significant long-term impact on a national economy, a cost that may invariably be underestimated.

Forgone domestic and foreign investment and reduced tourist arrivals are two other macroeconomic costs of war. Developing countries need foreign and domestic resources to grow their national economies. Tourism and foreign direct investment are both critical resources for a number of thriving economies, especially where there is the potential and capacity for growth. Conflicts and wars frighten tourists and the additional business risks associated with wars encourage the withdrawal of foreign investment and deter new foreign investment. These are real costs for belligerents and neighboring countries as war takes the risk of travel and investment in a region to another level.

Higher inflation rates, trade embargos and economic sanctions, and the higher costs associated with using alternative import and export routes are additional costs of conflicts and wars. Higher inflation rates restrain economic growth and prosperity. Trade embargos and economic sanctions shift the aggregate supply curve faced by a country upward, raising the cost of imports while lowering the demand curve for exports and reducing export revenues and, in turn, confining reduced economic output and its growth.

Another macroeconomic cost is the accelerated depreciation of military hardware. As Stiglitz and Bilmes suggest, there is a difference between the estimate of the budgetary and economic costs associated with military hardware. While the budgetary cost is focused on replacement expenditures, the economic cost is driven by the faster rate of depreciation of hardware and surprisingly does not stop when the war ends. The rate of utilization of military hardware increases during war—with material and equipment used up to five times the normal rate of utilization in peacetime (as assumed by the US Department of Defense).

One of the most critical macroeconomic costs of war is associated with the diverted government expenditures from investment and other more productive expenditures to the military and defense sectors. If a government does not spend on war and the preparations for war, it could spend the money on health care, infrastructure, science, education, and so on. One of the standard methodologies used to analyze different expenditure scenarios is "expenditure switching" (Stiglitz and Bilmes). Regarding different leakage and consequently multiplier effects of different government expenditures, one can simply estimate the effect of switching from one type of budgetary expenditure—war or defense expenditures in this case—to other more productive types of government expenditures. It is apparent that the fiscal multipliers of defense and war expenditures are lower than the fiscal multipliers of investment in infrastructure, science, or education. Ideally, we should isolate the opportunity cost of not investing in the public sector, but in our estimation in chapter 5 we are limited to assessing the costs associated with diverted aggregate government expenditures.

A final macroeconomic cost is that to the environment. What makes environmental damage important is first its enduring effect, and second the depth of its impact. It is almost impossible to get rid of many forms of environmental damage quickly and totally. However, environmental costs of war are routinely ignored in most assessments of the cost of wars. Oil spill in all three Persian Gulf wars, Iraq's use of chemical weapons in the Iran-Iraq War, the impact of the extensive oil well fires that were set, and the depleted uranium[4] used by allied forces in the last two Persian Gulf wars are just four examples of the extensive, enduring environmental damage of armed conflicts.

We now turn to a brief discussion of the budgetary and macroeconomic burdens on neighboring countries and on the rest of the world.

Cost to Neighboring Countries

In table 3.9 we delineate the major budgetary and macroeconomic costs to countries that are in the neighborhood of a conflict or war.

Table 3.9 Global Cost of War—Cost to Neighboring Countries

Budgetary Costs	1. Military and financial aid to the direct belligerents. 2. Higher defense budgets. 3. Costs associated with refugees. 4. Payment to global powers for war and military protection.
Macroeconomic Costs	1. Lost economic output (higher cost of trade, forgone domestic & foreign investment, and reduced tourist arrivals, higher energy prices, cost of higher inflation, cost of alternative import/export routes). 2. Costs associated with diverted government expenditures. 3. Environmental costs.

Budgetary costs: Neighboring countries invariably get involved in a war or conflict in their region, either directly or indirectly. Their involvement could be financial and/or military in nature. While neighbors could stand aside and be totally neutral, they tend to pick one or both sides of a conflict depending on their strategic regional game-plan, on specific economic benefits, cultural closeness to one side, fierce hostility toward another side, and so on. In addition to supporting one side in a war, neighboring countries could also increase their defense expenditures significantly during and after an armed conflict in a region.[5] A principal reason for increasing military expenditures is perhaps the sense of heightened insecurity due to current or past military conflicts and threats in the region.

Another budgetary cost incurred by nonbelligerents in a region is the cost associated with refugees. Also, weak countries may sometimes pay global military powers to protect their interests against regional threats.[6]

Macroeconomic costs: The national economy of non-belligerent neighbors, like that of direct belligerents, can be expected to suffer from the repercussions of a war in the region. Many factors may hinder normal economic growth, such as the higher cost of international trade, a higher risk for foreign and domestic investors, reduced tourist arrivals, higher energy prices, cost of higher inflation, and the costs of using alternative import/export routes. The initiation of war between two countries also usually leads neighboring countries to increase their military expenditures as the sense of security between countries deteriorates. As discussed earlier, almost all countries could easily feel the environmental damages to a regional ecosystem.

Cost to the Rest of the World

The budgetary and macroeconomic cost of war for the rest of the world depends on the economic importance of countries involved in the conflict

Table 3.10   Global Cost of War—Cost to the Rest of the World

Budgetary Costs	1. Military and financial aid to the direct belligerents.
	2. Increased defense budget due to higher global insecurity.
Macroeconomic Costs	1. Higher cost of trade due to higher risk and insecurity.
	2. Possible higher resource prices.
	3. Costs associated with diverted government expenditures.

or of the region. For example, Western military powers might simply ignore fierce, bloody armed conflicts in remote areas of sub-Saharan Africa but never hesitate to meddle in Persian Gulf affairs if a crisis or threat arises in the region, because of the strategic importance of the region for the rest of the world. In table 3.10, we list the main budgetary and macroeconomic war-related costs for the rest of the world.

Budgetary costs: In the world of politics and national interests, it is normal to take sides in a conflict. In armed conflicts, other countries around the world may militarily and financially support one or both sides to the conflict. However, the bottom line is always more budgetary burden for the supporting country's taxpayers.

For the rest of the world—especially global superpowers—to pursue their strategic goals and national interests in the region, it is almost impossible not to increase their military expenditures when a major conflict or crisis arises, especially if it lasts for a long time. Invariably, the first reaction of a global power to a threat is to ramp up its military presence, which immediately translates into higher defense budgets. In chapter 5, we discuss how the military expenditures of global powers increased at the time of the Persian Gulf War in 1991 and were sustained at a higher level for years after the conflict.

Macroeconomic costs: In addition to the higher cost of trade and the cost associated with diverted government expenditures, higher resource prices—energy and raw material prices—could inflict a critical macroeconomic shock to the rest of the world when an armed conflict takes place in a region, or between two countries, if they are major commodity exporters. Perhaps the prime example is the impact on energy prices from every conflict in the Persian Gulf.

Almost unquantifiable costs of wars:

> In addition to the categories of war-related costs discussed above (some of which we find already hard to quantify), there is a set of genuinely even harder to measure costs from wars that include:
> - higher dependency on resource export revenues—especially in developing economies,
> - cost associated with increased sense of insecurity,
> - cost associated with lower quality of life for citizens—emotional and psychological effects,
> - negative effects on financial markets,
> - long-term consequences of tighter monetary policies and weaker fiscal positions,
> - growth of extremism and absence of civil society, and
> - negative effects on the distribution of wealth and income.

Concluding Remarks

It is difficult, if not impossible, to include accurate estimates for every war-related cost. A number of the studies focus only on specific aspects of wars—effects on growth, productivity, and the like. The majority of studies include only the readily apparent budgetary costs of armed conflicts, and a few have a comprehensive perspective that includes the long-term macroeconomic damage of wars to national economies. An important and critical cost that is invariably ignored is that for neighboring countries and for the global economy as a whole. Some studies are limited to developing a descriptive framework and do not provide a quantitative approach for assessing the war-related costs of a military conflict. In our preferred framework, we have included the fallout for neighboring countries and for the rest of the world separately. We also include current and postwar budgetary and macroeconomic costs. But we recognize that we are still forced to omit a number of critical war-related costs, such as environmental damage and degradation, because they are difficult to quantify.

We should emphasize the need to recognize and incorporate all possible fallouts of conflicts and wars to come up with the true fallout price, or the most representative price, of aggression so as to dissuade would-be aggressors and those who support them. All parties to conflict, both the direct belligerents as well as those who have had a less direct role, must be assessed the damage they have caused on all those affected by the conflict. Thus, countries that have sowed the seeds of conflict, fueled conflicts, or have given or sold military equipment or provided financial support to a party in the conflict must be assessed damages. Similarly, companies that have sold lethal military equipment to a warring party must be assessed damages as well. These damages can be based on the same framework we have suggested but simply on a proportional basis. That is to say, if a direct belligerent's total military expenditures connected to a conflict was $10x over a certain period, and if a company sold $x of military equipment to the country during the same period that the country incurred the $10x in military expenditures, then the company would be assessed 10 percent of the total damages or reparations that were assessed on the country. Assessing damages in this way would, of course, mean that there would be double counting of some damages; in this case, the direct belligerent is assessed the full damage and the arms supplier is also assessed a proportional damage. Today, belligerents are not exactly lining up to pay reparations. If the day comes that every responsible party pays, such excess assessments could go into a special account to fund development projects around the world and to fund some of the projects connected to our proposed initiative discussed in chapter 6.

Finally, we should note that the more these calculations, their size, their payment (through the various means discussed in chapter 6), and the success of this initiative are advertised (named and shamed) around the world, the more citizens will embrace this effort and make acts of aggression less likely. Citizens around the world must become active participants and must bring pressure to bear on aggressors to create a world without war.

Chapter 4

The Seeds of Conflict and War: The Persian Gulf

Over the past 30 years, the Persian Gulf has witnessed three devastating wars, with a heavy price for the warring parties and with significant spillover effects for noncombatants in the region and for countries and regions much farther afield. The wars had historical roots and were interrelated. Both endogenous and exogenous dynamics fueled and sustained these wars. The full extent of the human toll, environmental degradation, destruction of property, and loss of economic output is still to be fully analyzed. There is little doubt that these devastating wars and the other ongoing conflicts in the region, if not reconciled amicably, will spawn more conflicts and wars in the future. For this reason alone, the economic costs of conflicts today understate actual costs that can be calculated only after the passage of time and with the definitive end of all resulting conflicts. Can a fourth war be avoided while the tragedies of past wars are still haunting the region and rubbing raw the wounds?

To see how a fourth war in the region might be deterred, we begin by briefly examining the history of the Persian Gulf wars, especially how these wars were sparked and fueled, how they might have been avoided, and what their human, financial, and economic toll has been? We examine the causes of these recent wars in the Persian Gulf, the efforts to deter them, and why these efforts in the cause of peace were not successful. We conclude with the lessons learned—lessons that might be instructive for avoiding future wars in this and other regions.

The history of the Persian Gulf is multifaceted. Arabs, Kurds, Persians, and Turks are the region's major ethnicities, with nuanced and important distinctions also along religious lines. Despite the region's deep historic roots, the emergence of nation-states is a relatively new phenomenon, created (with the exception of Iran) in the early half of the twentieth century by colonial powers. Persian Gulf countries sit atop a huge wealth of oil and natural gas, arguably the two most valuable traded natural resources in the modern world. The Persian Gulf boasts over 60 percent of the world's oil reserves and over 40 percent of its natural gas reserves. While oil and gas may appear to be the blessing of the Persian Gulf, they could just as well turn out to be its curse.

Historically, three components of geopolitical unrest can be identified in the Persian Gulf (Herrmann and Ayres). The first is the impact of global competition between major powers on the stability of the region. This global presence was evident during the imperial era when the British and other European powers conquered and occupied the region for more than 200 years, only to be replaced by the United States during the second half of the twentieth century. In turn, the cold war between the United States and the Soviet Union affected the development of the region. The second component of unrest is the relationship between the Persian Gulf states. The strong mixture of ethnic, religious, national, and dynastic tensions that shaped their foreign affairs has also characterized the relationship among them. The third component of unrest stems from each country's internal affairs, namely, the effect of domestic politics on regional affairs.

The countries affected by the three wars can be divided into two broad categories: those directly involved in the wars, such as Iraq, Iran, the countries of the Gulf Cooperation Council (GCC), and the United States; and those that are more peripheral, such as the other Arab countries and Israel. Those directly involved in the wars have behaved in a systematic pattern throughout the past 30 years. James Bill (1996) has called this pattern the "Gulf rectangle of tension," with only one collaborative relationship that developed between two actors, while the others remained confrontational. The collaborative relationship was between the United States and the GCC, the strongest and the weakest entities, respectively. Iran and Iraq were in a continuous struggle for regional hegemony from 1980 until the overthrow of Saddam Hussein, but could turn out to cooperate increasingly in the future. The absolute family rulers of the GCC, afraid of the spread of Islamic revolutions, confronted Iran and supported Iraq in its war against Iran. The United States supported Iraq and gave little consideration to limiting Saddam Hussein's excesses and the longer-term fallouts. The Iraqi dictator, after the end of his war with Iran, turned against the GCC and the United States and invaded Kuwait in 1990. The Clinton administration adopted a "dual containment" policy toward Iran and Iraq during the 1990s. The United States, under George W. Bush, invaded Iraq and toppled Saddam Hussein's regime in 2003, eliminating one regional power and indirectly opening the door for Iran's resurgence in regional affairs.

With the fall of Saddam Hussein's regime, the rectangle of tension was reshaped to form a "triangle of tension." The disintegration of Iraq has changed the pattern of tensions, eliminating some and creating others. For now, Iraq has been defanged as a rival to Iran and may play a new role in the simmering religious Sunni-Shia struggle in the region. But above all, the Iraqi quagmire has weakened US resolve and has dealt a severe financial blow to the United States. The US image in the world, and especially in the region, has been tarnished by distrust and aversion—especially after the revelations about the absence of Iraqi weapons of mass destruction (WMD), the treatment of prisoners at Abu Ghraib, and continued American duplicity supporting some regional dictators while espousing democracy and self determination—and stalled Palestinian-Israeli talks to establish a permanent Palestinian state. Although Iran has been seen as the major beneficiary of the decline in US power and prestige, it has not benefited as it could have because of its own self-inflicted economic mismanagement, pervasive corruption, and internal oppression.

The GCC was established in May of 1981 with six founding members: Saudi Arabia, Kuwait, Qatar, Bahrain, the United Arab Emirates, and Oman. The main purpose behind its formation was political—to enhance the security of the six countries in the wake of the Iranian Revolution and hostilities between Iran and Iraq. Saudi Arabia, the richest in oil reserves, accounts for 70 percent of the GCC population and enjoys the economic and political leadership of this country grouping (Bill, 1996). Saudi leadership of the GCC has, however, been challenged from time to time, especially by the much smaller, but more progressive, Qatar. The GCC's conservative dynasties have enjoyed close ties with the United States and host a number of US military bases (most importantly, a naval base in Bahrain) and a large contingent of US troops in Kuwait. Despite the GCC's enormous spending on weaponry, 7.5 times Iran's between 1997 and 2007, member countries still suffer from internal and external threats (Cordesman, 2008b). Anthony Cordesman has described the threats facing the GCC: "The primary threat that the Gulf Cooperation Council faces is the Gulf Cooperation Council" (Cordesman, 2008a, 3).[1] Cordesman was alluding to the intra-GCC conflicts and the lack of cooperation among the members. But the real threat to the GCC then, and even more apparent now in the aftermath of the "Arab Spring," is its members' inability to adjust and reform internally. They continue to do what they have always done, namely, "buy" support internally and externally. The failure of GCC rulers to tolerate increasing political participation, to develop a just social and economic structure, to afford minorities (especially Shia Muslims) equal rights, and to transform their economies into productive non-oil economies are important causes of resentment, sowing the seeds for future conflicts and upheavals in their countries and the region.

In revolutionary Iran, the natural regional hegemon, the theocratic regime has proven its strength and ability to survive despite an eight-year war with Iraq, economic sanctions, and international pressures and embargoes, and Iran was in 2011 stronger than at any other time since its revolution in 1979. Iran's population is significantly larger than that of all other Persian Gulf countries combined. By 2025, Iran's population is projected to reach 160 million, larger than that of Egypt or Turkey. Iran has an educated middle class, a battle-tested military, an institutionalized political system that some consider "liberal" (at least before the 2009 elections and in comparison to the GCC and even Iraq), and a long history as a nation. With the elimination of the Taliban to the East, Saddam to the West, and a financially weakened United States, the regime in Tehran has a new lease on life. But again, Iran's internal economic and political failures will continue to be a drag on its future role in the region.

The new triangle of tension between the United States and the GCC on the one side and Iran, supported by Iraq, on the other, holds the same causes of mistrust that existed before, and intervening wars have created the potential for future conflicts. In this chapter, we look into the three major wars and attempt to extract some lessons that would be helpful in reducing the likelihood of future conflicts and wars in the region. We start out by summarizing some of the critical events that predated these wars but which may have been its essential seeds.

A Collage of Important and Linked Events

Iraq and Iran were both under British influence for a large part of the early twentieth century. The British occupied both countries (although Iran only briefly from 1941 until the end of World War II, with Soviet collaboration and occupation in the north) and exploited their resources. British control of Iraqi and Iranian oil resources was, respectively, through the Iraqi Petroleum Company (IPC) and the Anglo-Iranian Oil Company (AIOC). Both companies enjoyed lucrative monopolies over the production and sale of Iraqi and Iranian oil, respectively. In 1901, Muzaffar Al-Din Shah sold William Knox D'Arcy, a British adventurer and financier, the "special and exclusive privilege to obtain, exploit, develop, render suitable for trade, carry away and sell natural gas [and] petroleum...for a term of sixty years" (Kinzer, 33). Because of the unjust exploitation of their oil resources, the Iranian people elected a parliament to address their complaint and the Shah appointed the populist Mohammad Mossadegh to power in 1951 (Kinzer). Mossadegh promised to regain control over the country's oil, throw the AIOC out of Iran, and free the country from British influence, domination, and exploitation.

Mossadegh, an Iranian hero, nationalized the AIOC and stood firm against all outside pressures, thus antagonizing Britain. Although the United States had been a low-profile actor in the Persian Gulf, the British, who had been trying to convince the United States to collaborate in the overthrow of Mossadegh, got their chance when Dwight Eisenhower was elected president in 1952. The British convinced the United States that Mossadegh was a communist threat. This was, however, not the first time the British and the United States conceived secret plans for Iran. In 1949 the US National Security Council (NSC) plotted with the British government and US and British oil companies, developing a plan that called for storing explosives in the Middle East to blow up oil installations and refineries in case of a Soviet invasion. This oil-denial policy remained in place through the 1960s (Telhami, 2002b).

After his inauguration on January 20, 1953, President Eisenhower authorized the Dulles brothers (Secretary of State John Foster Dulles and CIA Director Allen Dulles) to move against Mossadegh. Kermit Roosevelt (the grandson of President Theodore Roosevelt), a CIA officer, was sent to the region to direct a coup (codenamed Operation Ajax) in cooperation with the British Secret Intelligence Service (SIS). The coup took place on August 18, 1953, reinstating the unpopular pro-Western Shah, Mohammad Reza Pahlavi, in an intervention that would shape not only the future of US-Iranian relations but also the future of the whole Middle East through developments and events that are linked (Kinzer).

The 1953 coup signaled the beginning of a dramatic episode of events that unfolded one after the other. The reason for the coup, at least for the United States, was the containment of communism. Washington supported the Shah's authoritarian regime for the next 26 years, with all that went with it: corruption, mismanagement, rigged elections, and political repression, in turn alienating Iranians from the United States. The legacy of the 1953 coup was alive in the memory of the Iranian revolutionaries in 1979 when they seized the US embassy. Massoumeh Ebtekar, a spokesperson for the students who seized the embassy, said: "In the back of everybody's mind hung the suspicion that, with the admission of the Shah to the United States, the countdown for another coup d'état had begun" (Zahrani, 98). The embassy seizure encouraged Saddam Hussein to invade Iran in 1980, as he knew he could count on US support, while the GCC, worried about the spread of the popular revolution in Iran, afforded him all the financial support needed. The Islamic Revolution, with its potential effect on Afghanistan, was in turn a contributing factor in the Soviet decision to invade Afghanistan in December 1979. Mostafa T. Zahrani (93) summarizes this tragic history: "A lot of history, in short, flowed from a single week in Tehran."

The overthrow of Mossadegh in 1953 was in some ways analogous to the overthrow of the somewhat popular Qassim in Iraq in 1963. Qassim withdrew Iraq from the anti-Soviet Baghdad Pact. He nationalized part of the IPC and threatened to occupy Kuwait in 1961. The United States, antagonized by Qassim's policies, collaborated with the Baath Party. The CIA assistance "included coordination of the coup plotters from the agency's station inside the U.S. embassy in Baghdad as well as a clandestine radio station in Kuwait and solicitation of advice from around the Middle East on who on the left should be eliminated once the coup was successful"(Cockburn and Cockburn, 2002, 74). Later, Ali Saleh Sa'adi, the Baath Party secretary-general, admitted: "we came to power on a CIA train" (74). A counter coup in 1968 brought Ahmad Hassan Al-Bakr, Saddam Hussein's cousin, to power and made Saddam Hussein ostensibly the second-most powerful man in Iraq (while he was in reality the power behind the thrown). Ten years later, in July 1979, only months after the Islamic Revolution in Iran, Saddam Hussein replaced Al-Bakr as president of Iraq.

Saddam Hussein established his power with a bloodbath that eliminated all of his rivals and opponents in the infamous top-level party meeting of some 1,000 party members immediately after his inauguration (Miller and Mylroie). His reign of terror and brutality made such an impression that nobody in his inner circle had the courage to confront him again on almost any subject. This may, in part, explain why nobody in his leadership coalition dared to dissuade him from attacking Iran in 1980 and Kuwait in 1990.

The Root Causes of the Iran-Iraq War

During the 1970s, the Shah was the strong pillar of President Nixon's "Twin Pillars" policy in the Persian Gulf, with Saudi Arabia being the other pillar. US relationships in the region were intended to guarantee the free flow of oil and the containment of Soviet influence. The Shah received access to thousands of US military advisors, top-of-the-line nonnuclear weapons technologies, and hundreds of millions of dollars in loans from the Export-Import bank (Laipson). The relationship between the United

States and the Shah developed to such an extent that the monarch became known as "America's Shah" (Bill, 2004), while the United States was commonly referred to as *arbab*, or "boss," inside Iran. Iran under the Shah became the policeman of the Persian Gulf and the hegemon that faced little regional opposition. Iraq, all the while, suffered from a long-running Kurdish rebellion in the north supported by the Shah. Henry Kissinger and the Shah initially orchestrated support for the Kurds, and in 1972 the Kurds received US aid to destabilize the Baathist regime in Iraq. Iraq was weak, could not confront a militarily much stronger Iran, and had no choices but to offer Iran (supported by the United States) concessions to halt its support of the Kurdish uprising in northern Iraq.

In March 1975, at an OPEC meeting in Algeria, Saddam Hussein and the Shah of Iran met under the auspices of the Algerian President Houari Boumedienne. The meeting resulted in the Algiers Accord that was signed on June 13, 1975. Iraq recognized that Thalweg, the median course of the Shat-Al-Arab (named Arvand by Iran, as the two countries could not even agree to a common name) waterway, would be the border between the two countries. In return, Iran withdrew its support for the Kurdish rebellion, which, in turn, quickly collapsed. The two countries agreed to establish "friendly" relations and to exchange visits to finalize their border disputes. Neither side honored the treaty, sowing the seeds of war. The main point of contention was the shifting course of the Shat-Al-Arab and other disputed islands and territories. These disputes were not truly resolved even after an eight-year war that followed in 1980 (Isseroff).

Border disputes in the Persian Gulf are not unique to Iran and Iraq. Almost every country in the Persian Gulf has a border dispute with one or more neighboring countries. Iraq has had issues with Kuwait as to the status of the Bubiyan and Warba islands that block Iraq's access to the Persian Gulf. Iran has had an ongoing problem with the United Arab Emirates over the islands of Abu Musa and the Tumbs, and with Iraq. Saudi Arabia has had border disputes with Iraq, Kuwait, Yemen, Oman, and Qatar. These disputes have at times resulted in wars and at other times in border confrontations and skirmishes, but they have always resulted in hostile relations. Saudi Arabia fought with Yemen in the 1930s and the 1960s over territories in Jizan, Asir, and Najran (Cordesman, 1997). Similarly, Saudi Arabia fought with Oman over the Buramai Oasis. This dispute, coupled with Saudi concerns over British interference, encouraged the Al-Sauds to conclude a mutual defense assistance pact with the United States in 1951, which included a long-term lease of the Dhahran Airfield (Pollack, 2002). The Khaur-Al-Udiad area is a source of continuing contention between Saudi Arabia and Qatar (Cordesman, 1997). The paramount reason behind these disputes is the ambiguity of the agreements and the artificial borders drawn by the British in the beginning of the century, yet another legacy of the British role in the Persian Gulf. Importantly and ominously, border disputes that have been silent for decades, and thus might appear to be settled, can in an instant, and for no apparent reason, spark hostilities.

In January 1979, after 16 years in exile in Najaf (Iraq) and then briefly in France, Ayatollah Ruhollah Khomeini returned triumphantly to Iran. He had gone to France because the Shah had asked Saddam Hussein to expel Khomeini from Iraq and thus effectively out of the Persian Gulf region. Ironically, France afforded Khomeini a better platform and more freedom to spread his ideas inside Iran. The Iranian Revolution was not a surprise. The Iranian people had been demanding more political freedom and had contested the rule of the Shah and his brutal Savak (the security and information agency) for quite some time. Consequently, the popularity of Khomeini, who had opposed the regime, soared. Richard Cottam (14) summarized how Iran had developed in this way: "Iran is a dramatic example of the fruits of Cold War interventionist policies in strategically vital third world countries. The royal dictatorship in Iran has its counterparts throughout Asia, Africa and Latin America, in governments perceived by important sections of the public as loyal executors of U.S. policy." Further complicating conditions, on November 4, 1979, Iranian students took over the American embassy in Tehran holding 52 American diplomats hostage. The hostage episode ended with their release after 444 days in January 20, 1981. This event poisoned any possibility of building trust between the new revolutionary regime and future American administrations.

There were also fallouts from the Iranian Revolution in neighboring Iraq. Iraq and Iran have a majority of Shia Muslims (over about 90 percent and 60 percent, respectively); Iraq has the Shia holy cities of Najaf and Karbala, while Iran has the cities of Mashhad and Qum. Although Iraq had a more secular tradition than Iran, militant Iraqi Shia groups were tempted to repeat an Iranian-style revolution in Iraq (Cottam). Underground movements, such as Al-Dawa, gained momentum after the Iranian Revolution. One of the first attacks by the Al-Dawa party was against Tarik Aziz, then deputy prime minister, using a grenade at a student conference in Mustansariyeh on April 1, 1980. A series of other attacks followed. Saddam Hussein responded by executing a senior religious leader and one of the heads of the Al-Dawa party, Mohammad Bakr Al-Sadr (the father-in-law of Muqtada Al-Sadr), and his sister. He also expelled 30,000 Iraqis of Iranian origin. A media war started between the two countries; Saddam started referring to Ayatollah Khomeini as "that mummy" and Khomeini called on the Iraqi army to revolt against Saddam Hussein (Cottam).

Saddam Hussein probably believed that the disarray in Iran, the execution of a number of senior Iranian military officers, and Iran's international isolation because of the hostage crisis offered Iraq the once-in-a-lifetime opportunity to achieve its territorial ambitions. A declassified note from a Pentagon Defense Intelligence Agency agent (April 8, 1980) in Baghdad confirms much of this assessment of the situation. The note states that Iraq's plans to invade Iran had nothing to do with the Al-Dawa attacks. The agent's note reported: "There is a 50 percent chance that Iraq will attack Iran. Iraq has moved large numbers of military personnel and equipment to the Iran-Iraq border in anticipation of such an invasion." The agent added that Iraq believed that: "The Iranian military is now weak and can be easily defeated" (Cockburn and Cockburn, 2002, 80).

The United States not only knew of Iraq's aggressive intentions but also might have implicitly encouraged Saddam Hussein. Although there were no official channels of communication between the two countries, Iraq and the United States communicated through Saudi Arabia and, ironically, Kuwait. Gary Sick, then responsible for Persian Gulf policy at the National Security Council, explained the situation by saying: "After the hostages were taken in Tehran, there was a very strong view, especially from Brzezinski [President Carter's national security advisor], that in effect Iran should be punished from all sides. He made public statements to the effect that he would not mind an Iraqi move against Iran" (Hitchens, 51). In the fall of 1980, the *Financial Times* reported that a third-party Arab government gave Iraq US intelligence and satellite data showing that Iranian forces would not withstand an Iraqi attack (Hitchens). Again, the United States knew of Saddam Hussein's aggressive intentions, as did probably most of the permanent members of the United Nations Security Council (UNSC), and did nothing to dissuade him from his invasion of Iran.

While these events, going back to 1953, may represent the main roots for the Iran-Iraq War, it could be even argued that the seeds might have been planted still earlier in 1918 at the end of World War I. The winning allies drew artificial borders in the Middle East, Yugoslavia, and Northern Ireland, areas that had witnessed consecutive tragedies and wars (Fisk).[2] The settled border dispute between Iran and Iraq in the Algiers Accord unraveled with the fall of the Shah. Saddam Hussein manipulated the Arabs, Americans, and the world by gaining their support, political, military, and financial, to fight what proved to be a brutal and costly war. The world not only failed to prevent this war, especially the UNSC, which did absolutely nothing, but in our opinion even contributed to the fact that it lasted for eight years.

Some things are clear. We cannot today imagine, much less predict, the future fallouts of our ongoing policies and decisions. No one could have foreseen the full impact and fallout of the 1953 coup in Iran; no one could have foreseen how US support for Iraq in 1980 and the continued cooperation between the two countries for over a decade would play out over time. No one could have foreseen Saddam Hussein's invasion of Kuwait and the US invasion of Iraq. Policy makers must examine much more thoroughly possible future developments and all implications of today's decisions, possibly conducting even full "impact studies" of all policy decisions.[3] Today's wars and conflicts will in all likelihood lead to future wars and conflicts that we cannot even imagine. That is the natural order of things: conflicts beget conflicts. Conflicts must be stopped quickly and assertively, addressing the grievances of all sides, if we are to avoid, or at least limit, their future fallouts.

The Iran-Iraq War (1980–1988)

Saddam Hussein underestimated Iran's strength and the commitment of Iranians to defend their homeland. The population of Iran was three times Iraq's. The Iranian Revolution, initially popular but fractionated, was quickly solidified by Saddam Hussein's attack. Saddam Hussein thought that his army could overturn the 1975 Algiers Accord in quick order (Gettleman and Schaar). His miscalculations resulted in the longest conventional interstate war of the twentieth century. Iran regained virtually all of its lost territory by 1982, but Ayatollah Khomeini tragically (and we would add un-Islamically) did not accept the suggested terms for peace, and the war continued until 1988. Thus, many additional lives were lost in the name of "justice," and probably more for personal revenge (Khomeini having been deported from Iraq at the request of the Shah). Iraq achieved none of its objectives, but Iran was prevented from taking Basra because Iraq used outlawed chemical weapons, supplied by Western nations, against the Iranian forces. Iraq finally accepted Iran's terms for a settlement, again based on the 1975 Algiers Accord (Stork).

Saddam Hussein started his offensive on September 22, 1980, launching full-scale air and ground attacks across his 730-mile border with Iran, and capturing 6,000–8,000 square miles of the oil-rich and relatively heavily Arab-populated Khuzestan province (referred to as Al-Ahwaz by some Arab nationalists) without inflicting a major defeat on the Iranian army. Throughout this phase, Saddam Hussein was able to secure the political and financial support of oil-rich Arab states in addition to political and military support from Jordan and Egypt (Stork). Saudi Arabia and Kuwait loaned (or gave, depending on which side you are listening to) Saddam

$25.7 billion and $10 billion, respectively, during the first two years of the war (Cockburn and Cockburn, 2002).

The second phase of the war started in mid-1982 when an Iranian offensive pushed Iraqi forces out of most of occupied Iran and took the war into Iraq. When Iran pursued Iraqi forces into Iraq, Iraqi soldiers, mostly Shia, started to fight fiercely and the rate of surrender dropped significantly (Cockburn and Cockburn, 2002). A simple lesson of history that most aggressors never learn is that nationalism becomes the best defensive weapon when foreigners (even those of the same religious sect) threaten the defenders' homes. Around this time, Iraq and the GCC tried to convey the impression that the war was an Iranian-Arab war rather than simply a war between Iraq and Iran, in order to get wider support from Arab countries. When Saddam Hussein was forced out of Iran, the Saudis reportedly proposed a plan to end the war through complete Iraqi evacuation and $70 billion in war reparation. Ayatollah Khomeini rejected the proposal and demanded the removal of Saddam Hussein's regime, the repatriation of 100,000 expelled Iraqi Shia, and $150 billion in war reparations (Molavi). Iran tragically lost an opportunity to end the war. Khomeini probably thought he was fighting a just war and that he could remove Saddam's regime and establish a Shia revolutionary government in Baghdad. Iranians also overestimated their own capabilities while underestimating the West's commitment to supporting Iraq. This made for an additional five years of repeated and unsuccessful Iranian offensives, one after another. But what Khomeini did not appreciate was that the international community, and especially the United States, wanted to maintain the status quo, with Iran and Iraq continuing with the fighting and with no apparent victor. Henry Kissinger summed it up when he remarked, "It's a pity that they [Iran and Iraq] both can't lose." What Kissinger meant, and left unsaid, was that the United States would not allow either side to win a decisive victory.

The international community, rather than rushing to stop the war when Iraq invaded Iran, showered Saddam with military hardware and all other manner of support, including internationally banned weapons of war. The Soviet Union, after cutting off its arms shipments to Iraq at the beginning of the war, resumed its former position as Iraq's major military supplier. France supplied warplanes and missile systems that were used later in hunting Iranian ships, and with which Iraq even mistakenly hit the USS Stark on May 17, 1987 (Fisk). In addition to removing Iraq from the list of states supporting terrorism, the United States provided financial credits through the Export-Import bank and "agricultural" shipments that were used later to develop chemical weapons (Stork). Germany, France, Britain, and the United States also provided Iraq with banned chemical weapons, which were used as the decisive deterrent to thwart Iran's attack on Basra. The scars of outlawed chemical weaponry are still evident on the streets of Tehran today, providing ample incentive for further conflict in the future. The CIA provided Iraq with military intelligence and satellite imagery revealing Iranian positions and other useful military information (Cockburn and Cockburn, 2002). Ironically, in 1986, during the Iran-Contra affair, the United States gave Iran valuable intelligence on the Iraqi order of battle, which led to Saddam's defeat in the Fao Peninsula.

The interference of foreign powers to stoke and sustain the fires and an ineffective United Nations that is manipulated by its five veto-wielding members, saying and doing nothing when its all-important mandate is violated, are some of the tragic reasons that cause conflicts to continue for years and in turn beget future conflicts.

The third phase of the war started in 1984 when Iraq used French jets and missiles to halt Iranian oil exports (Stork). The "tanker war" initiated a stage in the war when the international dimension became much more apparent. It was oil and the flow of oil to the West that mattered. Iran had little choice but to retaliate after Iraq's assault. Since Iraq's exports had already been halted early on in the war, Iran attacked the oil shipments of Iraq's allies, namely, Kuwait and Saudi Arabia. When Kuwait requested international protection for its tankers, the United States responded by dispatching more than 50 warships to escort and reflag Kuwaiti and other ships through the Persian Gulf (Stork). The firm US response was triggered by a Soviet offer to undertake the reflagging mission.

The fourth and final phase of the war followed the unsuccessful Iranian "final offensive" of January through February 1987 (Stork). The Iraqi ground victories, the naval clashes with US forces in the Persian Gulf, and most importantly the US shooting down of Iran Air Flight #655, killing 291 innocent passengers, persuaded Iran to accept UNSC Resolution 598, which called for a ceasefire on Iraqi terms. Robert Fisk concludes: "In fact, Washington was fighting a war against Iran" (Fisk222). Washington's intervention in favor of Iraq forced Khomeini to "drain the bitter cup" and accept the ceasefire on August 8, 1988 (Cockburn and Cockburn, 2002). The US role in this bloody war may have also sown the seeds of future conflicts, both between countries in the region and also more directly with the United States.

Dimensions and Fallout of the Iran-Iraq War

The underlying factors that fueled the war revolve around oil and border disputes. Oil, and the border disputes that in turn affect the ownership of oil, is the central and common factor in all the Persian Gulf wars, to the extent that the First Gulf War could be named the first "oil war" (Stork). The British Empire's interest in the Persian Gulf region in the beginning of the twentieth century was primarily based on the region's abundant oil resources. The borders drawn by the British in those early years were the main reasons for future disputes and conflicts. British and American interventionist policies driven by oil interests restored the Shah's regime in Iran in support of the monarchy. Interventionist policies created a series of military regimes in Iraq. These same policies paved the way for the Islamic Revolution in Iran and for Arab nationalism in Iraq. The oil revenues of both countries and of other Persian Gulf states funded and sustained the war. A likely motive for US intervention and for delayed international support was a more fractionated and competitive oil market.

Iraq began its extensive use of poisonous gas on Iranians in 1984. The international reaction to Iraq's use of chemical weapons, including mustard gas and nerve gas (tabun and sarin), was shameful (Cockburn and Cockburn, 2002). Not only did world powers not discourage the use of these outlawed weapons, they in fact supplied and even encouraged Iraqi use of chemical weapons as the only way to thwart an Iranian victory. The deadly effectiveness of chemical weapons and the world's absence of concern encouraged Saddam Hussein to use chemical weapons against his own people in Halabja and in other towns in 1987 and 1988. Saddam Hussein must have felt that in the eyes of his foreign supporters he could do no wrong, a factor that must have surely played a critical role in his decision to invade Kuwait a few years later. To his mind, he must have questioned the world powers' serious concern for his supposed arsenal of outlawed chemical weapons when it was they who had supplied him with the weapons in the first place!

The active US role in the Iran-Iraq war set the groundwork for its further involvement during the following 20 years. The Reagan and Bush administrations were engaged in massive efforts to supply arms and weaponry to Saddam Hussein. Both US administrations assisted Saddam Hussein in obtaining chemical and biological weapons and their means of delivery (Waas). Again, these were the same weaponries that were later considered by the United States as a threat to regional and international stability in the 1990s. The American "tilt" toward Iraq started in 1983 and was sealed by the National Security Decision Directive 114, transferring billions of dollars in loan guarantees and credits to Iraq. It was formally established by Donald Rumsfeld's "friendly" trip to Iraq on December 20, 1983 (Hiltermann). The infrastructure of air and naval bases the United States built in Saudi Arabia and in other GCC countries during the Iran-Iraq War provided the helpful footprint for the war against Saddam Hussein in

1991. The United States not only armed Saddam Hussein but also covertly supplied arms to Khomeini's regime in Tehran in the controversial scandal known as the "Iran-Contra Affair" or "Iran-gate." By switching sides and supplying arms to both countries, the United States tried to master the same divide-and-conquer policy that the British had conceived, initiated, and practiced decades before. It created a market for US weaponry, established influence in the region with rulers, developed clientele in both Iraq and Iran, and prohibited the emergence of a rival power.[4] The goal of US policy was the mutual destruction of, and the continued rivalry between, Iran and Iraq.

The event that connected the Iran-Iraq War, the Persian Gulf War, and the Iraq War was the Iraqi invasion of Kuwait (Stork). After the Iran-Iraq War, Iraq faced an economic crisis with a devastated infrastructure, over $80 billion in debt, and a battle-tested army equipped with high-end weaponry. Iraq owed $25.7 billion to Saudi Arabia, $10 billion to Kuwait, smaller amounts to other Arab countries, and an additional $40 billion to the United States, Europe, and other countries. Saddam Hussein had literally used debt to launch his war and was militarily stronger at the end of the war than at its start; in 1980, the Iraqi army had only 10 divisions as compared to the 55 divisions it had in 1988 (Cockburn and Cockburn, 2002). In summary, the Iran-Iraq War had ended with a strong Iraqi war machine with no economic resources to sustain it, with a strong Iraqi regime burdened with overwhelming external debt but with continued international support; Iraq had thus become the hegemon of the Gulf.

Did the United States and the rest of the West comprehend how their decisions of the day would play out in the future, or were they just concerned with short-term results? Was morality a consideration in their decision making?

It would appear that global peace is thoroughly trumped by the short-term interests of global powers. Conflicts beget conflicts. The consequences of a mediated settlement are much more predictable than the fallout from a bloody and costly war.

Events Leading to the Persian Gulf War (Kuwait 1990–1991)

Before the era of British influence in the Persian Gulf region, Kuwait had been part of the Ottoman Province of Basra. The Al-Sabah ruling family concluded a protectorate agreement with the United Kingdom in 1899, granting the British all responsibility for foreign affairs. Because of

Kuwait's oil reserves (the world's fifth largest) and its strategic location in the Persian Gulf, the British had maintained a close relationship with the Al-Sabah family and protected the emirate's artificial borders. Britain intervened once in 1920 to protect the Jahrah area from being added to Ibn Saud's Najdi domain and then again in 1934 after Ibn Saud established his new Saudi Kingdom (Schofield). The British high commissioner drew the borders of Kuwait in a manner that restricts Iraq's access to the Persian Gulf and thus to the high seas; an access that Iraq desperately needed for unencumbered oil exports, especially with its narrow waterway in the Shat-Al-Arab. Kuwait became fully independent from the United Kingdom on June 19, 1961.

Due to the disputed status of the Shat-Al-Arab boundary with Iran and failure to undo the Algiers Accord after the eight-year war, Iraq developed an alternative port facility for Basra at Umm Qasr on the Khawr Zubayr. In order to secure a navigational access channel to the port, Iraq consistently pressed Kuwait for border concessions and the lease of the Warba and Bubiyan islands (Schofield). For a long time, Iraq-Kuwait borders and the status of the disputed islands remained unresolved. Iraq would not agree to the demarcation of the land boundary without Kuwaiti flexibility on the status of the islands. Kuwait, historically backed by and closely tied to Britain, did not feel sufficient pressure to concede to Iraqi demands.

Iraqi governments have historically viewed, and continue to view, Kuwait as an integral part of Iraq; thus Saddam Hussein's annexation of Kuwait in 1990 was in part a historical claim, similar to Iraq's claim of the Shat-Al-Arab. Iraq has historically pressured Kuwait on the islands whenever its differences with Iran over the Shat-Al-Arab have come to the fore, a scenario that prevailed in 1990 (Schofield). After the Iran-Iraq War, Kuwait tried to take advantage of Saddam Hussein's economic crisis and his huge financial debt to settle all territorial issues with Iraq. A report from Kuwait's director general of state security concerning his visit to the CIA in October 1989 says: "We agreed with the American side that it was important to take advantage of the deteriorating economic situation in Iraq in order to put pressure on that country's government to delineate our common border" (Cockburn and Cockburn, 2002, 83). The pressure the Kuwaitis exerted clearly did not meet its stated objectives! It was also naïve on Kuwait's part to think that concessions extracted from Iraq under such conditions would be long lasting and worth the effort. The tension between the two countries was apparent at the Arab Summit Conference in Baghdad in April 1990. Saddam Hussein confronted the Emir of Kuwait, accusing him of launching a war against Iraq through overproduction of oil and of exerting pressure over border issues (Cockburn and Cockburn, 2002). The irony is that in a similar Arab summit in Baghdad in 1978, when he was at least nominally the second in command, Saddam Hussein threatened to attack Kuwait if it did not break its ties with Egypt, after Egypt had signed a peace treaty with Israel. Iraq also accused Kuwait of pumping $2.4 billion worth of oil from the Rumaila oil field that rightfully belonged to Iraq (*Special Report: Persian Gulf War*).

Following the tilt toward Iraq during the Iran-Iraq War, the United States maintained a close relationship with Saddam Hussein and continued to support his regime. Until the spring of 1990, Saddam Hussein was an ally of the United States, with the common interest of containing Iran. At the end of his war with Iran, Saddam Hussein massed his military against Iraqi Kurds in the north and, on August 25, 1988, dropped chemical weapons on villages throughout Iraqi Kurdistan. This tragedy marked the first use of nerve gas against civilians in history (Waas). One month later, the United States received the Iraqi minister of state in Washington. He met with Secretary of State George Shultz. The United States "uncharacteristically" condemned the use of gas but the Reagan Administration vetoed the tough trade sanctions against Iraq passed by the US Senate (Waas). In addition, the United States continued to supply Iraq with aid that amounted to $1 billion a year when George Bush senior took over the US presidency. Saddam Hussein surely was led to believe that he could do no wrong in US eyes. Such favorable treatment of a brutal dictator and the duplicity that it represented, all in the name of *Realpolitik*, was sure to have dire consequences, something that Washington clearly did not foresee.

The incident that immediately preceded Iraq's invasion of Kuwait on August 2, 1990 was Saddam's controversial meeting with the US ambassador to Iraq, April Glaspie, on July 25. After Saddam Hussein had clarified his views about Kuwait, the ambassador replied: "But we have no opinion on the Arab-Arab conflicts, like your border disagreement with Kuwait. I was in the American embassy in Kuwait during the late '60s. The instruction we had during this period was that we should express no opinion on this issue and that the issue is not associated with America. James Baker has directed our official spokesmen to emphasize this instruction" (The Glaspie transcript, 68). Saddam Hussein apparently interpreted her words as a US green light to invade Kuwait. This proved to be the last high-level contact between the two governments before the Iraqi invasion of Kuwait, which Saddam Hussein undertook only one week later. After the invasion, Ambassador Glaspie told the *New York Times*: "We never expected they would take all of Kuwait" (Hitchens, 55). A number of prominent politicians in the Persian Gulf believe, even today, that there would have been no response if Saddam had annexed the disputed islands or occupied only a part of Kuwait. The decisions to take all of Kuwait and especially to threaten Saudi Arabia were Saddam Hussein's biggest political mistakes that ultimately sealed his fate.

One thing is certain: Ambassador Glaspie did not say that the United States was against aggression or that Washington supported dialogue and diplomacy as the only way to resolve differences between countries; she also did not try to dissuade an attack on Kuwait. Yes, misunderstandings can ignite conflicts and wars. While the presumed Glaspie "green light" might have pushed Saddam Hussein over the edge to invade Kuwait, the factors leading to the invasion of Kuwait had been apparent for some time, and, in our opinion, Kuwait would have been invaded even if Saddam Hussein had not had the meeting with Ambassador Glaspie. There were many reasons for the invasion of Kuwait; first and foremost was Iraq's long-standing territorial ambition, specifically, unhindered access to the Persian Gulf that would result only from Iranian or Kuwaiti concessions. Second was Iraq's annoyance with Kuwait's oil production policies. Iraq claimed that Kuwait was depleting (through directional or slant drilling) Iraqi oil from a disputed oil field. Iraq claimed that Kuwait was producing above its OPEC quota and thus driving down the price of oil. On this latter point, we have it from a high Saudi government source (directly connected to these matters) that, in fact, Kuwait was overproducing at the behest of Saudi Arabia, with an eye to reducing Iraqi (and Iranian) oil revenues, because Iraq had gone from being the defender of the GCC to its enemy. Third, Saudi Arabia, Kuwait, and the United Arab Emirates lent (or gave) substantial amounts of money to Iraq during the Iran-Iraq War. While Saudi Arabia unofficially forgave the loans (which it has since denied after the installation of a Shia government in Iraq), at an official meeting in Jeddah Kuwaiti officials negotiated for a higher rate of interest! Saddam Hussein felt that he had, in part, fought Iran for the GCC, and paying a high rate of interest to Kuwait apparently infuriated him. Fourth, Saddam Hussein's special treatment by foreign powers and by the United Nations led him to believe that he could do as he wished in the region, with little or no consequences. He was led to believe that there was no price to be paid for aggression as long as he had the support of those who mattered. In other words, he believed the price of his aggression would be low or even negative.

The Persian Gulf War (Kuwait 1990–1991)

On August 2, 1990, the Iraqi army marched into Kuwait claiming to be responding to a call for help from Kuwaiti revolutionaries who had overthrown the Al-Sabah ruling family. On August 8, Saddam Hussein declared the annexation of Kuwait, with the northern part of the country attached to the Basra province and the southern part becoming Iraq's nineteenth province (*Special Report: Persian Gulf War*).

The Iraqi foreign minister, Tariq Aziz, later testified that the original plan did not include an invasion of all of Kuwait. The plan was to seize the Bubiyan and Warba islands in addition to the disputed Rumailah oil field; the decision to take the whole country was made "at the last moment" (Cockburn and Cockburn, 2002, 85). Saddam Hussein's uncontested and hasty decision was "one of the greatest political miscalculations by any leader since Hitler invaded the Soviet Union in 1941" (Cockburn and Cockburn, 2002, 85). The United States and the rest of the world could not let Saddam control such a significant percentage of the world's oil reserves. By our figures, Kuwaiti and Iraqi oil would have given Saddam Hussein about 20 percent of the world's proven oil reserves as of 2008, with Saudi reserves slightly above this combined total. But what was even more worrying to the West was the fact that Saddam Hussein could have marched into Saudi Arabia and captured the major part of Saudi oil reserves in its Eastern Province in no time at all. This would have afforded Saddam Hussein close to 40 percent of world oil reserves and effective control over oil prices, with a stranglehold over Western economies.

Immediately after the invasion, the United States decided to come to the defense of Saudi Arabia, by then the most dependent and the most reliable US ally in the Persian Gulf. The United States was convinced at that point that Saddam was planning to occupy the Eastern Province of Saudi Arabia, something that raised red flags all over Washington (Pollack, 2003). President Bush dispatched his secretary of defense, Richard Cheney, to Saudi Arabia to convince King Fahd to agree to a US deployment of troops inside his country. Only after Cheney showed King Fahd satellite images of Iraqi army deployment along the Saudi borders did the King agree to Operation Desert Shield, allowing 250,000 American troops to be moved into Saudi Arabia (*Special Report: Persian Gulf War*). This US deployment within Saudi soil served as a recruiting slogan for militant groups, most notably Al-Qaida, to wage war against the "occupying infidels" in coming years. Again, man's limited minds could not foresee the full consequences of these actions.

When the United States had enough forces and weaponry in Saudi Arabia to defend the kingdom from an Iraqi invasion, it became clear that Saddam Hussein did not intend to attack but meant only to deter an American counterattack. It was then that the United States saw the invasion as an opportunity to neutralize Iraq's military power and to eliminate its weapons of mass destruction (WMD) program (Pollack, 2003). The

United States doubled the size of its forces in the Persian Gulf and started preparing for an invasion that would punish Iraq and prove its own indisputable hegemony over the Persian Gulf. Ironically, had Saddam Hussein immediately invaded Saudi Arabia, he would have had many more bargaining chips. The United States would not have had the option of landing troops and material at Jubail. He would have had a stranglehold on the world oil market and the world economy. He might have gotten away with what he originally wanted—the disputed islands and disputed oil fields. Instead, he was caught in the middle with no options and not that much bargaining power.

The United Nations, in a series of resolutions, condemned the occupation, called for an immediate Iraqi withdrawal, and imposed economic and air blockades. UN actions in defense of Kuwait should be contrasted with its total failure to act in defense of Iran in 1980. UNSC Resolution 678 set January 15, 1991 as the deadline for Iraq to withdraw from Kuwait (*Special Report: Persian Gulf War*). The resolution authorized member states to use all means necessary to enforce the Iraqi withdrawal. The United Nations issued 19 resolutions related to the war, with Resolution 687 as the most important. The resolution required Iraq to destroy its nonconventional weapons, both chemical and biological, which ironically had been supplied by the West. This was a precondition to the lifting of the UN-imposed sanctions. The implementation of this resolution and the complications that accompanied UN inspections provided the pretext for another war led by the United States against Iraq 12 years later in 2003.

Along with Operation Desert Shield, President Bush was committed to building an international coalition to oppose the Iraqi occupation of Kuwait, something that the United States did not even consider when Saddam Hussein occupied parts of Iran. It would appear that consistency, legality, and morality have not been considered as important elements of foreign policy. The objectives for building the coalition were to reduce the burden on the United States, enhance the effectiveness of sanctions, and legitimize the US presence on Saudi soil, especially in the Arab and Muslim world. Egypt and Syria were the two most important Arab nations contributing to the coalition forces along with two dozen other nations, with the United Kingdom as America's staunchest ally. The Bush administration stressed the Arab participation in the coalition in an effort to undermine Iraqi claims that the United States and its Western allies were waging an aggressive war against an Arab Muslim country (*Special Report: Persian Gulf War*). Throughout the war, Saddam Hussein counted on the fragility of the coalition and tried to exert pressure on the Arab public, by targeting Israel with Scud rockets, for example. The United States was successful in maintaining the unity of the coalition by containing Israel.

Immediately after expiration of the deadline for Iraqi withdrawal, on January 16, 1991, George Bush ordered the coalition forces to launch Operation Desert Storm by beginning a 38-day bombing of Iraq. On February 24, allied forces launched a ground offensive into Kuwait and Iraq. Only three days later, Kuwait was liberated and President Bush declared a ceasefire (*Special Report: Persian Gulf War*). The purpose of the ground offensive was not only to liberate Kuwait but also to destroy Iraq's army. In the words of General Collin Powell, the chairman of the US Joint Chiefs of Staff at the time, "Our strategy to go after this army is very, very simple. First, we are going to cut it off, and then we are going to kill it" (*Special Report: Persian Gulf War*, 17). More than 100,000 Iraqis were killed during the war, according to unofficial coalition estimates. Only 125 Americans were killed during the operation; this exceptional performance by US forces kicked "the Vietnam Syndrome" that had haunted the United States since Vietnam (Gettleman and Schaar, 271).

When Saddam Hussein realized that he might end up loosing his army, he began to negotiate his way out of Kuwait through Russian intermediaries. Because of the rebellion of the Shia majority in southern Iraq in mid-February, Saddam Hussein was afraid that his Republican Guard would be decimated and that he might not be able to defend his regime. President Bush ordered a halt to the ground offensive based on the advice of the Pentagon and the US Central Command (CENTCOM), believing that the Republican Guard had largely been destroyed (Pollack, 2003). The US decision to stop the war and to spare Saddam Hussein's regime was one of the major controversial issues of the war. Directly following the end of the war, Bush called on "the Iraqi military and the Iraqi people to take matters into their own hands—to force Saddam Hussein the dictator to step aside...and rejoin the family of nations" (Cockburn and Cockburn, 2003, 96). The Iraqis interpreted the words of President Bush as a call to join the fight against Saddam. The surviving Republican Guard divisions were sent to crush the Shia revolt in the south and the Kurdish uprising in the north, and the United States provided no support to either. The Kurds, being on the border with Turkey, were luckier than the Shia in attracting media attention and sympathy from the outside world. The ensuing massacres of the Shia in the south and the Kurds in the north by Saddam's Republican Guards were the direct consequences of US betrayal. The White House finally bent to public opinion and assisted the Kurds by sending food and medicine and later by providing air cover, under "Operation Provide Comfort," to deter Saddam from crushing the revolt a second time.

These tragedies are yet another testimony to how foreign interest has subverted quests for freedom and democracy in the Persian Gulf. Still, President Bush refused to admit that the United States should bear any guilt for encouraging the Iraqis to revolt and for failing to support them, stating, "That was not true. We never implied that" (Cockburn and Cockburn, 2003, 100). The United States did not want to remove Saddam Hussein. It was Iran that worried the United States, and Saddam Hussein could still be a useful instrument to contain Iranian ambitions. These perceptions defined the period after the war to liberate Kuwait.

By this time, US and UN policy was one of containing a weakened but still strong regime in Baghdad. In addition to maintaining strict US-backed economic sanctions against Iraq, the UN's mission was to find and destroy Saddam Hussein's arsenal of WMD (*Special Report: Persian Gulf War*). The implementation of UN Resolution 687 dragged the war for the liberation of Kuwait into an unsettled dispute over Iraq's military strength and its possible possession of WMD. The UN Special Commission (UNSCOM) was established to verify Iraqi compliance with the resolution. UNSCOM and the International Atomic Energy Agency (IAEA) first entered Iraq in 1991 and continued their inspections until 1998 (Graham-Brown and Toensing). The five permanent members of the UNSC had major disagreements over the process of inspections from 1994 onward. While France and Russia, with interests in Iraqi oil, pushed to lessen the sanctions over Iraq's exports and imports, the United States and Britain strongly opposed any softening of the sanction regime. In 1997, a UNSCOM and IAEA report stated that Iraq had destroyed its long-range delivery systems and had gotten rid of its nuclear stocks. Still, the United States and Britain rejected a Russian proposal to close Iraq's nuclear file and to establish a road map toward lifting sanctions. The stiff US and British position took the shape of a military operation coined Operation Desert Fox, an operation that was undertaken without the authorization of the UNSC (Graham-Brown and Toensing). Between December 16 and 19, 1998, the United States and the UK bombarded Iraq heavily, subjecting the already suffering Iraqi population to even more hardship. This pattern of consecutive military action without UNSC authorization was repeated on a regular basis by the United States and Britain. Operation Desert Fox led to UNSC Resolution 1284, creating a new arms monitoring body called UNMOVIC, but Saddam Hussein would not allow UNMOVIC into Iraq until November 2002, after great pressure and because he feared a US invasion. Indeed, the invasion came just months later, in 2003 (Graham-Brown and Toensing).

After the war, the United States maintained a policy to contain and isolate Iraq and Iran, while at the same time pushing peace talks between the Arabs and the Israelis. The Clinton administration's "dual containment" policy was designed to protect GCC allies and enable Israel and "moderate" Arab states to move toward a peace agreement without obstruction from the "rejectionist front" (Brzezinski, Scowcroft, and Murphy). The United

States had Iraq under control with a complicated net of international economic and military sanctions, including a no-fly zone in the south and a protected Kurdish enclave in the north. The Iraqi people were the tragic casualty of this policy. It is estimated that 1 million Iraqis, largely children, died as a direct result of internationally backed sanctions (Cockburn and Cockburn, 2002). This fact alone has surely sowed the seeds of hatred and future conflict.

The Iraq War (2003–2011)

Between 1995 and 2002, Iraq was living under the mercy of the "oil-for-food" program formulated in UNSC Resolution 986. This program came into operation at the end of 1996 and allowed Iraq to sell specified amounts of oil every six-month period. The financial proceeds were deposited into a UN-controlled account outside Iraq to be used to fill orders for humanitarian goods for the Iraqi people. The program was scrutinized by the United States and Britain under the assumption that some goods could have "dual use." By 2001, UN sanctions were fraying at the edges. Iraq's neighbors, including Syria, Jordan, Turkey, and some Persian Gulf states, were engaged in sanctions-breaching trade with Iraq (Graham-Brown and Toensing). The formal end of Arab participation in the sanctions and containment policies of the 1990s was reached during the March 2002 Arab Summit when Iraq formally recognized Kuwait's sovereignty. This summit called for the lifting of sanctions, and Arab diplomats tried to persuade Iraq to accept the return of the UNMOVIC weapons inspectors.

Despite the Arab-Iraqi breakthrough during the summit, it would appear that the United States and Britain had already set a new agenda for regime change. Long before the 9/11 attacks on the United States, neo-conservatives in the United States had ideological plans for change in the map of the Middle East. After 9/11, the same group of officials that had supported Saddam Hussein with chemical weapons, intelligence information, and loan credits during his war with Iran had the perfect opportunity to promote regime change in Iraq. Donald Rumsfeld had been President Reagan's special envoy to the Middle East when the US administration provided Saddam with biological materials such as anthrax, the West Nile virus, and botulinal toxin, facilitating Saddam's efforts to develop biological weapons (Mearsheimer and Walt, 2003). In 2003, the same Donald Rumsfeld, who had become the US secretary of defense, led a war against Iraq, claiming that Iraq's possession of WMD was a danger to regional and international stability.

The events of September 11, 2001 were of great significance and essentially divided recent world history into pre- and post-9/11 eras. After the 9/11 attacks, the United States found itself fighting an enemy who was not represented by national boundaries and existed everywhere. The enemy was terrorism, a vague word with an even vaguer meaning. The direct US response was to declare war on those who had planned the attacks and the states that funded and harbored them. Both categories could be stretched elastically to include organizations and states that had nothing to do with the attacks, such as Iraq, and to disregard states that funded extremist groups, such as Saudi Arabia, Pakistan, and the United States itself (one of the original benefactors of Osama bin Laden). The United States faced an enemy it had helped create, train, fund, and orient, but one it no longer controlled.

Religious fundamentalism and extremism, once perceived as an asset for the United States in its fight against communism, became an overriding liability. When asked if he regretted having supported Islamic radicalism against the Soviets in Afghanistan, Zbigniew Brzezinski answered: "What is most important to the history of the World? The Taliban or the collapse of the Soviet empire? Some stirred-up Muslims or the liberation of Central Europe and the end of the Cold War?" (Gettleman and Schaar, 274). Today, these "stirred-up Muslims" are a threat to the security of the United States. It would also appear that plans for toppling Saddam Hussein's regime predate the 9/11 attacks by years. In a letter sent to President Bill Clinton by the New American Century Foundation, a neoconservative nonprofit educational organization, on January 26, 1998, the authors urge the President to remove Saddam Hussein from power. Eighteen influential figures signed the letter, 11 of them held posts in the Bush administration as of March 2003 (Abrams et al.). Elliott Abrams, Richard Armitage, John Bolton, Zalmay Khalilzad, Richard Perle, and Donald Rumsfeld are some of the hawks that prepared, promoted, and launched the war that changed the Middle East. The change was meant to redraw the map of the Persian Gulf, as did the Sykes Picot Agreement of 1916 and the Balfour Declaration of 1917. The only difference is that the change was done the American way.

Dredging up the past to get at the true reasons for the US invasion of Iraq in 2003 is somewhat problematic. There is no doubt that Saddam Hussein's regime was abusive, but so were, and are, other US-sponsored dictatorships. The Iraqi regime was as brutal and undemocratic in 2003 as it was in the 1980s when the United States "tilted" toward Saddam and supported him against Iran with outlawed and illegal chemical weapons. Saddam's army was severely damaged by the Kuwait war, by repeated British and US attacks during the 1990s, and by the UN-led sanctions.

The UN weapons inspections were successful in eliminating Saddam's nuclear program and his stockpiles of biological and chemical weapons. The Iraqi regime had no connection to the 9/11 attacks or to their planners in Afghanistan and Pakistan (Mearsheimer and Walt, 2007b). Yet, after 9/11 the Bush administration decided to invade a country that had nothing to do with the attack. This was a decision that will, in all likelihood, continue to have many future repercussions—political, financial, and military. What forms and shapes those repercussions will take will be only revealed with the passage of time.

Eight years after the invasion, most, if not all, of the claims the US administration had used to promote its war in the UNSC and around the world were proven wrong. Even the director of policy planning in the State Department during Bush's first term, Richard Haass, who went on to preside over the Council of Foreign Relations, admitted that he would "go to his grave not knowing the answer" for why the United States had invaded Iraq (Mearsheimer and Walt, 2007b, 229). John Mearsheimer and Stephen Walt analyzed the war decision on three levels. First, the United States was the single most powerful country in the world after the cold war. It achieved consecutive military successes in the Gulf War in 1991, in the Balkans in 1995, in Serbia in 1999, and with its rapid defeat of the Taliban in Afghanistan after 9/11. Second, the 9/11 attacks convinced the United States that remote dangers couldn't be ignored, especially when there is the possibility of terrorists acquiring WMD. Third, advocates of the war believed that toppling Saddam's regime would be a strong message to other "rogue states" that the United States was too powerful to be messed with.

In summary, the United States was incomparably powerful, deeply worried about its own security, and confident of the deterring results of military action (Mearsheimer and Walt, 2007b). Mearsheimer and Walt argue that there was one more separate but decisive factor without which "the war would almost certainly not have occurred," namely, the Israeli lobby in the United States (Mearsheimer and Walt, 2007b, 230). The Israeli lobby and its neoconservative policy makers had pushed for an American invasion of Iraq well before 9/11. The lobby believed that removing Saddam and remapping the Middle East would be of mutual interest to Israel and the United States. Saddam's regime was not a threat to the United States but it was surely a major threat to Israel's security. Robert Novak calls the war "Sharon's war." He declared in April 2007: "I am convinced that Israel made a large contribution to the decision to embark on the war. I know that on the eve of the war, Sharon said, in a closed conversation with senators, that if they could succeed in getting rid of Saddam Hussein, it would solve Israel's security problem" (Mearsheimer and Walt, 2007b, 232). The invasion of Iraq in 2003 and Israel's role in promoting the war agenda is just another example of how the security and geopolitical fate of the Persian Gulf can be linked directly to foreign interests. Gary Sick calls the Arab-Israeli conflict "the ghost at the table" when speaking of the drafting of Persian Gulf policy, be it US policy, the West's policy, or that of the Gulf States themselves (Sick).

There are other factors that may have contributed to the US decision to go to war. According to some, Iraq has the second largest oil reserves after Saudi Arabia, with 11 percent of world reserves (Telhami and Hill); a figure we believe will eventually rise, possibly to a level comparable to Saudi Arabia's, after more extensive exploration in Iraq, the least explored country in the region and the world. Many believe that the Iraq War was a "war for oil" promoted by the major oil companies. The United States already had access to GCC oil resources. With its presence in Afghanistan, the United States secured access to Caspian and central Asian oil and gas. Occupying Iraq was a further step in controlling the world's energy resources and having leverage over China's economic ascension.[5] And finally, if it controlled Iraq, the United States would be in a position to bring Iran once again under its sphere of influence.

The United States invaded Iraq despite objections from some of its closest allies, such as Canada, France, and Germany, and from its adversaries, such as Russia and China. Millions of protestors all over the world took to the streets to demonstrate against the war. The United Nations did not authorize the invasion. None of this mattered because the Bush administration had adopted a new policy of "preventive wars" through preemptive attacks, or the Bush Doctrine. In a speech at West Point Military Academy, President Bush said that the "Cold War doctrines of deterrence and containment" had expired and that after 9/11 "we must take the battle to the enemy, disrupt his plans, and confront the worst threats before they emerge" (Lemann, 284). The United States was ready to topple Saddam's regime and it did so easily, but it was not ready for what came next, nor is it ready for what may come in the future.

The war propaganda machine persuaded Americans that the Iraqi people would greet US troops as liberators, waving flowers and American flags. After all, the war was waged to liberate Iraqis from Saddam's tyranny, to destroy his WMDs, and bring about democracy in the Middle East. The slogans proved to be devoid of fact. The Iraqis rejected the occupation in the same way they rejected the British occupation in the 1920s. In the 1920 revolt, the British had used the Royal Air Force to bomb Iraqi civilians, and now the United States used air power to bomb villages and towns. During the occupation in the 1920s, the British transferred Iraqi detainees to military bases in India where thousands were tortured and killed. The United States detained and tortured thousands of Iraqis in detention camps inside and outside of Iraq. The United States appointed a puppet government to rule Iraq under their supervision as the British had done when they established the Hashemite monarchy. All along, Iraqis have paid a heavy price. What made the toppling of Saddam Hussein even more confrontational than the earlier British efforts was that the Sunni minority who had ruled Iraq for decades were not willing to step aside in favor of their Shia compatriots. Eight years after the US-British invasion of March 20, 2003, Iraq still remains a devastated country. Iraqis in the hundreds of thousands have died and even more have been injured. Millions of Iraqi refugees have gone to neighboring countries such as Jordan and Syria. The once moderately rich country is now a battlefield divided and ruled by tanks, gangs, thugs, and religious fanatics. While the United States formally declared an end to the war on December 15, 2011, all of this has implications far into the future.

Weakened by the economic and military costs of the war and the global economic crisis of 2007–2010, the United States cannot afford to sustain its occupation. American military casualties (excluding military contractors and guards) have been significant in Iraq, 4,481 as of November 3, 2011 (antiwar.com). The US economic turmoil has put the administration under serious internal financial pressures. Public support for the war has plummeted and demands for focusing on domestic issues have risen significantly. The weakening argument that a total US withdrawal will launch Iraq into a civil war is a near exact repetition of the public debates in the British House of Commons when demands for withdrawal started pressuring the British government in the 1920s (Fisk).

Barak Obama won the 2008 presidential election based on the promise of a quick withdrawal from Iraq. In October 2011, he vowed that all US combat troops would be out of Iraq by the end of the year. Whether President Obama has in fact achieved a complete withdrawal remained an open question even in March of 2012, but what has been promised is that his administration will adopt a new approach toward Iraq and its neighbors. If it is to completely withdraw from Iraq, the United States needs the full cooperation of Iraq's neighbors. Violence will only be contained through a process of reconciliation. Engaging in talks with Iran and Syria to help end the fighting in Iraq was one of the recommendations of the Iraq Study Group, cochaired by James Baker and Lee Hamilton (Baker and Hamilton). The Obama administration has adopted a softer tone with Iran and has tried to initiate a dialogue on Iraq and other regional matters. The Saudis and other so-called moderate Arabs who fear that any improvement in the relations between Washington and Tehran will be at the expense of their own relationship with the United States do not welcome such a move. They mistrust Shia Iran and the Shia government in power in Iraq. The brutal suppression of human rights in Bahrain, supported by Saudi Arabia, during the Arab Spring has only deepened mistrust between Iran and Iraq, on the one hand, and between Iran and the GCC, on the other, with ominous implications for religious wars in the future.

International Deterrence to These Wars

Very little was done by the "peace loving" nations of the world or by the United Nations to deter these three wars. While pessimists might say that the wars were inevitable due to facts of history and the connection of events, such as the British occupation of Iraq, the overthrow of Mossadegh, Western support for the Shah, previous US backing for Saddam Hussein, the sale of lethal weapons to dictatorial regimes, and US and other foreign meddling in the region, we believe otherwise. The cycle of wars can be broken if the will exists and if effective institutions for intermediation to deter wars and to support peace are created. Aggressors, no matter who they are, must be confronted with the full human, social, economic, and political costs of their aggression. There is no room for duplicity when it comes to deterring conflicts and wars. There must be consistent and representative costs for aggressors and for those who support and supply them with lethal arms. The price of aggression must be allowed to rise to its real level.

Although the actions of a few Iranian students and the taking of American diplomats as hostages was deplorable, the West's reaction was disproportional in isolating Iran and encouraging and then supporting Saddam Hussein's acts of aggression. Again, the United Nations did almost nothing to condemn or stop Saddam's incursion into Iran. What good is the world's promoter of peaceful coexistence if it does nothing to stop acts of war that violate the most important clause in its charter? The major powers, one by one, said and did very little. In fact, they fueled the war by providing Saddam Hussein with illegal WMD. Ironically, even if they had discovered WMD in Iraq later during the Second Gulf War in 2003, it might have been the very weaponry the West had supplied. Such overtly duplicitous policies have bred contempt for the West and the United Nations in much of the Middle East, eroding almost every shred of credibility the West might have enjoyed. Western support for dictators in the Persian Gulf has become synonymous with corruption and is seen by Middle East intelligence services purely as the West's drive for economic gains. Where is the much-touted support for democratic reform and for social and economic justice?

Saddam Hussein's incursion into Kuwait may have been unstoppable because the major powers were perhaps actually surprised. While the United Nations condemned Iraqi aggression at the time, Saddam Hussein had previously been led to believe he could do no wrong when he invaded Iran. The West had gone along with his every horrific act, so why should this time be any different? If the West truly wants to reduce conflicts and wars, consistency must replace duplicity. Just imagine how much destruction and pain would have been avoided if Saddam Hussein had been indicted in the 1970s by an international court, if a court had existed, and if all countries had supported his indictment? Not only would Saddam Hussein's atrocities have ended but also a strong message would have been sent to other aggressors, and to would-be aggressors, around the world.

The Iraq War in 2003 was initiated by the United States and its allies and there was little anyone could say or do to deter this act of aggression. But the lesson is clear. No existing international institution can deter aggression if doing so is not in the interest of the veto-wielding powers of the UNSC. Illegal action by the UNSC's permanent members erodes UN credibility and encourages lawlessness and aggression around the world.

The three wars outlined above could have been contained, if not thwarted, had there been a strong institution that promoted and facilitated negotiation through intermediation. An institution that could identify and publicize the aggressor, calculate and enforce war reparations, and adopt crippling economic sanctions on the aggressor and on countries who support aggressors and supply them with arms, in short, an institution that could bring criminal leaders to justice and generally act as a nonaligned and impartial promoter of global peace. As is amply evident, the wars outlined above will in all likelihood beget more conflicts and wars in the future, wars and ongoing repercussions that we cannot even begin to fathom today.

Will There Be a Fourth Gulf War?

Three major wars and a number of smaller conflicts have haunted the Persian Gulf for the past thirty-some years. Their repetitive pattern makes a fourth major war within a decade or two at least plausible. Destruction, death, and misery have made the Persian Gulf a cursed region. This is the region that witnessed the birth of the first civilization and brought culture and knowledge to mankind. Is it destiny, divine will, or human nature that has turned the Persian Gulf into a battlefield? Can conflicts and wars be avoided in the future? Europe has overcome a number of wars, including two world wars most recently, and has been peacefully flourishing for the past 60 years. Can the rulers of the Persian Gulf and the world's powers learn from their past mistakes and turn the Persian Gulf into a second European Union?

After World War II, a number of enlightened Europeans realized that countries that benefited from economic cooperation with one another were less likely to engage in military conflict. Military conflict among countries that have significant economic relations (trade, capital flows, business ownership, human exchange, and so on) would be more costly than among countries that have no economic relations. European economies complemented each other (producing different goods and services), and today trade within the European Union represents significantly more than 60 percent of their total trade. The price of armed conflict within the European Union would be high today, much higher than if they had only limited economic relations with each other. Imposing internationally backed penalties against aggression and promoting economic cooperation among nations can increase the price of aggression. While this option was readily available to Western European countries, it has been more problematic for the countries of the Persian Gulf. Nearly all of these countries rely heavily on the depletion of oil and gas to run their economy, with oil also representing practically the entirety of their exports. This is why forming the GCC has done almost nothing to increase trade among its six member countries, whose trade with each other represents only about 5–10 percent of their total trade. There are regional economic projects that could benefit a number of countries, but economic progress and cooperation in the region has been seriously impeded by economic policies that are inconsistent and politically motivated. Still, vision and support, as contrasted with selfish meddling, from the outside could promote regional economic projects and cooperation.

One who does not understand history will never be able to build the future. History teaches us that foreign intervention in both its covert or overt form, whether direct or indirect, has impaired the normal process of nation building in the Persian Gulf, just as in other regions of the world. From Turkish to British to American interference, people of the Persian Gulf have been exploited and dominated because of foreign intervention. On the one hand, realistic political scientists argue that such interventions are normal behaviors of strong states and tend to expand their influence and extend their power. On the other hand, the logical reaction of exploited people and nations is to resent this fact and to rally against it, with ominous implications in the form of future conflicts and wars.

The United States and the rest of the West, Russia, and China should allow the people of the Persian Gulf to decide their own future. No state in the Persian Gulf poses a threat to US (or Chinese or even Russian) national security, because of geographic distance and military and economic disparity. Some argue that the United States needs to maintain its presence in the region to ensure undisrupted flow of oil. The question is not whether the United States should be dependent on Middle East oil, because there is no scenario where it would not be for the foreseeable future, the question is whether the United States needs a huge military presence in the Persian Gulf to secure a continuous flow of oil. A fact that is almost always forgotten is that these countries need to sell their oil to finance their import needs. Oil will flow at market-based prices unless one country takes over another and increases its monopoly power. Such an eventuality can be easily thwarted if the United Nations and the veto-wielding members of the UNSC guarantee the sanctity of each country's borders. Shibley Telhami, in his quest to understand the American oil strategy in the Persian Gulf, asks: "why oil economics should be mixed with oil politics or what necessitates a military strategy at all?" (Telhami, 2002a, 1). He argues that many countries, such as China and Japan, are heavily reliant on imported oil and they base their policies on market demand rather than on political or military intervention. Even political alliances do not determine who gets oil and who is denied. Libya exported the same amount of oil to the Soviet block both before and after the rise of pro-Soviet President Gadhafi in 1969 (Telhami, 2002a). Oil is like any other commodity accessible through the market and its price is linked to its supply and demand. Oil should not be the pretext for continuous American military and political intervention in the Persian Gulf.

Foreign intervention will fuel extremism and undermine moderation and pragmatic governance. The underlying argument for extremists is to fight imperialism and its "puppet regimes" in the region. After World War II, we might not have seen dictators in the guise of shahs, kings, princes, sheikhs, and clerics in the Persian Gulf if there had been no foreign intervention, covert or otherwise. After a period of struggle, we might have, instead, seen more modern and representative governments emerge from the likes of Mossadegh and Qassim; we might have seen governments that served the interests of their own people rather than those of their foreign patrons. We would not have to study border disputes between Persian Gulf states, kingdoms, and sheikhdoms. We might have seen better and more efficient institutions developed and more oil revenues invested in education, economic development, and human welfare rather than in military buildup and outrageously wasteful spending to satisfy the outlandish wishes of a few. Examples from around the world have proven that foreign interventions have invariably generated misery and deprivation. A glimpse into the history of Latin America, Africa, and Southeast Asia tells a similar story. The natural resources of the Persian Gulf, if used efficiently and justly, could provide a prosperous life for all the people of the region. Unfortunately, foreigners have sowed the seeds of conflict and have used corrupt dictators to serve their own short-term interests, making it more difficult for the region to achieve its potential.

People of the Persian Gulf, especially Iranians and Iraqis, understand the horrors of war, and if given a choice they would surely avoid it. Iranians and Iraqis remember how the West and Russia have played them against each other. Almost every family in Iraq or Iran has lost a loved one in the war. More than 100,000 Iraqis have died since the US invasion in 2003 and even more have been injured. From the horrors and sorrows of war, peace can still emerge. Europe needed more than two wars, millions of dead, and massive destruction to learn that peace is the only solution to any and every problem. France and Germany have no more disputes over their Alsace and Lorraine border regions. When will the Persian Gulf follow the European model of reconciliation? Hopefully it won't require a fourth war. Political and economic cooperation is the only fruitful road forward.

Conclusion

It would appear that the human mind cannot fully comprehend what today's conflicts, if unresolved, will lead to in the future. One thing is for sure, the fruit of mediation, reconciliation, and settlement is far more predictable than the aftermath of war, not only in terms of human fatalities, injuries, and destruction, but also because conflicts can spawn more conflicts in the future.

Dictatorships are invariably the enemies of peace. Decisions made by one man—to go to war or to accept peace—are never as measured as group decisions. In a moment of anger, one man's decision can be the basis for many years of conflict and millions of casualties. One man cannot understand all the facets of conflicts and its resultant aftermath. A dictator does not internalize the fallout of war, especially the pain and human suffering. A dictator is not answerable to anyone and has no future election to force him to adopt better policies. Most importantly, the pain and deprivation that he causes do not reverberate back to him. He faces a low, or even a negative, price for his acts of aggression and injustice.

Dictatorships are invariably less popular than democracies, with higher degrees of social, economic, and political injustice. Dictators do not support and nurture efficient institutions—necessary for economic prosperity—because these institutions would in turn undermine their corrupt rule. Dictatorships are more likely to pit one group, whether religious, ethnic, or tribal, against another—to divide and conquer—and sow the seeds of internal conflict.

Some speak of just wars and revenge for wrongs, but the pursuit of justice and revenge invariably brings more unhappiness and pain than the momentary, fleeting joy of a just victory. If Khomeini had accepted peace in 1982 or 1983, hundreds of thousands of lives would have been saved and hundreds of billions of dollars in destruction would have been avoided. Both Iran and Iraq would most probably be much more prosperous. But Khomeini wanted personal revenge against the one man who had kicked him out of Iraq and who had later invaded Iran.

Border disputes and disputes over natural resources are fires that continue to smolder. They continue to plague a number of regions around the world and should be urgently addressed. These disputes are easily identifiable and must be mediated before conflicts escalate and differences become more difficult to resolve.

Importing lethal weaponry, especially arms banned by international conventions, into conflict regions only makes conflicts more devastating, in turn breeding more hatred and resulting in more devastation and future conflicts.

Foreign powers in pursuit of their own short-run aims miss the bigger and longer-term picture as they adopt policies that are invariably devastating for the people they choose to dominate. In the end, policies that foreign powers consider to be in their national interest may in fact turn out to be exactly the opposite, with significant human and economic costs. US support for Middle East dictators affords ample examples in support of these assertions. Today the United States finds itself unpopular and distrusted in much of the Muslim world and has limited options to influence events in the Middle East.

Foreign support of dictators and autocratic rulers lowers their perceived price of aggression. Dictators may be given the impression that they will be supported no matter how egregious their acts. This can but only fuel aggression and conflict around the world.

Economic prosperity, economic cooperation, and economic projects among countries sow the seeds of peace by elevating the price of all conflicts.

The United Nations cannot hope to be credible if it acts duplicitously, caters to the major powers in a biased way, and unquestioningly does their bidding. The United Nations must act impartially and must not be used by global powers as yet another instrument to pursue their own selfish interests around the world. All members of the UNSC, especially the permanent members, must conduct their own policies in the letter and spirit of UN resolutions.

Maybe, just maybe, it is time to interject a small dose of morality into the foreign policy mix. The absence of morality in foreign affairs may become increasingly apparent in a world of Internet and social media.

Finally, we should note that a single person scarred by war and with a burning hatred can, unfortunately, be the source of another war a generation later. But at the same time we should note that, fortunately, one principled and committed human being could also affect positive change that may have been thought impossible. Conflict is a cycle that must be broken, not by revenge but by reconciliation, with forgiveness at its core.

Chapter 5

The Global Cost of Three Wars in the Persian Gulf

The Persian Gulf region has been in a state of war for the past thirty or so years.[1] The world's most significant and costliest wars since the Vietnam War have been fought in the Persian Gulf: the Iran-Iraq War from 1981 to 1988, the Persian Gulf War in 1991, and the Iraq War, which was launched in 2003 and although officially over in December of 2011 is still taking a toll. In chapter 3, we discussed our preferred framework for calculating the global cost of wars. In this chapter, we use this framework to estimate the cost of the three major conflicts in the Persian Gulf region during the 1980s, 1990s, and 2000s. We should emphasize that almost all the estimates provided here are based on conservative assumptions and are in constant US dollars. Data limitations have prevented us from estimating every cost attributable to these wars.[2]

Global Cost of the Iran-Iraq War

The Iran-Iraq War was the longest conventional war of the twentieth century, lasting from 1980 to 1988. The war not only devastated the economies of the direct belligerents but also affected the global economy with the resultant higher energy prices and higher sense of insecurity. Moreover, this war profoundly changed the geopolitics of the Persian Gulf region forever.

Cost to the Direct Belligerents

To estimate the budgetary costs of the Iran-Iraq War to each country, we depended on two previous studies (Amirahmadi; Mofid) and used many of their available numbers. Both studies give estimates for the direct and indirect costs of the war to Iran and to Iraq but do not include a number of critical macroeconomic costs of the war. Moreover, the estimated cost is not summed up in constant dollars in either study; the estimate is a simple summation of costs in each year throughout the eight-year war, but there was inflation in the United States and the dollar depreciated significantly in the 1980s—by around 50 percent from 1980 to 1988—affecting costs that were denominated in other currencies. For our estimate, we converted values in current US\$ to constant 1988 US\$ wherever possible. Table 5.1 shows the elements of the budgetary and macroeconomic cost categories of the Iran-Iraq War.

For budgetary costs of the war for Iran, we depended on the estimates provided by Amirahmadi. He used official values extracted from a report prepared by the Iranian government two years before the 1988 ceasefire. Assuming the same rate of accruing costs for the last two years of the war, we estimated the total budgetary cost of the war. For damage to Iranian infrastructure, we used the same estimates used by Amirahmadi. The total damage to Iranian infrastructure was more than \$210 billion.[3] The cost of combat and support operations was about \$49 billion, and another \$6 billion was paid to veterans, the families of the fallen, refugees, martyr foundations, and the like. Furthermore, we conservatively estimated that at least \$12 billion was needed at the end of the war to support veterans and the families of the fallen for the next two decades, namely, the1990s and 2000s. For Iraq, we relied on estimates provided by Mofid. He estimated the damage to Iraq's infrastructure at about \$67 billion. Iraq spent at least \$55 billion for combat and support operations during the war. Since there were no estimates for the costs associated with veterans, and also considering Iraq's human losses and injuries,[4] we conservatively assumed (assuming some proportionality to Iranian costs) that Iraq needed more than \$10 billion to cover such costs. The total budgetary cost of the war for Iran at the end of the war was \$277 billion and for Iraq it was \$132 billion in current US\$. However, if we assume that all these costs were incurred at a constant rate during the eight-year war, we can provide a better estimate in constant 1988 US\$. Thus we estimated a budgetary cost of \$329 and \$157 billion to Iran and Iraq, respectively. We should emphasize that our estimate still does not include increased postwar military expenditures and war financing costs

Table 5.1   Cost of the Iran-Iraq War to the Direct Belligerents

	To Iran	To Iraq
Budgetary Costs	• $210 billion in damage to infrastructure (including resettlement costs). • $49 billion for combat and support operations. • $6 billion in payments to refugees, veterans, the injured, and the Martyrs Foundation during the war and a minimum of another $12 billion for the next two decades.	• $67 billion in damage to infrastructure. • $55 billion for combat and support operations. • $10 billion in payments to refugees, injured, veterans, and the families of the fallen.
Total (current US$)	$277 billion.	$132 billion.
Total (1988 US$)	$329 billion.	$157 billion.
Macroeconomic Costs	• $112 billion in lost economic output (excluding forgone oil revenues). • $147 billion in forgone oil revenues. • $49 billion in costs associated with diverted government expenditures.	• $20 billion in lost economic output (excluding forgone oil revenues). • $144 billion in forgone oil revenues. • $55 billion in costs associated with diverted government expenditures.
Total (1988 US$)	$308 billion.	$219 billion.
Total Budgetary and Macroeconomic Costs to both Countries	$1,013 billion.	

Source: Author's estimates; estimates for budgetary costs are derived from data provided by Amirahmadi, H. "Economic Reconstruction of Iran: Costing the War Damage." *Third World Quarterly* vol. 12, no. 1 (1990): 26–47. Mofid, K. "Economic Reconstruction of Iraq: Financing the Peace." *Third World Quarterly* vol. 12, no. 1 (1990): 48–61.

on war-related debt—chiefly due to the lack of accurate data—and also war reparation costs.[5]

To calculate the macroeconomic costs of the war, we intentionally separated the oil sector from the rest of the economy in both countries. Our reason for doing this is that the oil industry is the backbone of both economies and can be better assessed on a stand-alone basis. Before the war, the oil sector accounted (in terms of GDP) for around 20 percent and 60 percent of the economy of Iran and Iraq, respectively. Iran and Iraq were, respectively, the second biggest and third biggest oil exporters in OPEC prior to the war. Iran was exporting more than 5 million barrels per day before its revolution and Iraqi oil exports were more than 2.5 million barrels per day. Iraq was expected to increase its exports to 3 million barrels per day by the early 1980s, while Iran's recovery (after a decline in exports) to an export capacity of about 4 million barrels would have been a reasonable expectation—since such a capacity had already existed—if there had been no war. So we assumed that in the absence of war Iran would have succeeded in increasing its export capacity gradually, reaching 4 million barrels per day by 1983, and Iraq's oil export would have reached 3 million barrels per day by the end of 1980.

In the counterfactual analysis, we also needed a hypothetical price for oil. The spot price of oil jumped from $13 a barrel in 1978 to $30 in 1980 due, in large part, to Iran's revolution in 1979 and the instability in its oil exports. In 1980, the border conflict escalated between Iran and Iraq, pushing prices as high as $35. In spite of the global economic downturn in the first half of the 1980s, oil prices were hovering above $25 until 1986 when they fell sharply to slightly above $13. If there had been no war, we believe oil prices would have retreated to their pre-1979 levels. So, as a reasonable scenario, we assumed at least $5 of the increase in oil prices from 1980 to 1985 and $3 of the increase from 1986 to 1988 were due to the war.[6] We then subtracted these values from the Dubai oil basket average annual spot prices and used the adjusted values in our counterfactual analysis. As for both countries' realized oil exports from 1980 to 1988, and given our counterfactual assumptions, the forgone oil revenue for Iran and Iraq were highly significant, namely, $147 and $144 billion in constant 1988 US$, respectively.

Because of data limitations, we used two different methods to calculate lost economic output for Iran and Iraq. Amirahmadi provided partial estimates of lost economic output for Iran. Total forgone economic output was estimated at around $382 billion, of which the lost economic output in oil and gas industries accounted for almost 75 percent or $287 billion. To avoid double counting we first excluded the lost economic output in the Iranian oil industry from the calculation. The balance, or $94 billion, was considered forgone economic output in the principal economic sectors excluding oil and gas in current US$. If we simply assume the Iranian economy incurred this loss at a constant rate during the war, the total value could be as high as $112 billion in constant 1988 US$. For Iraq, we did not have detailed data to estimate its lost economic output. We first subtracted

Iraq's oil revenue from its GDP for the period from 1980 to 1988. Then, as suggested by Alnasrawi, we assumed a 6.5 percent economic growth rate—the average growth rate for non-oil exporting developing economies in the 1980s—for Iraq in the absence of war. The value of forgone economic output excluding lost oil revenues based on our calculation was $20 billion, a figure that is very close to Mofid's estimate. Iraq also saw all of its $35 billion in foreign exchange reserves vanish in the early stages of the war. We did not include this loss in our calculation because it had been accounted for elsewhere.[7]

For the cost associated with diverted government expenditures, we assumed that government expenditures in a developing country, such as Iran and Iraq, in any sector other than military—namely, education, health care, transportation, and so on—would at least yield a multiplier of 2. The Stiglitz and Bilmes estimate for the US economy was 1.5, but we believe for developing countries in the 1980s, which were operating below their potential (production capacity), a multiplier of 2 is a more appropriate figure. Also, regarding the fact that a considerable share of the budget for combat and support operations was allocated for importing weapons and replenishing military arsenals—fighter jets, ammunitions, missiles, warships, helicopters, and spare parts—one could reasonably assume a high leakage. The Stiglitz and Bilmes estimate for the United States' military expenditures multiplier was 1.1, with the lion's share of war-related spending in Iraq channeled back to US defense contractors. Therefore, we believed that a somewhat lower military expenditures multiplier of 1 would be appropriate for Iran and Iraq.[8] The difference between these two multipliers—which was 1 for Iran and Iraq—multiplied by the budgetary costs of the combat and support operations yielded the opportunity cost associated with diverted government expenditures. This opportunity cost was $49 billion for Iran (spent directly on war in the form of the combat and support operations) and $55 billion for Iraq. Thus, based on our estimates, the total macroeconomic cost of the war for Iran was $308 billion and for Iraq it was $219 billion. These figures do not include the environmental cost of the war[9] or the long-lasting destructive effect of brain drain[10]—both of which will last far beyond the period of war and will have profound negative effects on the national economy—and the costs associated with accelerated depreciation of military hardware.

As presented in table 5.1, the total cost of the war for Iran was at least $637 billion and for Iraq it was at least $376 billion, resulting in the minimum (because a number of cost items were omitted due to data limitations and because we assumed conservative estimates all along) total cost of $1,013 incurred by both countries—all in constant 1988 US$.

Cost to Other Persian Gulf Countries

During the eight-year war between Iran and Iraq, three other Persian Gulf countries, namely, Saudi Arabia, Kuwait, and the United Arab Emirates, were at least financially involved in the war. Their unequivocal backing for Iraq was accompanied by around $40 billion in financial support, according to the Iraq Survey Group Final Report.[11] Iraq received this financial assistance throughout the war, thus the real value of this support in constant 1988 US$ was higher than $40 billion. Unfortunately, the military expenditures data was not readily available for all the countries in the region before 1979, so we were not able to estimate the increase in the Persian Gulf countries' defense budgets during and after the Iran-Iraq War. However, the evidence of an increase in military expenditures was strong in the 1988 military expenditures data provided by the Stockholm International Peace Research Institute (SIPRI). Kuwait's military expenditure was $3.3 billion, Oman's was $2.1 billion, and Saudi Arabia's was a staggering $17.8 billion—all in constant 2008 US$—which suggests that the whole region became more heavily militarized during and after the war. In our opinion, the Iran-Iraq War initiated the trend leading to the Persian Gulf region becoming the most militarized region in the world. And finally, given the absence of data on the cost of caring for refugees and payments to global powers for military protection,[12] our estimate of the budgetary costs of the war to the other Persian Gulf countries again underestimates their true budgetary costs.

As for the macroeconomic costs, we only had financial aid data, so we were only able to estimate the macroeconomic costs associated with this category of diverted government expenditures.[13] We assumed that the $40 billion in financial aid to Iraq provided by the GCC was drained almost fully from their economies—full leakage. Therefore, one could reasonably assume that if these countries spent that amount on nondefense sectors, assuming a multiplier of 2 for nondefense expenditures, their macroeconomic gain would have been as high as $80 billion. Apart from this, we did not have sufficient data to calculate other macroeconomic burden to the other Persian Gulf countries. Although looking directly at the economic output of each country does not show that their economies suffered significantly from the war (as they had large current account surpluses), it is reasonable to assume that all national economies in the region were affected by the higher cost of trade, forgone domestic and foreign investment, reduced tourist arrivals, higher energy prices (for energy importers), higher costs for alternative import routes, and lower economic confidence for the future. As we have already mentioned, we did not have sufficient data on military expenditures prior to 1979, and we did not have data on

Table 5.2 Cost of the Iran-Iraq War to Other Persian Gulf Countries and to the Rest of the World

Cost to other Persian Gulf Countries	Budgetary Cost	• $40 billion in financial aid to Iraq.
	Macroeconomic Cost (limited)	• $80 billion in costs associated with diverted government expenditures.
	Total (1988 $U.S.)	$120 billion.
Cost to the Rest of the World	Budgetary Cost	• $35 billion in financial aid to Iraq.
	Macroeconomic Cost (limited)	• $256 billion in the macroeconomic effect of higher oil prices. • $35 billion in costs associated with diverted government expenditures.
	Total (1988 $U.S.)	$326 billion.
Global Cost of the Iran-Iraq War		$1,384 billion.[1]

Source: Author's estimates; estimates for financial aid to Iraq are provided by International Court of Justice. "Case Concerning Military and Paramilitary Iraq Survey Study Group Final Report (2004)." Retrieved from http://www.globalsecurity.org/wmd /library/report/2004/isg-final-report/

Notes: [1]This includes the cost to direct belligerents, other Persian Gulf countries, and the rest of the world. It is adjusted for $75 billion in financial aid transferred from neighboring countries and the rest of the world to Iraq.

environmental damage to the Persian Gulf ecosystem. Thus our analysis excluded other costs associated with diverted government expenditures in other Persian Gulf countries and also the environmental costs. All in all, we believe that our conservative estimate of the total costs incurred by other Persian Gulf countries is considerably below the actual costs incurred by these countries during the eight-year war, for the reasons mentioned above. We believe that the true cost of these factors (for which we had no data) to Iran's and Iraq's neighbors during and after the war could plausibly be estimated in the hundreds of billions of dollars (see table 5.2).

Cost to the Rest of the World:

According to the Iraq Survey Group Final Report, Iraq's foreign debt at the end of the war consisted of Western credit provided for military assistance, development finance, and export guarantees. Roughly $35 billion was loaned to Iraq between 1980 and 1989. Although the destructive role that the Iran-Iraq War played in deteriorating security conditions in the Persian Gulf region and in the global energy market is apparent, we did not have the required data to show how this heightened sense of insecurity was translated into higher military expenditures, not only in the Persian Gulf but also in the rest of the world, especially among global superpowers. The total budgetary cost of the war to the rest of the world was $35 billion, which we again believe to be an underestimate of the true cost.

The heightened sense of insecurity also resulted in higher cost of international trade and higher risk of domestic and foreign investment, undoubtedly affecting global economic growth negatively. We did not include these costs due to the lack of data. For the cost associated with government expenditures, again we were limited to the negative effect of direct financial aid to Iraq by the rest of the world. Since almost all the financing was from European or East Asian developed economies, we assumed multipliers of 1.5 and 0.5, respectively, for their nondefense spending and for financial aid to Iraq.[14] Based on our assumptions, the cost associated with this category of diverted government expenditures was estimated at $35 billion.

The most important part of the global cost of the Iran-Iraq War was its effect on energy prices paid by the rest of the world for eight years and its consequent macroeconomic shock to global GDP. If we again assume that at least $5 of the increase in oil prices from 1980 to 1985 and $3 of the increase from 1986 to 1988 were due to the war, the total amount of the increase spent on oil by the rest of the world would be estimated at $991 billion. The direct effect of higher oil prices, namely, higher oil import bills, benefited oil exporters to the same degree as higher oil export revenues. While one group incurred a cost, another received the same in benefit, a windfall that was enjoyed by all oil exporters around the world. Therefore, this extra cost was just a transfer of revenue from oil-importers to oil-exporters around the world, and should not be included in the aggregate calculation, but this was still a considerable benefit to some and a cost to others and had to be included as benefits or costs for subgroups of countries.

Moreover, higher energy prices had a significant macroeconomic impact on the global economy. As Mussa suggested, higher oil prices affected the global economy through a variety of channels: such as the rise in the cost of production, impact on the general price level, and direct and indirect effect on financial markets. Mussa investigated the energy price surge in the late 1990s and showed that each 20 percent sustainable increase in oil prices would have led to a 0.25 percent decline in global output for the ensuing four years. We believe that since the dynamics of the global economy in the 1970s and 1980s was very different from what they were in the late 1990s and early 2000s, these measures could hardly be applied in this analysis. It is clear that in the early 1980s even developed economies were far more vulnerable to oil price volatilities. While the oil price surges of the 1970s and 1980s had destructive effects on both developed and developing countries in the form of deep recessions and double-digit inflation rates, recent oil price shocks have by no means had the same devastating effect, even on weaker developing economies. So we can be reasonably certain that a 20 percent increase in oil prices in the 1980s would have caused far more than a 0.25 percent decline in global output for a period longer than four consecutive years. If we assume that a 20 percent increase in oil prices[15] leads to a 0.5 percent decline in global output for the ensuing four years (still yielding conservative estimates), the negative effect of higher oil prices on the rest of the world would be as high as $256 billion in constant 1988 US$.

The total estimated cost to the rest of the world during the Iran-Iraq War, based on our conservative (and omitting a number of important costs for which we had insufficient data) estimation, is $326 billion.

Total Cost of the War

The estimated cost of the war was $637 billion to Iran, $376 billion to Iraq, and $326 to other Persian Gulf countries and the rest of the world, all in constant 1988 US$. The estimated global cost of the Iran-Iraq War, based on our conservative assumptions and methodology (while omitting a number of significant costs due to the lack of data), is almost $1.4 trillion in constant 1988 US$.

Global Cost of the Persian Gulf War

Beside Iraq, Kuwait, and Saudi Arabia, who were directly involved in the Persian Gulf War, countries from around the world, from Western and Eastern Europe, from Africa and the Muslim world,[16] were also participants. Other than for a few budgetary and macroeconomic cost items, we rely heavily on estimates and data provided by Cranna. For the rest, we have made our own estimates.

Cost to Direct Belligerents

Different estimates were available for damage to Iraqi and Kuwaiti infrastructure and for reconstruction costs, namely, between $100 and $200 billion for Iraq and between $50 and $100 billion for Kuwait. In this analysis, we assume that the reconstruction cost for Iraq was $150 billion and for Kuwait it was $75 billion—or an average of the available estimates. Iraq was also held responsible for the war and was assessed $53 billion in war reparations to Kuwait. Although Iraq incurred reparation costs after the war and by the end of 2010 had paid more than $18 billion to Kuwait, we exclude the war reparation payments from our total or aggregate cost calculation (although a benefit to one and a cost to the other, they cancel out when we add the cost to Iraq and Kuwait) because the sum is simply a transfer between direct belligerents. As for combat and support operations, different sources give different estimates. Some claim Saudi Arabia alone spent more than $60 billion on the war. Based on data provided by Cranna, we assume Saudi Arabia and other Persian Gulf countries paid a total of at least $50 billion to the allies for combat and support operations, with Kuwait alone paying $22 billion. For Iraq, there was no available data on combat and support operations. Based on our estimates, the total budgetary cost to Iraq—excluding the cost of combat and support operations, but including war reparations—was at least $203 billion, which is high for a 210-day war for a developing economy. For the allies, the budgetary cost does not stop here.

After the war, the military expenditures of almost all Persian Gulf countries skyrocketed, especially those of Saudi Arabia and Kuwait. It is difficult to isolate the amount of increase in military expenditures specifically attributable to the Persian Gulf War. We must also remember that a significant share of almost any increase in the military budgets of Persian Gulf countries is translated into higher military sales and profits for the world's major arms exporters, namely, the United States, France, and the UK, already considered direct belligerents in this analysis.[17] So to avoid counting this transfer of cost/profit between direct belligerents, we first need to calculate the additional, or unusual, increase in Saudi and Kuwaiti arms imports and subtract that figure from the unusual increase in the countries' total military expenditures. What is left could be considered the unusual increase in defense expenditures independent of unusual increase in defense imports. We believe this is the best way to avoid counting the transfer of cost/profit between direct belligerents and at the same time to detect the unusual increase in military expenditures. For Saudi Arabia, we conservatively assume that the figure of $17 billion military expenditure in 1988 is normal.[18] Then we assume that any further increase in the amount of military expenditures in the next five years was actually due to the Persian Gulf War and the higher sense of insecurity in the region. For the period of 1993–1997, we estimate that at least $5 billion in constant 1991 US$ increase in Saudi Arabia's postwar defense budgets was due to the Persian Gulf War and its associated repercussions.[19] Applying the same technique for Kuwait, we estimate that Kuwait's postwar increased military expenditure was at least $5 billion higher in 1991 constant US$.

A different approach was needed to estimate the higher military expenditures of France, Britain, and the United States resulting from the war. The cold war was practically over by the end of 1989, thus, one would reasonably expect that the military expenditures of the major military powers would have declined in the 1990s to a lower equilibrium level. However, this did not happen until after the mid-1990s[20] in these countries, and we believe that the major reason for this delay was the Persian Gulf War. One reason behind this delayed decrease in military budgets could be the higher depreciation rate of military hardware and consequently the demand for replenishing military arsenals and replacing old or lost hardware.[21] Based on our estimates, in 1994 and 1995 at least $45 billion of the US military expenditures in constant 1991 US$ was due to the 1991 war. For Britain and France, our conservative estimates are $7 billion and $4 billion, respectively.

The last two budgetary costs are associated with the no-fly zone and veteran benefits. According to John Amidon of the Air War College, the cost of the no-fly zone is estimated at $15 billion per year, while Wallsten and Kosec suggest a figure of around $11 billion (Stiglitz and Bilmes). Here we assume that the cost from 1991 to 2003 (when the Iraq War began) was $10 billion annually in constant 1991 US$. Therefore, we arrive at a figure of $120 billion for no-fly-zone costs to the United States and its allies. As for the cost associated with veteran benefits, the annual estimate of this cost to the United States is about $2 billion (Hartung). If we assume that the US government has been incurring this cost from right after the end of the war and will continue to pay these veteran benefits for 25 years after the war, our estimate of the total cost for veterans would be $35 billion in constant 1991 US$. For Iraq and other direct belligerents, we either do not have an estimate for total veteran costs or it is not significant. We know Iraqi combat casualties were estimated at 20,000 to 35,000 and Iraqi civilian casualties were estimated at 3,500 (Fisk). Also, more than 75,000 Iraqi soldiers were wounded in the 210-day conflict (Conetta). We do not include budgetary and macroeconomic costs of the Iraqi casualties and injured in our calculation, although one can be reasonably certain about the significant, devastating effect of Iraq's human loss on its economy.[22]

Based on our estimation and recalling the fact that a number of important cost items are excluded from our calculation due to the lack of accurate data, the total budgetary costs of war to the allied forces is $368 billion and to Iraq it is $203 billion. We estimate the total budgetary cost of the war—excluding $53 billion in war reparations—to the direct belligerents as $518 billion. It is important to note that we could not include costs associated with refugees, Iraqi combat and support operations, Iraqi and allied veterans (except for the United States), and environmental costs (see table 5.3).

Estimation of the macroeconomic cost to Iraq is relatively straightforward. Iraq's GDP dropped from $66 billion in 1990 to almost zero. Based on our calculation, $10 billion of this decline in GDP was due to forgone oil revenues. Since we did not have any estimate for Iraq's direct war expenditures, we could not provide any estimate for the costs associated with diverted government expenditures. Also, we did not have any estimate for the long-term macroeconomic loss associated with Iraq's human losses— between 20,000 and 35,000 combat fatalities 3,500 civilian casualties, and 75,000 wounded soldiers.

For the allies, we had Kuwait's $13 billion decline in economic output—of which we estimate $10 billion as forgone oil revenues. For the cost associated with diverted government expenditures, we had two groups of countries: Western developed countries and the Persian Gulf countries. For the Persian Gulf countries, we first summed up all direct war expenditures incurred and, as in the case of the Iran-Iraq War, we assume a multiplier of 2 for government expenditures in nondefense sectors and a multiplier of 1 for defense-related expenditures.[23] For the developed countries we apply the estimates used by Stiglitz and Bilmes for the US economy for the 2003 Iraq War: 1.5 for government expenditures on nonmilitary sectors and 1.1 for war-related government spending in Iraq. Therefore, we estimate the costs associated with diverted government expenditures for Western developed countries and the Persian Gulf countries at $70 billion and $82 billion, respectively.

Here again a number of critical macroeconomic cost items are excluded from our calculation due to lack of data, the most important being the environmental costs. According to the Government Council of the United Nations Environment Program, the total amount of Kuwaiti oil spills and fires during the Persian Gulf War in 1991 were higher than all other recorded oil spills and oil fire incidents around the world combined.[24] We do not provide any monetary estimate for this catastrophic damage to the Persian Gulf ecosystem due to lack of data.

We finally arrive at a minimum of $66 billion in macroeconomic costs to Iraq and at least $165 billion in macroeconomic costs to the allies.

Cost to Other Persian Gulf Countries

We have already included the financial transfer to the allies—mainly for combat and support operations—by other Persian Gulf countries in the

Table 5.3 Cost of the Persian Gulf War (1991) to the Direct Belligerents

	To Iraq	To the Allies
Budgetary Costs	• $150 billion in reconstruction costs. • $53 billion for war reparations (excluded from calculation-transfer between direct belligerents).	• $75 billion for Kuwait's reconstruction costs. • $72 billion paid directly by Saudi Arabia, Kuwait, and other Persian Gulf countries to the allies for combat and support operations (a cost not included below in the cost to allies, to avoid double counting); the total cost included $17 billion paid by Japan (see table 5.4). • $14 billion borrowed by the governments of Saudi Arabia and Kuwait after the war due to budget deficits (excluded from calculation to avoid double-counting). • $10 billion increase in Saudi Arabia and Kuwait's military expenditures within the next five years after the war. • $45 billion in extra military expenditures by the United States. • $11 billion in extra military expenditures by Britain and France. • $35 billion in additional US veteran costs for the next 25 years after the war. • $120 billion cost of the no-fly zone to the United States and its allies for the next 12 years.
Macroeconomic Costs	• $56 billion in lost economic output (excluding forgone oil revenues). • $10 billion in forgone oil revenues.	• $3 billion in lost economic output (excluding forgone oil revenues). • $10 billion for Kuwait's forgone oil revenues. • $82 billion in diverted government expenditures for Saudi Arabia, Kuwait, and other Persian Gulf countries. • $70 billion in diverted government expenditures for the United States, Britain, and France.
Total	$269 billion.	$533 billion.
Total Cost to Direct Belligerents		$749 billion.[1]

Source: Author's estimates.

Notes: [1]War reparation payments are not included as they are a cost to the aggressor and a benefit to the recipient.

Table 5.4   Cost of the Persian Gulf War to Other Persian Gulf Countries and to the Rest of the World

Cost to Other Persian Gulf Countries	Budgetary Cost	• Included in the calculation of the cost to direct belligerents.
	Macroeconomic Cost	• Included in the calculation of the cost to direct belligerents.
	Total Cost	—
Cost to the Rest of the World	Budgetary Cost	• $17 billion paid by Japan and Germany to the allies for combat and support operations.
	Macroeconomic Cost	• $17 billion in costs associated with diverted government expenditures.
	Total Cost	$34 billion.
Global Cost of the Persian Gulf War (1991)		$783 billion.[1]

Source: Author's estimates.

Notes: [1]To avoid double counting, it is adjusted for the reconstruction and relief costs to Iraq funded by the rest of the world.

previous section. Again, it is reasonable to assume that all national economies in the region suffered macroeconomic damage through higher cost of trade, forgone domestic and foreign investment, reduced tourist arrivals, costs associated with diverted government expenditures, and, finally, calamitous environmental damages to the Persian Gulf ecosystem due to oil spill, which was about 300 times bigger than the 2010 oil spill in the Gulf of Mexico (see table 5.4).

Cost to the Rest of the World

Twenty-seven countries from four different continents were directly involved in the Persian Gulf War. The war-related costs incurred by these countries are already included in the "direct belligerent" category. But, besides the coalition or allied countries, Germany and Japan also made significant contributions—solely financial—to the war. They paid the allies $17 billion for combat and support operations.

As for macroeconomic costs to Germany and Japan, we again assume a multiplier of 1.5 for spending on nondefense sectors and of 0.5 for granting financial aid to the allies. Therefore, the costs associated with diverted government expenditures are estimated at $35 billion. Here again the lack of appropriate data has forced us to exclude other macroeconomic cost items from our calculation.

Total Cost of the War

In contrast to the Iran-Iraq War, this short war did not have a profound long-term impact on oil prices, so we exclude the effect of higher energy prices from our calculation. However, inevitable exclusion of the environmental costs of the war from our calculation results in an underestimate of the burden on Persian Gulf countries.

The cost of the Persian Gulf War was $269 billion for Iraq, $533 billion for the allies, and $34 billion for the rest of the world. The global cost, based on our conservative assumptions and calculation, is at least $783 billion in constant 1991 US$, far above the initial estimations and highly significant, by any standard, for a 210-day military conflict.

Global Cost of the 2003 Iraq War

What seemed to be a certain military victory at the end of a 42-day military campaign turned out to be one of the costliest military interventions in recent history. Before the war, the conflict was estimated to cost anywhere between $50 billion and $100 billion according to official preliminary US estimates, but by 2011 the United States had squandered $816 billion[25] of American taxpayers' money in combat and support operations alone and continued to spend great sums till late 2011. In this section, applying our framework, we use data and estimates provided by the Eisenhower Study Group[26] as well as those by a number of other studies to estimate the global cost of the Iraq War.

Cost to the Direct Belligerents

Although many countries[27] were involved in the invasion of Iraq, almost all of them except the United States and the United Kingdom participated marginally and pulled out their small number of troops between 2004 and 2009. The United States and Iraq are the two countries most heavily involved in the war and have suffered the most in terms of human losses, budgetary costs, and macroeconomic burden from the war. In our calculation, we focus mainly on the costs incurred by the US, the UK, and, of course, Iraq. In table 5.5 we present our estimates of the budgetary and macroeconomic costs inflicted on the direct belligerents.

As for combat and support operation costs, the Pentagon has allocated $758 billion for combat and support operations alone in Iraq since

Table 5.5   Cost of the Iraq War (2003–2011) to the Direct Belligerents

	To Iraq	To The Allies
Budgetary Cost	• $44 billion in international aid allocated for reconstruction and relief.	• $816 billion spent by the United States for combat and support operations. • $20 billion spent by the UK for combat and support operations (excluding troops' basic salaries and veteran cost). • $200 billion in projected combat and support operation costs (through 2020). • $21 billion spent by the United States for veteran care (through 2011). • $412 billion in future veteran costs. • $217 billion for increase in US defense expenditures attributed to the Iraq War (through 2011). • $45 billion spent by the United States on financial and security assistance to Iraq and on reconstruction and relief.
Macroeconomic Costs	• $13 billion drop in economic output in 2003.	• $334 billion for social-economic costs for veteran and military families. • $424 billion in costs associated with diverted US government expenditures. • $8 billion in costs associated with diverted UK government expenditures.
Total	$57 billion.	$2,497 billion.
Total Costs to Direct Belligerents		$2,509 billion.[1]

Source: Author's estimates.

Notes: [1] It is adjusted to avoid double counting for parts of US costs for reconstruction, relief, and security assistance to Iraq.

the start of the war in 2003, according to the Congressional Research Service (Wheeler). We estimate the present value of this amount in 2011 US$ at $816 billion. The UK had spent more than £9 billion by mid-2010 on combat and support operations, according to various official reports. Our calculation suggests that the present value of this amount is about $20 billion, a figure that does not include the base salaries of UK troops and long-term veteran benefit costs. For future budgetary costs of the war to the United States, we rely on estimates provided by the Congressional Research Service (CRS) and the Congressional Budget office (CBO). The total amount projected as future (through 2020) war spending for Iraq and Afghanistan by the CRS and CBO is $441 billion. So far, Iraq War costs account for 65 percent of the total budgetary cost incurred by the Pentagon in Iraq and Afghanistan. If we reasonably presume that in this decade the Pentagon will focus more on Afghanistan, we can assume that the share of costs for the Iraq War will decline to around 50 percent of the Pentagon's budgetary costs. We estimate the present value of the projected war expenditure budget for the Iraq War at roughly $200 billion for the next nine years (through 2020). The present value of the total costs incurred and the projected budgets allocated by the allies to combat and support operations in Iraq is at least $1,036 billion—noting the fact that we have not included all direct budgetary costs incurred by other allied countries except the UK, and that the CBO and CRS almost always underestimate and ignore some critical US defense department costs.

As of June 2011, there were 4,457 US soldiers, 418 non-US soldiers, and 1,537 American contractors killed in Iraq. More than 32,000 US soldiers, 426 British soldiers, and 40,688 American contractors have been wounded during the Iraq War (Lutz). For the costs of veteran care, we have access only to US data, so our final estimate here would be conservative by omission. The United States has already spent more than $31 billion since 2001 on medical care and disability benefits to Iraq and Afghanistan veterans (Bilmes). By 2011, some 70 percent of the injured were from the Iraq War. Also, until recently the majority of 1.2 million US servicemen and servicewomen engaged in the war against terror in the Persian Gulf region were serving in Iraq. So we can reasonably assume that 70 percent of the veteran care budget was, and will be, allocated to Iraq War veterans. Based on our assumption so far, $21 billion in 2011 US$ has been spent by the United States on Iraq War veteran care—medical care and disabilities. According to Bilmes, veterans from Iraq and Afghanistan are utilizing Veterans Affairs (VA) medical services and applying for disability benefits at much higher rates than in previous wars. She estimates that the present value of future medical, disability, and social security costs of the wars in Iraq and Afghanistan to the United States for the next 40 years is in the range of $589 to $934 billion. We pick the conservative number and estimate the present value of future veteran care costs of the Iraq War to the United States at $412 billion.[28] Thus, the total veteran cost of the Iraq War to the allies would exceed $433 billion in 2011 US$. This is, of course, a fairly conservative estimate, since we have taken a conservative approach to estimating the US cost and have added to this only the UK's veteran budgetary costs.

According to the Pentagon's budget baseline plan, the defense budget was supposed to increase slightly from $386 billion in 2001 to $417 billion in 2011—both values in constant 2011 US$. However, the difference between the planned and the actual Pentagon expenditures, excluding war spending budget allocations, is $667 billion in higher spending in constant 2011 US$ (Wheeler). We can reasonably attribute half of the allocation over the projected baseline spending to the wars in Iraq and Afghanistan—due to the accelerated rate of military hardware depreciation, costs associated with replenishing arsenals, and the natural tendency of defense spending to inflate during a war. From that $334 billion, we estimate the total increase in the defense budget specifically tied to the Iraq War at $217 billion.[29]

Moreover, since 2003, the Pentagon, the Department of State, and USAID have administered roughly $41 billion in war-related economic assistance, expenditures that are not included as a part of the Pentagon's budget for the military cost of the war (Dansc). Of that amount, $18 billion was allocated to, and spent in, Iraq in 2003 and 2004 for reconstruction and relief. The rest was mainly used for security (military) assistance. The present value of the $41 billion in assistance over the past eight years is estimated as $45 billion. We should note that there has been some controversy over the effectiveness of this economic assistance. For example, the Special Inspector General for Iraq Reconstruction (SIGIR) conducts audits and has found anomalies, which include duplicate payments and fictitious contractors. By the fourth quarter of 2010, SIGIR had opened 53 criminal investigations (Dansc).

According to our fairly conservative estimates presented in table 5.5, the total amount of realized and projected budgetary costs of the Iraq War to the allies is at least $1,731 billion in 2011 US$.

The Iraqi economy was almost completely destroyed even before the 2003 invasion. Iraq's infrastructure, once one of the better ones in the region, was annihilated by the Iran-Iraq War, the 1991 Persian Gulf War, and the following 12 years of crippling economic sanctions. However, the country still had something left before the 2003 invasion. Unfortunately, there is almost no data available on Iraqi combat and support operation expenses, veteran costs, and defense expenditures. The only relevant budgetary data that is available is about Iraq reconstruction needs that were estimated in 2003 by the United Nations/World Bank Joint Iraq Needs Assessment Report. According to that report the total reconstruction fund needed for Iraq was $36 billion in 2003, or $45 billion in 2011 US$. Half of this amount was pledged by the United States, which is already accounted for in our figures and must be excluded here to avoid double counting US reconstruction and relief assistance to Iraq.

More than 3.5 million Iraqis are still internally displaced (Crawford), more than 1 million have fled the country since the invasion, and the number of casualties—mainly civilians—ranges from 105,000 to more than 1 million according to various studies and leaked official reports. Sadly, we do not have enough data to estimate the past, current, and future budgetary burden of this scale of human tragedy in Iraq.

For the macroeconomic costs of the war to the allies, we include the social-economic costs to American veterans and their families and also costs associated with diverted government expenditures. This cost category includes all macroeconomic costs inflicted on a national economy due to the loss of life, serious injury, mental health disabilities, quality-of-life impairment, and strain on veteran families. In 2008, these costs were estimated at between $295 and $415 billion for the wars in Iraq and Afghanistan (Stiglitz and Bilmes). Although we acknowledge that it is not easy to translate the value of life to purely monetary terms, governments commonly use this approach and determine the value of statistical life (VSL), based to some extent on the value of foregone earnings and contributions to the national economy. If we adopt the same assumptions and method[30] and use the latest data on the number of veterans, injured, and dead, the total social-economic cost of the Iraq War to the United States would be at least $334 billion in 2011 US$.

As for the cost associated with diverted government expenditures, again we assume a multiplier of 1.1 for war spending in Iraq and 1.5 for nondefense spending at home. Thus, we estimate the lost economic output due to switching from spending at home to spending in Iraq at $424 billion for the United States and at least $8 billion for the UK. As for the macroeconomic effect of higher oil prices on the economies of the United States and UK, we have already included these figures in the macroeconomic impact of higher oil prices on the global economy, which will be discussed later. Our estimate of the total macroeconomic cost of the Iraq War to the allies is at least $766 billion—this is a low estimate because the macroeconomic burden on other allies are omitted from our calculations.

Iraq's GDP (in real terms) stagnated in the first decade of the twenty-first century. In 2000, Iraq's GDP stood at $25 billion, while by the end of the decade it had declined to $24 billion in constant 2000 US$.[31] During this period, Iraq's oil exports fell precipitously to around 850,000 barrels per day in 2003, but then quickly returned to prewar export levels—1.5 million barrels per day—by mid-2004 and reached even 2 million barrels per day in early 2011. Therefore, one cannot simply attribute the real decline in Iraqi GDP to the performance of the oil sector, which, of course, dominates the national economy. Since Iraq's economy had already been crippled by

sanctions for 12 years prior to the war, we cannot simply assume a counterfactual no-war growth scenario to capture possible lost economic output
attributable to the war. However, we can still reasonably attribute the $13
billion (in 2011 US$) sudden drop in Iraq's 2003 GDP to the war.

As already discussed, we did not have sufficient data to accurately
estimate the budgetary costs to Iraq attributable to those who died, were
injured, or were displaced. We have the same problem estimating the
macroeconomic costs of human tragedies of the war for the Iraqi people,
although a few researchers provide some rough techniques to capture a part
of the socioeconomic cost. For example, Stiglitz and Bilmes suggest $3.5
million for the VSL for Iraqis, based on estimates provided by Wallsten
and Kosec.[32] In our analysis, we do not include the VSL cost to Iraq, since
we are not certain about the real macroeconomic effect of Iraqi casualties on the already crippled economy of Iraq. Although we do not have
detailed data on Iraqi casualties, one could be reasonably certain that the
socioeconomic cost to Iraq could be as high as several hundreds of billions
of dollars.[33] And finally, we must mention the environmental damage to
Iraq—mainly due to the war-accelerated destruction and degradation of
forests and wetlands, and 1,000–2,000 tons of depleted uranium used in
US ammunitions—for which no monetary estimate is available.

As presented in table 5.5, the total budgetary and macroeconomic cost
to Iraq is estimated at $57 billion. However, this does not include a number
of key budgetary and macroeconomic expenses. Our estimate of the total
budgetary and macroeconomic cost to the allies is simply breathtaking—
$2.497 trillion—and the estimated total past and future budgetary burden
and macroeconomic cost to the direct belligerents (allies and Iraq) is in
excess of $2.5 trillion, after adjustments to avoid the double counting of the
US fund for security assistance, reconstruction, and relief for Iraq.

Cost to Neighbors and Other Persian Gulf Countries

A direct effect of the Iraq War on the other Persian Gulf countries is their
soaring military expenditures. In addition to the general sense of insecurity throughout the region due to two ongoing military campaigns, the
US military presence in Iraq and Afghanistan has encouraged Iran to pursue ballistic missile and nuclear weapons programs as deterrence factors. In
response, GCC countries began spending extravagantly on military and
defense, ordering the latest, most advanced weapons systems from the West.
According to the World Bank's World Development Indicators (WDI)
data on military expenditures in the period between 1998 and 2002, total
military expenditure of the neighboring countries—Iran, Saudi Arabia,
Bahrain, Syria, Jordan, the United Arab Emirates, and Oman—was on

average almost $51 billion in 2011 US$, ranging from $46 billion in 1998 to $56 billion in 2001. Total expenditures skyrocketed one year after the invasion of Iraq and reached $81 billion in 2009. If we assume $51 billion in constant 2011 US$ as the military expenditure baseline for the region—which is already significant for a group of eight developing economies—the total amount of the extra budgeted spending on the defense sector from 2003 to 2009 would be estimated at $139 billion in 2011 US$. We believe at least half of this extra spending could be attributed to the war in Iraq. Also, taking the same multiplier assumptions that we already used for the first two wars, we arrive at $70 billion as the estimated macroeconomic cost associated with diverted government expenditures. The total budgetary and macroeconomic cost to the neighboring countries is thus $140 billion (table 5.6). Again, a number of categories of budgetary and macroeconomic costs for which we had no data have been omitted from our calculation.

Cost to the Rest of the World

Table 5.6 shows our estimates for budgetary and macroeconomic costs incurred by the rest of the world. The amount pledged to Iraq's relief fund in 2003 by the rest of the world was $44 billion in 2011 US$; this includes roughly $22 billion from the United States and the remainder from the rest of the world. Thus the estimated total budgetary cost to the rest of the world is $22 billion. We did not have data on other budgetary burdens incurred by the rest of the world.

As for macroeconomic costs, there are two major cost categories—the direct cost of higher oil prices on the rest of the world and their consequent macroeconomic effect on the global economy. For the first of these, we assume 20 percent ($5) higher oil prices in 2003 because of the war. Stiglitz and Bilmes assume 20 percent higher prices for the five-year period after the war, but as Edwards (2011) suggests, there is no clear evidence of the long-term impact of the war on energy prices. Since the direct cost of higher energy prices is not considered a global cost (in the aggregate), we only focus on its macroeconomic impact on global economy, while noting that some countries benefited from higher oil prices (higher oil export revenues) while others incurred a cost (higher oil import bills). As we have already mentioned, higher oil prices affect the global economy through a variety of channels, such as increased production costs, impact on the general price level, and direct and indirect effects on financial markets. Recalling Mussa's conclusion that a 20 percent sustainable increase in oil prices would lead to a 0.25 percent decline in global output for the ensuing four years, we estimate the total macroeconomic loss for the global economy—including for the United States—at $498 billion in 2011 US$.

Table 5.6 Cost of the Iraq War to Other Persian Gulf Countries and to the Rest of the World

Cost to other Persian Gulf Countries	Budgetary Costs	• $70 billion increase in military expenditures by neighboring countries.
	Macroeconomic Costs (limited)	• $70 billion in costs associated with diverted government expenditures.
	Total	$140 billion.
Cost to the Rest of the World	Budgetary Costs	• $22 billion for Iraq's reconstruction and relief.
	Macroeconomic Costs (limited)	• $498 billion in macroeconomic effects of higher oil prices. • $11 billion in costs associated with diverted government expenditures.
	Total	$531 billion.
Global Cost of the Iraq War		$3,158 billion.[1]

Source: Author's estimates.

Notes: [1]To avoid double counting, it is adjusted for the reconstruction and relief costs to Iraq funded by the rest of the world.

And finally, we have to add $11 billion in macroeconomic costs associated with diverted government expenditures—from domestic nondefense sectors to reconstruction and relief aid to Iraq.[34]

Our estimate for the total budgetary and macroeconomic costs to the rest of the world exceeds $531 billion in 2011 US$.

Total Cost of the Iraq War

When President Bush made his famous "Mission Accomplished" speech on May 1, 2003, he probably never imagined that US combat and support operations expenses alone in Iraq would exceed $1 trillion by 2015.

In our calculations, we did not include some key budgetary and macroeconomic costs of the war, such as costs to Iraq associated with the loss of life, injuries, and displaced people, environmental costs to Iraq and its neighbors, and various types of budgetary and macroeconomic costs to other allies. Also, in almost all cases we took the most conservative assumptions and estimates. In spite of these, our final figures are still large.

The total cost inflicted on the direct belligerents, neighbors, and the rest of the world is estimated at $2,509 billion, $140 billion, and $531 billion, respectively. These bring the global cost of the Iraq War, after adjustments to avoid double counting, to almost $3.2 trillion in 2011 US$.

Other Studies on the Cost of the Three Persian Gulf Wars

For the Iran-Iraq War, there are a few studies that provide numerical estimates for the cost of the war. However, none of these studies assess the global cost of the war. Their focus is on the direct belligerents and on the budgetary costs, rarely including even limited macroeconomic costs. Alnasrawi, two years before the ceasefire, claimed that the total cost of the war to Iran and Iraq already exceeded $500 billion. His study is incomplete, because it excludes the last two years of the conflict and also focuses only on the direct belligerents. The most comprehensive study on the cost of the war to Iraq puts the total budgetary and economic costs as high as $453 billion (Mofid). For Iran, the most complete analysis suggests a figure of $592 billion (Amirahmadi). But as mentioned earlier, these studies do not provide estimates in constant US$, are not based on very conservative assumptions, and do not consider the regional and global costs of the conflict. In our estimates, we have tried to address some of these deficiencies.

Many studies discuss the economic consequences of the 1991 Persian Gulf War but only a few provide actual estimates. Among these studies, Cranna is the most comprehensive, assessing budgetary, economic, and reconstruction costs inflicted on the major belligerents, although he does not give an estimate for the total cost of the war. His estimate for the total cost of the war for Kuwait, Iraq, Saudi Arabia, and the West is in the range of $300 to $450 billion in current US$. However, he does not include some key budgetary and macroeconomic costs—increased military expenditures and costs associated with diverted government expenditures—and does not look at the other long-term consequences of the war—such as no-fly zone and veteran benefits—in his calculations. Our $769 billion estimation of the global cost of the Persian Gulf War in constant 1991 US$, although based on some conservative assumptions, includes some of the key elements of budgetary and macroeconomic costs that were not addressed in previous studies.

As for the 2003 Iraq War, at least two comprehensive studies, Stiglitz and Bilmes and the Eisenhower Research Project at Brown University, include a number of costs inflicted on the United States, Iraq, and the rest of the world. However, both of these studies estimate the aggregate cost of the combined Iraq and Afghanistan wars. Moreover, the Eisenhower Research Project does not provide a monetary estimate for the macroeconomic impact of the war on the United States and on the global economy, while Stiglitz and Bilmes ignore the impact of the war on neighboring economies. Prior to these two studies, Wallsten and Kosec also provide some estimates for the cost of the Iraq War but fail to capture all budgetary and macroeconomic aspects of the conflict from a global perspective. None of the mentioned studies provides its estimates in constant US$. In our case, we had access to the latest available data on the war, we focused on the Iraq War (excluding the war in Afghanistan) and its budgetary and macroeconomic impacts on the global economy, and all our estimates are in constant 2011 US$.

A Further Look at the Economic Consequences of Wars in the Persian Gulf

Almost two-thirds of the $1.4 trillion global cost of the Iran-Iraq War was born by the direct belligerents. Prior to the war, Iran's oil revenues were roughly $30 billion in 1988 US$, while Iraq's oil revenues were around $37 billion in 1988 US$. The total cost of the war to Iran was equivalent to almost 19 years of Iran's oil export revenues. For Iraq, its burden represented 13 years of its prewar oil revenues. Iran's cumulative GDP between 1980 and 1988 was $739 billion in constant 1988 US$. Thus, the total damage to Iran's economy during the war was equal to about 77 percent of Iran's cumulative economic output during the war years. Iraq's aggregate output between 1980 and 1988 was $363 billion in constant 1988 US$. Thus, its total war-related cost was equal to about 136 percent of its cumulative economic output during the same period. These are staggering costs.

The Iraqi and Kuwaiti economies suffered the most damage during the 1991 Persian Gulf War. Given that Iraq's oil revenues before the invasion of Kuwait were $15 billion, Iraq would have needed almost 18 years of its prewar oil revenues to pay for the total damage inflicted on its economy. On the other side of the conflict, Kuwait suffered at least $130 billion in budgetary and macroeconomic losses during the invasion and occupation by Iraq. Kuwait also needed 13 years of its prewar oil revenues to cover the budgetary and macroeconomic damage to its economy.

The Iraq War inflicted severe budgetary pain on the United States, perhaps for the first time since the Vietnam War. More than half of the total estimate for the global cost of the war was, and will be for some more time, incurred by the United States—a figure exceeding $1.7 trillion. Moreover, the human cost for the United States has been unmatched since the Vietnam War. The deficit spending,[35] coupled with the spending on the wars in Iraq and Afghanistan, has raised the ratio of debt to GDP by about 10 percent. This will eventually put upward pressure on interest rates and impede future economic growth (Edwards, 2011). At the same time, the human cost of the war for Iraq from fatalities, injuries, and displaced population has already exceeded hundreds of billions of dollars according to very rough and conservative estimates.

Apart from the total losses to the direct belligerents, the most profound effect of the three wars on the region may be found in the composition of government expenditures in the Persian Gulf (see table 5.7 and table 5.8).[36] According to WDI data, in the period between 1989 and 1995, Bahrain's armed forces quadrupled, Saudi Arabia's more than doubled, and the UAE's, Qatar's, and Oman's increased by 50–75 percent. The number of armed forces in other countries—except Iraq and Jordan—either increased or did not change significantly. The result of this far-reaching trend of militarism in the region is the high share of military expenditures in almost all countries of the region. In all of them—except in Iran, where the quality of data, especially for military expenditures, is highly disputable—the share of military expenditures, in total government expenditures, is either higher than or equal to the share of public education and health care combined during the 1990s and 2000s. Also, military expenditures (columns in table 5.7) are the only expenditure category where all Persian Gulf countries "outclass" other developing countries, OECD countries, and the global average. Add to these facts and figures the $60 billion arms sales contract announced in 2011 between Saudi Arabia and the United States,[37] the UAE's $7.1 billion contract to purchase 80 of the most advanced F-16 fighters in the past decade,[38] the $35 to $40 billion contract in 2011 with the United States to purchase and upgrade the UAE's antimissile defense systems, Oman's $12 billion and Kuwait's $7 billion contracts with the United States to buy new warplanes,[39] and Washington's reported[40] agreement to sell bunker-busting bombs to the UAE. This is a breathtaking set of numbers associated with arms transactions. As for government expenditures as percentages of GDP (table 5.8), the story is pretty much the same.

Another revealing fact about the region's conflicts and wars is that almost all Persian Gulf countries are trailing the OECD, the world average, and other developing countries when it comes to public spending on health care as a percentage of GDP. While it is widely accepted that long-lasting economic and human development requires emphasis on health care and especially on education, the Persian Gulf countries seem to be

Table 5.7 Composition of Government Expenditures

Percent of Total Government Expenditures

Country	Public Education %		Public Health %		Military %	
	1990s	2000s	1990s	2000s	1990s	2000s
Bahrain	10	12	11	10	20	18
Iran	18	20	8	9	13	15
Iraq	6	-	1	3	-	-
Kuwait	12	13	7	7	31	17
Oman	15	24	7	6	45	45
Qatar	-	-	5	8	-	-
Saudi Arabia	15	23	7	9	-	-
UAE	-	25	8	9	-	-
Yemen	-	-	7	6	30	-
Middle Income Countries	15	15	-	8	-	13
OECD	13	13	-	-	-	10
World	14	14	-	15	-	11

Source: Author's estimates.

Table 5.8 Government Expenditures as a Percent of GDP

Government Expenditures as percent of GDP

Country	Education %		Health Care %		Military %	
	1990s	2000s	1990s	2000s	1990s	2000s
Bahrain	3	3	3	3	5	4
Iran	5	5	2	2	2	3
Iraq	-	-	0	2	-	4
Kuwait	5	5	3	2	13	6
Oman	4	4	3	2	14	11
Qatar	4	4	2	2	-	3
Saudi Arabia	7	6	2	3	11	9
UAE	-	1	3	2	9	7
Yemen	-	7	2	3	7	5
Middle Income Countries	4	4	3	3	2	2
OECD	5	5	6	7	3	2
World	4	4	5	6	3	2

Source: Author's estimates.

going in the opposite direction. Again, and as already mentioned, these wars did not only inflict heavy budgetary and macroeconomic damage to direct belligerents and to other countries in the region, they have also had a major role in turning the Middle East into the most militarized region in the world over the past three decades.[41] The future may not be bright, because conflicts beget conflicts, unless leaders in the region can adopt bold measures, such as those adopted in Europe in the aftermath of World War II.

These are staggering costs that all residents of the Middle East must be made aware of, costs that are a testament to the folly of their leaders and the duplicity of the powerful nations, who back different sides in the conflicts and supply them with lethal weaponry. The question that must be answered is simple. Would these wars have occurred if leaders and countries knew the global price of their aggressive actions and believed that they would have to pay for them in full—for countries, full reparations (based on calculations as above); and for leaders and their cronies, forfeiting their ill-gotten wealth, being subject to arrest and trial by the International Criminal Court, with no free passage to a life of luxury?[42]

Chapter 6

How Conflicts and Wars Can Be Ended

Recalling what President Ronald Reagan famously said, "History teaches that war begins when governments believe the price of aggression is cheap," our goal is to develop a framework, initially in the private sector, to increase the price of aggression to its full cost or fallout, a level that makes it expensive and painful for aggressors, be they leaders or countries, to engage in acts of aggression—sowing the seeds of conflict and war, instigating them, and being a belligerent party.

We live in a world where powerful countries use their military, economic, and political might along with organizations such as the United Nations, the International Monetary Fund, and the World Bank to pursue their perceived short-term and narrow interests. They use force and the threat of force to interfere in the internal and regional affairs of others and to bring corrupt and autocratic rulers under their influence, invariably fueling human misery, if not conflict, around the world. They use the United Nations Security Council (UNSC) to serve their own ends and bribe weak members of the UNSC to do their bidding, as they sanctimoniously denounce corruption and espouse support for effective institutions and democratic values. They express their support for a world at peace but adopt policies that do the opposite. In such a world, no realistic leader of a powerful country would unilaterally relinquish the perceived, or imaginary, political, economic, and military advantage his or her country enjoys, while practical and opportunistic leaders of weaker countries vie for the support of powerful countries to keep their hold on power and to reap financial gains.

Illegitimate leaders of many undemocratic developing countries, who invariably care more for their own personal interests than those of their people, have little or no incentive to change the status quo in their country as long as they have the needed foreign support or domestic military might to keep a tight rein on power. Autocratic leaders around the globe do little to develop good institutions that are at the foundation of economic and social progress but that might, in turn, undermine their own absolute rule. As a result, the citizenry are oppressed and deprived of economic progress. These autocratic rulers invariably favor their families, the military, the small band of supporters who benefit from them, or their religious sect, ethnic allies, or tribe. The classical divide-and-conquer and us-against-them mentalities are at work.

Under such conditions, religious, ethnic, tribal, and social conflicts thrive. Leaders, regime backers, and cronies benefit from conflict and all that it entails. While the average citizen, especially in the most unfortunate countries, suffers, is economically deprived by failed policies, and pays a heavy price for the internal divisions and conflicts that emerge and for the wars initiated by the country's leadership, wars that may have been instigated, fueled, and sustained by outside powers.

Thus, intrastate and interstate conflicts and wars are afforded fertile ground to develop and to spawn even more conflicts in the future. All the while, conflicts and wars take a heavy toll on global economic output, on the environment, on the sustainability of our planet, and ultimately on the well-being of billions of individuals with marginal livelihoods around the world. This vicious circle is almost impregnable; conflicts spawn new conflicts. The end result is that the vast majority of conflicts are, in fact, renewed conflicts. The only imaginable way to break the circle would be if, by magic, every leader in the world simultaneously realized the utter waste of human and economic resources caused by conflict and developed the courage to renounce all aggression. Even we, naïve as we may be, realize that this will never happen without a truly significant outside force.

There may be little incentive for the autocratic leader of a developing country to be independent and nonaligned. The Non-Aligned Movement (NAM) was envisaged in part as the way around this dilemma. NAM was founded in April 1955 and its official purpose as formally stated in the *Havana Declaration of 1979* is to ensure "the national independence, sovereignty, territorial integrity, and security of nonaligned countries" in their "struggle...against all forms of foreign aggression, occupation, domination, interference, or hegemony as well as against great power and bloc politics." The members of NAM represent nearly two-thirds of the membership of the United Nations and about 55 percent of the world population. While NAM was a noble idea, it has done little to enable the nonaligned to stay nonaligned or to be safe from external aggression. It has also not done anything to end the support of advanced countries for unsavory regimes that do their bidding, to deter armed conflicts and wars between countries, or to deter interethnic, intertribal, or interreligious conflicts and wars. NAM was more effective when its moral father, the late Indian prime minister Jawaharlal Nehru, was alive. His moral sway and international stature gave NAM enhanced standing in global affairs, but today NAM is viewed as little more than a large gathering of developing countries who feel left out of global decision-making or who want to pretend that they are nonaligned.

In the final analysis, it is the citizenry, not the leaders or their powerful backers, who pay dearly for acts of aggression. In failed countries, an autocratic leader can destroy the lives of millions and deprive them of hope for a better life. In this connection, today's Somalia, Zimbabwe, and the Sudan may be the three countries that first come to mind, but a number of other examples abound—oil-rich countries such as Nigeria, Iraq, and Libya are a few others.[1] Citizens are duped in the name of religious, ethnic, and tribal solidarity and nationalism to defend their leaders when they pursue policies that divide their country and initiate conflicts.

There is no formal system of enforcing penalties on instigators of aggression even if penalties or reparations were to be assessed. There is nothing that affords the many parties to most conflicts a significant incentive, much less the obligation, to sit down and resolve their differences before taking up arms and thereby making reconciliation even more difficult. Countries can, if they choose to, seek mediation from one of the NGOs that we have already mentioned in chapter 1, but they are not given strong incentives to do so. Yes, there are NGOs devoted to nuclear and conventional arms reduction, but there is no method to force countries to reduce their acquisition of the instruments of aggression, namely, increasingly lethal weapons. Similarly, there are many outstanding NGOs devoted to improving human rights and supporting democratic reforms, but, again, there are few or no compliance mechanisms.

The prevention of armed conflict is at best an ad hoc process with a number of contradictory policies. Governments espouse peace but their major efforts are focused on preparing for conflict and war.[2] Countries have even realized that the apparent economic pain of interstate wars may be reduced for today's voters if wars are financed by debt instead of through current taxation. Debt allows governments to postpone the financial burden of everything into the future, to be suffered by future generations who have little or no say in the matter.

Although conflicts and wars take a heavy human, social, economic, and environmental toll, their legacy may be far more ominous. Today's armed conflicts beget tomorrow's armed conflicts. As mentioned in chapter 2, all available studies indicate that the vast majority of armed conflicts are, in fact, renewed conflicts with a past and from the past. Most recent armed conflicts have been in the developing world, and the developed world has also used them to fight their surrogate wars. Intra-religious, ethnic, and tribal conflicts pave the way for hatred and conflict for years, for generations, and in some cases for centuries to come. Such a legacy magnifies the cost of conflicts and wars manyfold and makes reconciliation ever more difficult, despite the fact that the cost of reconciliation would be insignificant in comparison to the cost of aggression.

As the world waits for enlightened leaders and true statesmen, especially from the powerful countries, to set up a global institution that truly has the means to deter conflicts and wars, private citizens and NGOs have little choice but to develop an interim solution. We, and future generations, must initiate such a process and then wait for nation-states to join the effort to put an end to conflicts and wars—for a world without war.

Governments, especially those that are powerful, will not voluntarily adopt the pursuit of peace and conflict resolution as a central mission. Therefore, we are putting forward a step-by-step approach for creating a global institution of the future to deter conflicts and wars. We propose to initiate our effort with an NGO that assumes the role of a global institution designed to deter conflicts and wars and that is equipped with the necessary tools. Thus the private sector, with widespread support of citizens around the world, would substitute for governments to initiate the process to reduce conflicts and wars. This NGO would expose, name and shame, the role of those who sow the seeds of conflicts—corrupt autocratic rulers, their foreign supporters, the exporters of lethal arms, and individuals and corporations that benefit from acts of aggression around the world. The NGO would put pressure on governments by exposing the role of all aggressors in fueling conflicts and wars and would publicize the economic and social costs of their aggressions. Damages would be assessed against all aggressors; this information would be publicized through all available means, especially the Internet, Social Media, Twitter, and other forms of mass media. In this way, we hope to nurture the seeds of peace. We hope that this NGO's demonstrated success will motivate citizens across the world to increasingly support its efforts. Our goal would be that the less powerful nation-states would see the merits of this approach and lend their support to it. In time, the powerful nation-states would realize that such an initiative is also in their long-term interest. Ultimately, the global community would come to accept the premise that the world cannot afford to pay for conflicts and would embrace the notion of a world without war as the best way forward for humankind. In time, we hope that the world would demand an international institutional structure that deters and ends all conflicts and wars.

The Basis of Our Approach to End Conflicts and Wars

Limitation of Governments

As we have said many times before, with the world as it is, governments will not embrace, much less establish, a framework to increase the price of aggression, either in the form of an effective international organization or as a group of collaborating countries with the goal of eliminating conflicts and wars. Thomas Jefferson said: "Governments constantly choose between telling lies and fighting wars, with the end result always being the same. One will always lead to the other."

We must begin the process of bringing peace to the world through private sector channels, because governments are unable and unwilling to end conflicts and wars for many reasons: (i) powerful countries that meddle in global affairs and whose cooperation would be critical to eradicate conflicts will not relinquish what they perceive as their advantage over others; (ii) powerful countries use conflicts and wars in other countries (largely in the developing world) to fight surrogate wars with those they perceive to be their adversaries; (iii) a change in the status quo would require that all countries simultaneously forsake their military and perceived short-term international interests in favor and of peace, something that is highly unlikely; (iv) arms production and its international trade, and, more generally, military expenditures, benefit special interest groups that governments and the media appear reluctant to oppose; (v) lobbyists push the interests of special interest groups who benefit from the arms industry and from conflict, be they nationals or foreigners; (vi) governments resist establishing institutions that would assess reparations and require their payment, be those reparations aimed at direct parties to conflict or at those who support them; (vii) although the International Court of Justice (ICJ), an organ of the United Nations, was established in part to settle disputes between countries, its enforcement authority and effectiveness are at best limited, which is how the powerful countries prefer to have it; (viii) a number of governments are reluctant to promote the reach of the International Criminal Court (ICC), an entity whose effectiveness we believe is essential for the prevention of conflicts and wars,[3] with the

United States even unsigning itself from the agreement, arguing that the court impinges on sovereign rights and exposes US government officials to biased international justice, while the ICC's meager resources and a few of its unqualified judges have limited its effectiveness; (ix) powerful countries will not support initiatives that would reduce the projection of their international power in organizations such as the United Nations; (x) the process of mediation or its facilitation, an integral and essential component of the framework to reduce conflicts and wars, is both trust and time intensive; trustworthiness is not normally a trait attributed to governments; and individuals whose continuous involvement may be required for a decade or more are rarely uninterrupted members of most elected governments; (xi) governments will not support initiatives that may put them in conflict with other governments and that require funding at a time of serious budget constraints; (xii) many governments now finance wars through debt, not current taxation, reducing the protests of current generations and postponing the financial pain for future generations; (xiii) future generations have no say in ending today's conflicts and wars; and, perhaps most importantly, (xiv) leaders, those who invariably instigate, initiate, and fuel conflicts and wars, pay almost nothing for their acts of aggression (a zero price for aggression unless the conflict is unpopular and leaders are voted out of office, something that may occur only in a limited number of democracies around the world) and may even pay a negative price, with the burden instead falling on the general citizenry, both current and future.

The Promise and Limitations of NGOs

Because of these and other limitations of governments, we have to turn to the private sector as our best hope to initiate and develop our proposed initiative to significantly increase the price that is paid for aggression. NGOs are invariably more principled, are not tied to conventions, and are less likely to be manipulated by powerful special interest lobbies. Realistically, NGOs represent our only hope for beginning to truly increase the price of aggression.

As we mentioned in chapter 1, many of the elements that help reduce conflicts and wars are already in place in the private sector and have operated for many years with great success, but they are not focused on the goal of reducing and eradicating conflicts and wars by increasing the price of aggression. A partial (because there are hundreds of outstanding NGOs) list of these elements that are already in place and a few of the outstanding NGOs include the following: (i) mediation and reconciliation

(Crisis Management Initiative (CMI), Centre for Humanitarian Dialogue (HD), Carter Center's Conflict Resolution Program); (ii) promotion of human rights (Human Rights Watch, Amnesty International, Carter Center, Committee to Protect Journalists, Helsinki Watch, Committee for Human Rights); (iii) support for democratic governance (Freedom House, Open Society Institute, Council for a Community of Democracies); (iv) disarmament and international arms trade (Global Zero, Union of Concerned Scientists); (v) human welfare (Oxfam, Red Cross, Red Crescent, Doctors Without Borders); and (vi) environmental preservation (Nature Conservancy, Worldwide Fund for Nature, Sierra Club, Friends of the Earth, Greenpeace).

While countries currently refuse to embrace the cause of peace, substituting NGOs for governments will not be without its own problems, they face issues that include their operational efficiency, conflicts of interest, accountability, and legitimacy to their ability to achieve fundamental reform and change.

Although better adoption of modern business tools may improve the operational side of NGO performance (Walsh and Lenihan), this does not address other questions surrounding the role of NGOs. In his review of UK NGOs, M. Edwards identifies four major weaknesses: "an overall absence of clear strategy, a failure to build strong alliances, a failure to develop alternatives to current orthodoxies, and the dilemma of relations with donors." He goes on to elaborate these four points:

> In summary, what is needed is a proper, multi-layered, and multi-faceted strategy for NGO advocacy which relates themes, targets, objectives, activities, roles, and responsibilities together in a coherent way; which is monitored carefully and evaluated at regular intervals; which integrates detailed policy work with public campaigning; which is rooted in real experience; and which embraces the whole organization in pursuit of a common cause...Rather than arriving at a consensus based on the lowest common denominator, a more creative approach to alliances would be to recognise and build on the differences which exist among the NGO "community." The aim should be synergy (working individually but in a mutually supportive way), not standardization (all doing the same thing)...However, genuine, credible, and sustainable alternatives must emerge from local debate and action in both North and South, even if the results are more complex and less comfortable than we expect...Increasing competition for funds may press NGOs into accepting ever more money from official donors, and so bring about a creeping compromise in their advocacy agendas.

Cavill and Sohail assess the performance of international development NGOs by assessing "practical accountability," namely, how they do their activities and "strategic accountability," or how well they perform relative to their mission. They conclude that while international NGOs (INGOs) use quality control mechanisms to assess practical accountability, this does not necessarily mean that they will achieve their mission of reducing poverty, suffering, and injustice. They conclude: "One way to explore how INGOs can enhance their strategic accountability is to establish a conceptual framework that enables them to integrate their mission and values into policies and practice." Charnovitz explores the various aspects of accountability of NGOs and concludes that governments should not directly regulate the performance of NGOs. Instead, governments (and indeed international organizations) could help indirectly "by establishing mechanisms that give NGOs an incentive to upgrade their own performance. NGOs are very likely to be criticizing governments and it will be difficult for governments to appear to be objective were they to insist that NGO statements be honest and fair."

The core issue facing NGOs is their conflict with governments: "A new question and a new challenge face those who look for the accountability of NGOs in the public sphere—are NGOs doomed to fail by the environment that made them necessary? In other words, are they doomed to fail because they are unelected and unaccountable, and unlikely to rise above the limitations of the current system that made them necessary in the first place?" (Lehman). To be successful, NGOs must move beyond addressing the symptoms of problems at hand (for example, poverty) and push for fundamental reforms. In his introduction to a number of articles looking into these issues, Mathangi Subramanian says:[4] "Because reformist agendas that NGOs are now pursuing may undermine the authority and power structure of institutions that provide them with financial and political support, scholars and activists question whether NGOs can ever truly pursue reformist agendas (Edwards and Hulme, 1998; Mundy and Murphy; Wils)...Additionally, funders demand greater and more specific accountability for data representing 'results and impact'" (Wils, 60). These reporting requirements place greater value on quantifiable activities (such as the provision of direct services) rather than efforts that are best captured qualitatively (such as the communication of new ideologies and reform measures). While such accountability measures have rewarded NGOs that achieve impressive results (Stromquist), they may also penalize those that pursue agendas considered too radical or progressive (Edwards and Hulme, 1998).

Critics argue that as a result of these pressures, NGOs often feel more accountable to funders than to the constituents they purport to serve (Edwards and Hulme, 1995; 1998; Mundy and Murphy; Wils). Not only does such questionable allegiance detract from organizations' motivations to work toward widespread change, Wils claims that NGOs that lose touch with the communities they serve tend to advance policy agendas that are inadequate or ineffective.

Can NGOs convince entire nations to engage in substantial social reform? Can NGOs receive private funding while remaining primarily accountable to those they serve? Can NGOs be trusted to work for political reform that may disrupt the status quo that provides them with their financial and political power? In short, can NGOs actually change the status quo?

Powerful economic and political forces—governments, corporations, and lobbyists—oppose the work of some NGOs. This is especially problematic when the NGOs are small and have a low profile. A number of NGOs simply criticize but do not always present viable options. Realistically, they are not staffed as major international institutions, in large part because of their limited funding and their constant need to look to future funding; they lack the diversity and number of needed staff; many do not have the depth and the detailed technical capabilities to be credible; and unlike government organizations, most do not have access to privileged information and to key decision makers around the world. Moreover, because NGOs need publicity to raise money and to survive, they sometimes resort to slogans and pursue activities that generate publicity as opposed to activities for the reconsideration of policies based on careful analysis.

The most fundamental questions about NGOs may have deep roots in political theory (Wapner). What is the NGOs' source of legitimacy for representing the global public interest? Do they understand the differences in public interest across the world? Who elects and appoints them? To whom do they respond? Are they held accountable for their actions? Is there an institution that regulates them?[5]

It is in large part because of these issues, especially funding and the need for fundamental reform challenging the role of governments, that we would hope a credible philanthropist or a number of such philanthropists will be so convinced of our initiative as to adopt it as their own, establish it, ensure its funding, and oversee its governance for at least five to ten years, hopefully immunizing it from these oft-quoted limitations and failures of some existing NGOs.

The Foundation of Our Proposal

What we are proposing is different from the ongoing efforts to reduce and to end conflicts and wars, or the status quo, in at least three important ways. Ours is a coordinated effort on a number of fronts to increase the price of aggression for all leaders, countries, and companies, encompassing every channel that affects their behavior and the price that they face for their acts of aggression, and targeting all parties to aggression and conflict (those who sow its seeds, fuel and enable it, as well as all the direct belligerent parties).

We cannot overemphasize the fact that we are not simply focused on the direct combatants, who are invariably the focus of most NGOs operating in this arena. We are instead recommending the adoption of a number of simultaneous initiatives that affect the price of aggression for all parties involved (both directly and indirectly), to increase its price closer to the market level (the true fallout of a conflict) and thus impede conflicts and wars. We believe that only such a comprehensive effort could succeed because of the many factors in play, factors that are frequently mutually opposing. Most existing NGOs are focused on a narrow agenda that undoubtedly affects conflicts and wars, be it arms control, human rights, democratization, economic development, mediation, or reconciliation. While we applaud the work of these NGOs, we believe that there is no global institution in place today that has the structure and resources to significantly, and in the course of a generation, reduce and eliminate conflicts and wars.

What good is it to promote economic cooperation to increase the cost of conflict when the same parties to a conflict are given lethal arms by foreign powers? What good is it for international organizations to give developing countries development assistance if a significant portion of the aid is channeled into arms? What good is it to adopt conventions against corruption when the ill-gotten gains of rulers are welcomed by international banks in developed countries? What good is it to espouse human rights when the most egregious rulers are welcomed in powerful capitals around the world and if the deposed rulers are guaranteed a life of luxury in the most envied safe havens? What good is it to leave it to conflicting parties to seek mediation and reconciliation if they have no strong incentive to do so? While ongoing efforts at mediation and reconciliation are to be applauded, they should offer sufficient incentives for reconciliation and cover all conflicts, be they ongoing, potential, dormant, or between countries or groups that are of little importance in global affairs; and these efforts should be supported by a number of other initiatives that increase the likelihood of success.

How specifically can our proposed NGO go about reducing and ending conflicts? We propose ten major operational principles: (i) all potential and actual conflicts be mediated (or mediation facilitated), with any party refusing to negotiate automatically declared the aggressor; (ii) the comprehensive costs of all conflicts and reparations be calculated on a transparent basis and their payment be enforced through every possible means;

(iii) leaders be held accountable for their crimes against humanity (through the auspices of the International Criminal Court (ICC) and bringing pressure on all countries, especially China, Russia, and the United States, to sign and ratify their accession thereto) on a consistent basis, whether the said crimes are committed in their own country or against other countries, through countries who are willing to cooperate with this initiative or through other venues such as judges in third countries; (iv) all illegally acquired wealth that has been invested and deposited domestically or abroad by rulers, their families, and their cronies be exposed and seized and returned to the legitimate government of the country; (v) leaders, would-be leaders, and dissidents accused of crimes against humanity be barred from living a life of luxury in foreign lands, they would instead be referred to the ICC or to judges in third countries; (vi) a global effort to simultaneously reduce and eliminate the international arms trade (and reduce military expenditures) be adopted; (vii) the structure of the UNSC be modified to eliminate the privileged veto powers of the permanent UNSC members ; (viii) in addition to the direct adversaries, all countries and groups that spawn, incite, fuel, and sustain aggression around the world be held accountable for their actions and be subject to referrals to the ICC; (ix) a transparent effort to promote democratic reforms in all countries around the world be adopted; and (x) global efforts (with a significant percent of global development assistance to be channeled through the World Bank) be focused on promoting economic projects that specifically increase economic interdependence of countries within regions in order to further increase the price of aggression.

All of these principles, or channels, are important in addressing conflicts and wars, to increase the price of aggression sufficiently for all parties to capture most of its negative effects and interject positive economic effects to enhance the chance of success.

Such a private sector approach can be effective only if the global citizenry is made aware of, and educated about, the economic and welfare issues that are at stake for them, their children, and their grandchildren, and how the future of the world will be shaped by our success or failure today to reduce, and one day end, all conflicts and wars. It is the citizenry, not the leaders, who in the end pay the terrible costs of aggression. The global citizenry must become active participants in the worldwide effort to inflict sufficient pain on would-be parties to a conflict by publicizing their transgressions and shaming them into mediation and thereby ending other aggressive behaviors. Citizens would participate in the enforcement of reparations through boycotts and the like. Our world will never get on the right track if citizens stand by and accept things as they are today.

On the bright side, we must say that the task before us is becoming easier by the day because of an increasingly connected world of social sites such as Facebook and Twitter supported by the Internet. If Facebook membership exceeded 800 million in early 2012, is it not possible that a billion citizens across the world could become connected in a matter of a few years in the quest for world peace?

Our Proposal to End Conflicts and Wars

Specifically, we propose the establishment of an NGO to adopt and implement the principles outlined above to increase the price of aggression to its full market level. The NGO would adopt all possible means to promote formal mediation and reconciliation efforts before disputes lead to armed conflict, calculate the cost of conflicts and wars, publicize the heavy toll of military expenditures, document and publicize the aggressors to a conflict and those who will not negotiate, recommend reparations to be paid and sanctions to be placed on those who are classified as aggressors, and expose the harmful policies of autocratic regimes and the role of foreign powers that support them.

We hope that public pressure will, in time, motivate the weaker nation-states, especially those that have embarked on the road to establishing democratic rule, to see the benefits of such an effort, to embrace this work, and to become an integral part of a network to end conflicts by supporting our NGO. They could do it by giving their official endorsement and by joining this effort. The union of informed and active citizens around the globe, other concerned NGOs, and weaker nation-states would, in time, persuade the powerful to see the benefits of generalized peace in a holistic framework, that is, when they consider all the ramifications of their actions on their own long-term economic conditions, on global poverty, human misery, and environmental degradation. An effort such as this will take time to establish the credentials and effectiveness of our proposed NGO; enlist the active participation of millions of citizens around the world; experience the benefits of peace and imagine its future potential; develop confidence in such an approach, initially among the weaker countries; and encourage simultaneous reductions in all acts of aggression by all nation states.

Given below is the preliminary list of entities (and their missions) needed to implement our proposed initiative.

1 UNNGO

A foundation, a philanthropist, or a number of philanthropists working together establishes an international umbrella NGO, say "UNNGO" (in essence a privatized United Nations or a united global network of citizens whose goal is to end conflicts and wars), that would mimic the role of a truly effective United Nations. If a credible philanthropist or foundation establishes the UNNGO, it will be afforded immediate credibility; it would not have to spend time and possibly make compromising concessions to fund its initial operations; it would stand a better chance of starting out with good governance in place; and it would be easier to attract the needed technical staff and management with strict ethical requirements.

UNNGO would be an umbrella organization in the sense that it would coordinate all the specific initiatives, described in this book (and constituted as a stand-alone NGO, see below), to increase the price of aggression. UNNGO would not have any legal standing but would instead rely on moral sway and public pressure to persuade nations and parties to conflict to resolve their disputes and differences. While UNNGO would not possibly take a case to the ICC, it could take a case to a judge who is willing to hear it in any country, or it could collaborate with a nation-state that would refer the case to the ICC. It would establish (or work with existing entities that have the same goal, where appropriate) and orchestrate all activities to reduce conflicts and wars. Many of these efforts would reinforce each other. UNNGO would be an impartial standard bearer for all nation-states to develop confidence that peace is in the long-term economic interests of all countries, the weak as well as the powerful. As we have stated above, UNNGO would start out as a private sector entity, but, in time, it would be joined by nation-states as its success is established and nation-states see the benefits of a world without war.

The structure of UNNGO would be:

1. An eminent international board of directors, with no conflict of interest and no affiliation with any government, international (such the United Nations, the IMF, or the World Bank), or regional institution (such as the Asian Development Bank) supported by governments, to guide all operations of UNNGO. To promote transparency, nominations for board members would be solicited from Nobel laureates, democratic governments, international organizations, business leaders, and NGOs; all nominations would be made public; and all elected board members would disclose their past and ongoing business and government relationships and would agree to drop any relationship that might be problematic. The quality and commitment of this board would be critical in determining the credibility and the success of UNNGO's work.

2. A management team, with the same strict ethical requirements as for the board of directors, to carry out day-to-day business, including a professional staff to coordinate major activities.

3. A development division to raise funds for the UNNGO's future activities; funding is to be obtained from entities and individuals who gain nothing from their financial support (and are promised nothing for their support), to reduce the likelihood of conflict of interest between the funders and the mission of UNNGO. This division would also oversee the financial accounts of the UNNGO. To further reduce the negative impact of issues broadly classified as conflicts of interest, the development division would have no contact with the operational side of UNNGO.

4. UNNGO would establish an eminent and appropriately constituted advisory board for each of its major initiatives (each with a distinct NGO, see below), with prior experience in the activity area of the NGO (for example, in the case of MediationNGO, with experience in mediation; or in the case of ArmsControlNGO, with experience in disarmament). In essence, these boards of directors would be more narrowly constituted to be more focused and to reflect the activity to be directed.

5. UNNGO would, in turn, create (or possibly, as mentioned earlier, cooperate with an existing NGO that is focused on the same goal as the NGO to be established) a number of other NGOs with specific missions—facilitating mediation and reconciliation, calculating reparations, supporting arms control, promoting economic and social policy reforms, developing and encouraging economic cooperation and integration, mobilizing the global citizenry in the cause of peace, and disseminating information. In this pursuit, an interactive website promoting and publicizing the work of the UNNGO to enhance citizen participation would be indispensable.

2. MediationNGO

For the first of these NGOs, UNNGO establishes an NGO, say *"MediationNGO,"* to initiate negotiations (perhaps, more correctly, facilitate negotiations) at the first sign of conflict between countries (between all conflicting parties), with the explicit goal that countries enter negotiations in earnest, that countries and groups who refuse to negotiate or walk away from negotiations be automatically declared the aggressor, be pressured to pay reparations in the event of armed conflict and war (calculated as described in chapter 3 and implemented as discussed in chapter 5), and be subject to international economic boycotts and sanctions during the war and until all reparations are fully paid.

Again, as the MediationNGO would have no legal standing to enforce reparations and sanctions, it would rely on the mobilization of citizens and institutions to bring pressure on aggressors (see below). We propose to set up a permanent and eminent group of men and women from countries that have gone through such traumas and have later gone through a reconciliation process—Ireland, South Africa, Iraq, and so on—as the critical staff of MediationNGO to facilitate negotiations and mediations.

In cases where neither party agrees to mediation or where aggression follows, MediationNGO would examine the conflicts that ensue, determine the aggressor in each case, name the aggressor, recommend economic boycotts, and do everything to publicize the amount of reparation and to motivate aggressors to pay the reparations. It would also document and publicize the criminal acts of individuals or parties to the conflict and endeavor to have them indicted in any court that would hear the case, with the expectation that the case might later be referred by a cooperating nation state to the ICC. These—the naming of aggressors, recommendation of economic boycotts, calculation of the costs of conflicts, size of reparation payments, and referral of criminal acts to the ICC—would be heavily publicized to expose aggressors and those who refuse to negotiate (see below). Initially, the MediationNGO's preferred weapons would be boycotts, pressure, and moral suasion.

In time, and with demonstrated success of MediationNGO, it is hoped that this NGO would begin to look into "dormant" conflicts, such as border disputes, and try to facilitate mediation and reconciliation before a flare-up occurs.

3. ReparationNGO

The UNNGO then establishes another NGO, "*ReparationNGO*," to undertake the technical calculations on the cost of actual and potential conflicts and wars on a continuous basis, based on a transparent framework that is further scrutinized and endorsed by those respected in the field. These calculations would be used for a system of automatic and globally "pressure-enforced" reparations to be paid by aggressors. ReparationNGO would rely on individuals who have experience in developing effective economic sanctions in order to devise targeted sanctions against aggressors responsible for conflict and against those who refuse to pay assessed reparations.

ReparationNGO would calculate the comprehensive cost (human, economic, and environmental) of conflicts and wars (and of their aftermath, such as medical care of the injured) on the direct combatants, on peripheral countries, and on the rest of the world, using the suggested framework in chapter 3. This calculation would be initially limited to ongoing major conflicts and wars, but, in time, it would cover all ongoing conflicts and those that are dormant but imminent. Costs would be calculated for parties directly involved in a conflict and for third parties, including parties that support either side in the conflict or supply arms and funding or act in any way that fuels the conflict. These costs would be related to major benchmarks including, among others, population affected, death-by-disease category, and GDP, and would be publicized in every way to reach the widest audience around the world to demonstrate the continued harm that will befall humanity if we fail to eliminate all armed conflicts.

ReparationNGO's calculation of the costs of imminent conflicts would be publicized to mobilize the citizenry. This information would fully inform the general citizenry of warring countries and would put pressure on governments to undertake negotiations instead of taking aggressive action.

4. ArmsControlNGO

UNNGO establishes another NGO, "*ArmsControlNGO*," to monitor military expenditures and the international arms trade, and to expose arms dealers and rulers who benefit from arms trade through bribes and other corrupt practices. ArmsControlNGO would also calculate the cost and the implied burden of military expenditures and international arms trade. Again, these costs would be related to major benchmarks such as the affected population, death-by-disease category, GDP, and the like. Every year, the cost of conflicts, the impact of military expenditures and arms imports on national economies, and the names of those who benefit from arms trade, including companies that manufacture and sell arms and companies that train armies and elite forces, would again be publicized in every possible way to reach the widest audience, demonstrating the senselessness of military expenditures and how they limit our economic and social welfare.

ArmsControlNGO would also undertake two global initiatives to achieve simultaneous reductions in (i) military expenditures and (ii) arms trade. These initiatives would be structured on confidence building and verification and would be time intensive.

With the rising power of China, predicted to become the largest economy in the world before the end of the decade, the United States and China could very well embark on a new arms race. This could be an arms race that accelerates a US decline, given America's economic outlook, its debt problems, and its urgent domestic, social, and economic needs. The United States could take a closer look at its own future and ask an important question: is it advantageous to enter disarmament negotiations with China from a position of strength (which it now enjoys), or wait and do so from a position of weakness (which, if history is any guide, will be the case in the not too distant future)? Although China's broad economic outlook is bright, its average per capita income would still be well below that of the United States for many more years. Thus, is this not the best time for China to preempt a senseless new arms race? While China today professes its peaceful intentions, is this not the best time for the United States to challenge China to a mutual military expenditures reduction accord? If the United States and China cannot see the light, isn't it an opportune time for NGOs to step in and stop a new arms race in its track?

Most military superiorities are likely to be temporary and fleeting. The case of drones (or what some refer to as UAVs, unmanned aerial vehicles, or RPAs, remotely piloted aircrafts) may be only the latest case in point. The United States has enjoyed a distinct global superiority in drones since their inception. But recently a number of countries, including Iran, are showing signs of catching up. This low-cost military capability may in time also become readily available to terrorists. While the United States may still be safe from the threat of drones for a number of years to come, the future prospects look very different now and is much more uncertain than it was only five years ago.

5. ReformNGO

UNNGO establishes "ReformNGO" to monitor and publicize policy reforms, credentials, and practices—economic as well as political—of all countries and their leaders. It would not only shed light on the policies of countries but also examine and expose their support from foreign powers and the details of these relationships. While all corrupt rulers and their foreign supporters should be exposed, special attention must be paid to rulers in the Middle East North Africa Region (or MENA, as defined by the World Bank) as they have been in the "limelight" in 2011, invariably showing how they have failed their people and countries.

Rulers in the MENA region, as a number of rulers elsewhere, have, by and large, created little of value (wealth), namely, sustainable economic progress and, in the case of the countries endowed with significant oil resources, economic progress that would continue once the oil and gas runs out in their countries. Per capita economic growth has been low and unemployment generally high in many of these countries, with subpar education and health services. Most importantly, effective institutions that are the foundation of development and rapid sustained economic growth have been *expressly and deliberately* undermined because effective institutions, such as an independent legal system with the rule of law or a democratic system of governance, would impinge on an autocratic ruler's own corrupt activities. Dictators have robbed their citizens and all future generations of

their birthright, namely, the limited oil and natural gas reserves that right-
fully belong to all citizens, and have produced little in its place. The practice of depleting natural resources to finance lavish lifestyles is not limited
to the MENA or to the exploitation of oil and natural gas. Rulers in developing countries all over the world, rich in other depletable resources such
as diamonds and copper, are guilty of the same crime. Such a setting pres-
ents fertile ground for conflict, both intrastate as well as interstate.

Greed, theft, and corruption at the national level must be exposed more
consistently and widely and the practice ended, if for no other reason than
that they provide fertile ground for conflicts. Two measures that should
be taken by advanced countries might help to reduce the theft of national
wealth by rulers in a number of autocratic developing countries. First is
the adoption of an international treaty barring lobbying on behalf of foreign governments and rulers in all countries. Individuals and corporations
could have financial dealings, but these would have to be fully disclosed
and the parties must be barred from contacting government officials to
discuss anything that might be interpreted as support for foreign governments and rulers. While some may find such a measure in contravention
of the right to free speech, it is not so. Lobbyists can write what they want.
They can also express themselves on the radio, on television, and in any
public forum, but not to government officials, including members of the
legislature, in private, to solicit support for foreign leaders and governments. Second is the adoption of an international treaty to disclose all
assets of rulers in every country. Dictators want absolute power not for the
sake of power but, in large part, for a life of luxury and the accumulation of
unimaginable wealth. Control over wealth allows them to buy the support
of their military and cronies at home, and the support of influential foreigners. Domestic cronies and foreign backers, whose support is absolutely
necessary for the autocrats to hold on to power, become greedier by the day;
their numbers keep growing, and their continued support for the regime
in power is dependent on ensuring that the status quo is maintained—an
unjust economic system that supports the corrupt lifestyles of a few and
fuels popular rage at the ruling elite and the foreigners who prop them up.
Once a tyrant comes to power and goes down this road, conflict will be
inevitable. The only questions are when it will happen and how.

As mentioned above, the most debilitating fallout of such corruption
and theft of national wealth is that rulers have no incentive to establish or
to nurture efficient institutions. The result is utter economic injustice—
theft, deprivation, and no hope for a better future. It would be better for
the future of such countries to even give huge salaries to rulers if they
then agreed not to undermine the development of effective institutions.
How can democracy and peace emerge in a system where everything is

organized around promoting corruption and theft? If true democracy and the rule of law were to emerge, the raison d'être for the regime would be trumped. Even after a successful revolution, new rulers will be tempted to go back to the old system but with them at the helm. Consider Iran after the revolution or Iraq after the overthrow of Saddam Hussein. Egypt will follow suit, unless this simple fact is addressed. On the one hand, if grand theft can be reduced, democratic reform will be more likely to follow once the rewards of autocratic rule are expunged. On the other hand, simple regime change will not usher in democratic reforms if the rewards of autocratic rule are still in place. At a minimum, corruption, theft, and cronyism must be addressed simultaneously with regime change and democratic reforms.

This may all sound well and good, but how can ReformNGO help reduce support for autocratic rulers in important foreign capitals? Here is where ReformNGO should lobby the United States and other powerful governments. Here is where the United States and other powerful governments can prove how serious they are when it comes to human rights, democratic reforms, and improving relations with the Muslim world. The US administration has in-depth information and can get all the details needed very quickly (from commercial banks, investment banks, hedge funds, and the like) about the assets and financial holdings of foreign leaders, their families, and cronies. The United States should simply release these figures. Yes, just release the details. Doesn't this violate all privacy laws? No it does not. First, the United States requires full financial disclosure of its elected and sometimes unelected officials. Isn't it even more reasonable to demand this of foreign leaders, especially foreigners who have robbed their own people? Second, under the Dodd Frank financial reform legislation enacted in 2010, all hedge funds are required to register with the Securities and Exchange Commission (SEC) by March 2012 if they manage more than $150 million in assets. This law calls for all funds to report information about the assets they manage, about potential conflicts of interest, and information on investors and employees. Again, the holdings of American investors will be reported and exposed. Is it not reasonable to expect the same of foreigners? It is for this reason that billionaire investor George Soros will only manage his family holdings (exempted under the law). Shouldn't the United States require the same of foreigners who by robbing their own citizens have increased the likelihood of future conflicts?

These two simple measures will seriously undermine autocratic rulers around the world and give tangible support to those who struggle for democratic reform and economic justice. While the ReformNGO would lobby for the two initiatives mentioned above, especially in the powerful countries, it would also press for other reforms to reduce the likelihood of future conflicts. In this regard, we should note that a reform that could reduce the likelihood of armed conflict is to bring about a change in how armed conflicts are paid for. As mentioned before, many countries, especially in the West, finance wars by issuing debt. This is a less painful way to pay for wars than taxation. By issuing debt, the financial pain of wars is passed on to future generations who have no say about the matter. ReformNGO would propose a global initiative to persuade all countries to adopt a policy to exclude the financing of wars through debt. Such a proposal should be popular with conservatives in a number of countries as they seek balanced budget amendments to their constitutions, such as in the United States.

6. CooperationNGO

UNNGO establishes *"CooperationNGO"* to devise and promote projects that are specifically designed to enhance economic collaboration between countries and groups, and thus raise the price of future conflicts. These economic initiatives could include free trade areas, joint oil and gas development projects, joint transportation and pipeline projects transiting a number of countries, joint tourist development projects, joint educational projects such as major regional universities, and the like. In these efforts, CooperationNGO might do well to collaborate with the World Bank, regional institutions, and multinational corporations as they have shared interests in these pursuits. With the passage of time, economic interdependencies would grow in a number of areas, such as labor, capital, and trade in goods and services. Most importantly, increased contacts, tourism, business dealings, educational and cultural exchanges, and the like will help reduce suspicion between neighboring countries.

7. MobilizeNGO

UNNGO establishes *"MobilizeNGO"* to coordinate and organize all activities that involve mobilizing citizens around the world to support (and, yes, help enforce) the mission of the UNNGO and its affiliated NGOs. The mission of MobilizeNGO is essentially to bring pressure on aggressors and on those who support them. Because none of these NGOs have official standing, MobilizeNGO's major weapon is likely to be global economic boycotts targeting the economic and financial interests of aggressors, organized hunger strikes, mass protests, and the like. Even one determined individual can affect changes that might have been considered unimaginable. The hunger strike of Anna Hazare against corruption in India in 2011 (whether one agrees with the specifics of Hazare's proposal or not) and the supreme example of Gandhi much earlier for independence are examples of what can be peacefully achieved by a single individual with strong convictions. In February 2012, a video depicting the atrocities of Joseph Kony and the Lord's Resistance Army (LRA) in Uganda was uploaded on YouTube and was seen by over 60 million people in just five days. The outrage generated by this 30-minute documentary may have prompted President Obama to commit 100 US troops to the capture of Joseph Kony.[6] Dedication and modern technology can work wonders!

8. InformationNGO

UNNGO finally establishes "*InformationNGO*," whose primary function would be to publicize the activities of the UNNGO and of all the other NGOs that work with it, and to garner international support for all their activities. InformationNGO would essentially be the arm of UNNGO that publicizes all the activities discussed in this book in order to solicit global citizen and corporate support, support that will be essential to bring pressure for reducing conflicts and wars. Close collaboration between InformationNGO and MobilizeNGO would be an essential element for success.

These efforts will be targeted toward facilitating mediation and reconciliation in ongoing conflicts and in those that are imminent, and even in those that may be considered "dormant." Again, the majority of conflicts are not new but, rather, recurring ones, such as the border disputes between Iraq and Kuwait. While direct efforts to facilitate mediation and reconciliation may appear to be the major activity of UNNGO and its affiliated NGOs, this is not really the case. Reconciliation will be successful only if all other initiatives are simultaneously adopted and pursued to give conflicting parties the incentive to reconcile by increasing the price of aggression and, equally important, reducing the likelihood of conflicts developing in the first place.

The activities of these NGOs will be enhanced by an effective International Criminal Court (ICC). The court needs more resources and all countries, especially China, Russia, and the United States, as members. InformationNGO could initiate an international campaign to strengthen the ICC and especially lobby citizens to require their country to join the ICC, a membership that could afford ordinary citizens around the world additional protection against all manner of injustice.

Some Remaining Questions

Given the earlier discussion on the changing form of global conflicts and the preponderance of intrastate as opposed to interstate conflicts, is our proposal likely to be as effective in reducing intrastate conflicts and especially those that are classified as acts of terrorism? We believe so. Most non-state actors, even some terrorists, have financial interests that can be exposed and sanctions imposed if there is an effective global agreement; many non-state actors are supported by states or state entities, which can be identified and targeted by NGOs; and non-state actors would be just as concerned as government officials by the reach of an impartial, respected, and effective ICC.

What does our proposal portend for national sovereignty? The Peace Treaty of Westphalia, the series of treaties signed in 1648, established the exclusive sovereignty of each country over its people and its territories, and responsibility for the aggressive actions of its citizens. Clearly, our proposal and the mission of UNNGO limit this long-standing treaty firmly establishing the rights and obligations of state sovereignty. We foresee a period of challenge to national sovereignty, but, in time, as nation-states increasingly acknowledge the benefits of global peace and replace the UNNGO by an international institution that is committed to the same mission, the Treaty of Westphalia would have to be modified by a normative framework to recognize the limitations of national sovereignty when conflicts and wars are at issue.

What if the higher price of aggression does not deter an aggressor? Is international military intervention an acceptable option? No, it is not. During the period when this initiative is being established and expanded, many aggressors may ignore the price of their actions, but, in time, when the system is firmly established, especially when the success of the NGOs motivates nation-states to embrace this solution to end conflicts and wars, we are confident that all potential aggressors will seek mediation and reconciliation. In the meantime, the use of military intervention as a means of enforcement is both risky and against the foundational principle to end conflicts and wars, namely, that conflicts beget conflicts. Thus, we are not eliminating but rather limiting the scope of the Peace Treaty of Westphalia.

There are a number of important reasons why we must, and can, make a success of such an initiative to reduce and eradicate conflicts. Debt has become a major constraint to almost any global economic initiative. The world can no longer support such high levels of military expenditures and damage from conflicts and wars. Environmental considerations may require significant restructuring of energy consumption, which will, in turn, have considerable economic costs. The United States and China are at a tipping point, and we will soon see the beginning of another costly arms race. There are likely to be new tensions and conflicts over the next couple of decades as fast-growing Asian economies challenge the rich

Western countries in North America and Europe. And, on a more positive note, it is becoming easier to mobilize the global citizenry into action to increase the price of aggression and end conflicts and wars in the age of the Internet and social networking sites.

Final Words

Can our proposal to reduce, and in time eradicate, conflicts and wars succeed? It must. There is no choice. The cost and burden of military expenditures, conflicts, and wars can no longer be supported. Again, conservative estimates indicate that the eradication of conflicts, wars, and military expenditures would increase global economic output by about 10 percent and add another 5 percent by freeing up military-related resources. In other words, we would have roughly 15 percent more resources to address the legitimate and desperate needs of humankind. The world is in dire need of these repurposed resources. The poor need food and shelter; the world's aging population need health care; the disadvantaged need education; however, our environment is slowly being destroyed by a multitude of human demands and abuses, including conflicts, wars, and the destruction and degradation they bring. In the face of these global challenges, some nation-states find themselves in the middle of a fiscal squeeze that threatens, or will threaten, their very social fabric. All of this is in addition to the millions of people, combatants and civilians alike, who are killed or seriously injured, the millions who lose their loved ones, and the millions who are relegated to refugee status and whose lives are impaired by the direct and indirect horrors of conflicts and wars.

While the United Nations and the international community should be lobbied to adopt an effective international organization, similar to the NGO outlined above, to implement a program of deterrence to wars, we realize that nation-states will not embrace such an initiative. A number of countries believe, in our opinion, falsely, that they benefit from conflicts because of their power to dominate and dictate to others, while others legitimately and understandably will not forsake their military preparedness unless every country does the same to eliminate the likelihood of external threats. In such a setting, we cannot rely on governments to undertake such an initiative. Thus the only choice is to initially pursue the goal of reducing, and, in time, ending, conflicts and wars through the private sector NGOs. We recognize that NGOs have not received universal acclaim, but they are our only hope to initiate the process to achieve a world without war. We will avoid the often-voiced criticism of NGOs.

We hope that the success of UNNGO will be a positive force for formal change at the global level. Once the success of UNNGO is proven, it would motivate weaker countries to join this effort. In time, as more and more countries see promise in this initiative and embrace its policies, powerful countries will have little choice but to join. The speed of success of this endeavor would be enhanced if a credible philanthropist or foundation embraced, adopted, and took over such an approach for eliminating conflicts and wars.

We have seen the toll of recent wars in the Persian Gulf: the human toll; the toll in monetary terms relative to GDP, to GDP per capita, to oil revenues; and the toll in damages in every other way imaginable, such as the environment. Wars have brought misery, increased poverty, impeded the availability of modern education and health care, and significantly impaired the quality of human life. If we fail today, future generations will be haunted by our inaction and will ask: "what were our ancestors thinking and how could they have been so shortsighted?"[7]

The increasing number of deprived and disenfranchised people in the Persian Gulf may have given rise to extremism and fueled conflicts that are not between states but are, instead, between individuals or groups against other groups or individuals, against rulers, and against foreigners who have interfered in regional affairs in the past and still continue to do so. Conflicts will always spawn more conflicts. Take, for example, the CIA coup in Iran in 1953. Who could have imagined then what we can today realistically attribute to that episode in history? No one can predict all the interconnected developments that will follow an event in history. While the costs from the three wars in the Persian Gulf are stunning, such costs and pain are not restricted to this region. These costs are repeatedly suffered by almost every region the world over, especially regions that are developing and need economic growth; these costs will continue to be borne by these regions unless something radical is done.

Rich countries tout their support for the disadvantaged around the world and point to the aid they give. Yet the global costs of military expenditures, conflicts, and wars dwarf the amount rich countries give as financial and economic assistance to the developing world. Even in the spring of 2012, the world is still besieged by the financial crisis that erupted in 2007–2008, a crisis that is likely to continue for a number of years. But even the economic fallout of this crisis is dwarfed (possibly by about a factor of ten) by the global burden of conflicts and wars, to say nothing of military expenditures.

Although powerful countries think they benefit from military power because they can dictate to others and pursue their strategic economic interests, in our opinion any perceived gain has to be balanced with the cost of military expenditures, the cost of present and future conflicts, and of the resulting human toll. When all of this is calculated, we believe that the perceived gains will evaporate for the powerful countries as well as for the weak. We hope to demonstrate this to the global citizenry.

It is understandable that no country would give up its arms, disband its military, and disavow all wars unless all other countries do the same simultaneously. Don't we already have some success along these lines in other areas? Have we not followed such a path to reduce and eliminate nuclear warheads, with confidence-building measures to achieve simultaneous and verifiable reductions? Did we not adopt the same type of process to establish the GATT and later the WTO with a system of liberalized trade? Does it not make sense to follow a similar path to reduce conflicts, wars, and military expenditures if every country's perceived gains due to conflicts are really not net gains once all costs, including future costs, are included? Has the United States received a net benefit from the wars in Iraq and Afghanistan? Was there a better approach, not just in 2001 but also in the years before?

Our aim is to make the price of shunning negotiations and of initiating, stoking, and fueling conflicts and wars prohibitive for all leaders, governments, countries, and companies. Leaders and countries must be afforded significant incentives to negotiate their differences and to reconcile them without resorting to armed conflict. Citizens must realize that it is they and their descendants, not their leaders, who end up paying for conflicts and wars. Again, President Reagan was correct when he said, "History teaches that war begins when governments believe the price of aggression is cheap." We cannot rely on the market for a solution, even financial markets need regulations and supervision. The only way to assimilate President Reagan's lesson of history is to acknowledge the market failure and elevate the price of aggression to its full global fallout, a price that is, without a doubt, prohibitively expensive.

Notes

1 INTRODUCTION AND OVERVIEW

1. While the increased availability of economic resources could alleviate poverty and increase welfare around the world, it may not do so in practice if human greed and corruption get in the way and limit the benefits of these released resources to a select few. Ending conflicts and wars and increasing the availability of economic resources will not change the basic nature of man. Still, such a vast increase in resource availability could but only help. An end to conflicts and wars will also not eliminate competition among countries, but, again, is it not better to compete in economics, education, and the like instead of in war?

2. The secretary-general at the time, Perez de Cuellar, was not about to go against the wishes of the UN's powerful members until his term in office just about ended!

3. In the face of a transparent and uniform system of international justice, the military, political, and business cronies will be less willing to back a corrupt tyrant.

4. As mentioned just above, some of these initiatives may be specifically adopted by existing NGOs, and in this regard the mediation function would be an obvious candidate. As noted in "Privatising Peace," *The Economist*, July 2, 2011, 50–51: "certain types of diplomacy are becoming privatised. Non-governmental organizations (NGOs), some with roots in aid-giving and disaster relief are playing an ever-greater role in conflict resolution. In what has become a crowded field, the biggest players are: the Crisis Management Initiative (CMI) based in Helsinki and founded in 2000 by Martti Ahtisaari, a former president of Finland; the Carter Center's Conflict Resolution Program, which helped win Jimmy Carter the Nobel peace prize in 2002; the Congress-funded but independent United States Institute of Peace (USIP); and HD [Humanitarian Dialogue], which was established in 1999 by Martin Griffiths, a British diplomat and former UN assistant secretary-general." We should add another name to this illustrious list, Robert Bendetson, a former student and dear friend, who as a private citizen has spent time and resources as a facilitator between opposing factions in Iraq. In our case, we hope that the mediation (facilitation) NGO would mediate many more conflicts, including

potential conflicts that have not yet even erupted, such as dormant border disputes, as well as conflicts that have been inflamed for many years, such as the Kashmir and Kurdish conflicts.

2   A Glance at Recent Conflicts and Wars

1. A time sandwiched between the war with England in 1812–15 and the Mexican War in 1846–48.
2. http://www.correlatesofwar.org/.
3. For a complete list of all wars since the beginning of the nineteenth century, refer to the COW project.
4. Battle-related deaths are civilians and soldiers killed in the course of combat. Nonviolent deaths caused by war, such as those occurring through starvation or disease, and deaths due to unorganized violence (such as riots) or one-sided violence (such as genocide or execution of detainees) are not included in this study, because consistent time series data on one-sided violence and nonviolent deaths due to war do not exist.
5. http://news.brown.edu/pressreleases/2011/06/warcosts (accessed on August 10, 2011).
6. Regimes can be categorized into three types: personalist, centrist, and polyarchic. Individuals or small groups of people, invariably with a military background, are in control in personalist regimes. Centric regimes are totalitarian and authoritarian, with a larger number of people with more diverse interests in charge. Groups who change periodically through different mechanisms such as elections govern polyarchic regimes.
7. The Kimberley Process or *The Kimberley Process Certification Scheme (KPCS)* is a joint government, industry, and civil society initiative to stem the flow of conflict diamonds—rough diamonds used by rebel movements to finance wars against legitimate governments. The trade in these illicit stones has fuelled decades of devastating conflicts in countries such as Angola, Cote d'Ivoire, the Democratic Republic of the Congo, and Sierra Leone. The process can limit the trade of diamond as a way to finance conflicts. Its success has been questioned in some quarters.

3   Estimating the Price of Conflicts and Wars

1. For instance, if a country gives financial assistance (gift) to a warring party, the gift is a direct cost. At the same time, war damage to the warring party is a direct cost. But to sum both of these (the war damage and the gift that paid for it) as war-related costs would simply double the real cost.

2. For example, in all three major Persian Gulf conflicts, the belligerent parties experienced all three types of refugee flows.

3. For example, during the 1980s, Iraq received tens of billions of dollars in loans from other Persian Gulf countries—mainly Saudi Arabia and Kuwait—as well as from the West and the Soviet Union. These were loans Iraq was apparently not willing or able to pay back at the end of the Iran-Iraq War.

4. According to media reports, in 2003 in the first three weeks of the Iraq War alone, allied forces used (mostly in Iraqi cities) between 1,000 and 2,000 tons of depleted uranium munitions.

5. For example, the increasing trend of military expenditures throughout the whole region has made, in our opinion, the Middle East the most militarized region in the world over the past 30 years, according to Global Military Index (GMI) as reported by Bonn International Center for Conversion (BICC). Small countries of the Persian Gulf region, relying on the free flow of petrodollars, have been spending billions of dollars buying the most sophisticated weaponry systems chiefly from the West.

6. For example, during the Iran-Iraq War the presence of Western superpowers, especially the United States, became somewhat permanent in the region. The United States and Britain, and recently France, have set up permanent military bases in the region at the expense of their host countries.

4 The Seeds of Conflict and War: The Persian Gulf

1. The 17th Annual Arab-US Policy makers Conference in October 2008.

2. Although this was not exactly the case for Northern Ireland, which was unilaterally partitioned by the UK in 1921 and not as a direct result of World War I (the division of the Ottoman and Austro-Hungarian empires).

3. As is required for environmental impact in the United States.

4. Although the United States may have garnered support with some rulers in the region, it surely alienated the ordinary citizens of the entire region for years to come.

5. We believe that this—the containment of China's economic ascendancy— may in time become the most important factor in the formulation of US foreign policy toward the Persian Gulf region.

5 The Global Costs of Three Wars in the Persian Gulf

1. Although the Iran-Iraq conflict was actually ignited right after the Iranian Revolution of 1979 (see chapter 4), there were significant border conflicts even during the 1970s.

2. In reporting all estimates in constant US$, we calculate the present value of all costs at the end of each war, and as such we do not need to add interest expenses.

3. The estimates include damage to agricultural, manufacturing, transportation, telecommunications, oil and gas, health care, real estate, banking and financial sectors, public safety institutions, labor force, and resettlement costs.

4. There are many casualty estimates for Iraq with a huge variance—from the official estimates of 150,000 to more than 500,000—and almost no estimate for the numbers injured. We assume at least 300,000 casualties and estimate at least 300,000 seriously injured for Iraq.

5. Iraq was held responsible for initiating the conflict, according to UN Security Council Resolution 598.

6. For the 2003 Iraq War, Stiglitz and Bilmes (2008) assume that 20 percent of the increase in oil prices was due to the war. Our estimate is a slightly smaller (more conservative) increase in oil prices due to the Iran-Iraq War.

7. We believe that part of the $35 billion that was spent on military or other war-related imports is already counted in the budgetary cost to Iraq, so we do not count it again, because this would amount to double counting.

8. The literature on the effect of military expenditures and higher defense budgets on economic growth is extensive. The results of a number of empirical studies suggest that there is no significant, or a very weak, relationship between military expenditures and economic growth in less developed economies, and even in developed economies such as the United States (Dunne, 2000; Dakurah et al., 2000; Kusi, 1994; Wilkins, 2004; Deger and Sen, 1983; Chowdhury, 1991; Abu-Badr and Abu-Qarn, 2003; Dunne, 2010; Pieroni et al., 2008). Some of these studies even suggest that military expenditures have a negative effect on national economies. The result of an empirical study on the government expenditures multiplier in the member states of the Gulf Cooperation Council by the IMF (Espinoza and Senhadji, 2011) suggests that the value of total government expenditures multiplier declines drastically—falls significantly below 1—when military expenditures are included in the estimations. Regarding the negative or neutral effect of military expenditures on economic growth, supported by the main strand of literature, we believe that assuming the difference of 1 between nondefense and defense expenditures multiplier—2 and 1, respectively—for developing economies such as Iran and Iraq is reasonable.

9. More than 15 percent of the world's palm trees were wiped out between the late 1970s and early 2000s mainly due to the Iran-Iraq war (Waslekar and Futehally, 2009). In the late 1970s, between 17 million and 18 million palm trees, a fifth of the world's 90 million, were on the two sides of the Shatt Al Arab waterway between Iran and Iraq. By 2002, almost 80 percent of them had vanished.

10. Iran ranks first in brain drain among 91 developing and less developed countries, according to IMF reports. Iran has been losing tens of thousands of its most talented and educated citizens, incurring annual economic losses that amount to tens of billions of dollars. This destructive trend started after Iran's 1979 revolution and the onset of the Iran-Iraq War. Iraq also has lost a considerable number of its educated workforce, beginning with the Iran-Iraq War and continuing thereafter.

11. After the war, they claimed that the financial assistance they provided was a loan, but Iraq refused to consider it as a loan.

12. Other Persian Gulf countries, specifically Kuwait, paid the United States hundreds of millions of dollars, especially in the later stages of the war to protect their oil tanker fleet from Iran's retaliatory attacks.

13. These GCC countries had large current account surpluses, and their financial support of Iraq did not restrict their other expenditures; thus the effect may not be a cost.

14. Here we reasonably assume that the financial aid granted by the rest of the world was not fully drained from the national economies of the donors. Iraq defense and nondefense imports chiefly from the West increased significantly during the eight-year war, so virtually some part of the financial aid was channeled back to the donors' economy. We believe that a multiplier of 0.5 is a plausible factor to capture this macroeconomic effect.

15. The dollar value of this 20 percent assumption is smaller than $5.

16. More than 27 countries were directly involved in combat and support operations.

17. Including Germany, which was not a direct belligerent.

18. In constant 2008 US$.

19. We reasonably believe this is a very conservative estimate, since the number of Saudi armed forces more than doubled between 1989 and 1995—from 82,000 to 177,500—according to WDI data.

20. For example, US military expenditures reached a steady state—$360–370 billion—in 1996 and did not change until the 9/11 attacks.

21. Coalition forces lost 43 aircrafts and had their cruise missile arsenals almost depleted.

22. Daponte (1993) estimates that about 56,000 Iraqi soldiers and 3,500 Iraqi civilians were killed in the war. Also, 35,000 Kurds and Shiites were killed by Saddam Hussein's regime right after the end of the war and another 111,000 civilians died due to postwar adverse health effects, raising the total Iraqi war-related death count to more than 205,000.

23. This is clearly a conservative assumption, since the majority of the costs for combat and support operations incurred by Kuwait and Saudi Arabia were actually in the form of payment to the allied forces. So it does make sense if one assumes that the bulk of these expenditures were practically drained from the national economy of these two countries, yielding a very low multiplier effect.

24. The equivalent of between 1 billion and 1.5 billion barrels of Kuwaiti oil were set on fire and 25 million to 50 million barrels were spilled into the Persian Gulf and on Kuwaiti soil during and after the war.

25. In 2011 US$.

26. A number of studies organized and directed by the Watson Institute for International Studies at Brown University.

27. Besides the United States, the UK, Australia, Poland, Korea, Italy, Georgia, Ukraine, the Netherlands, and Spain, who were directly involved in the invasion, there were 30 more countries that were a part of the Multi-National Force-Iraq (MNF-I) active from 2004 to 2009.

28. Or 70 percent of $589 billion.

29. About 65 percent, which is the share of Iraq War spending in total spending on the Iraq and Afghanistan wars, multiplied by $334 billion.

30. Assuming $7.2 million as the value of statistical life (VSL) for the dead and the seriously injured and 20 percent of the VSL for other wounded, and including the economic cost of the loss of life, the seriously injured, mental health disabilities, quality-of-life impairment, and strain on veteran families.

31. Assuming 2000 oil prices.

32. Wallsten and Kosec (2005) estimates the VSL for different countries based on their GDP per capita relative to US GDP per capita and an elasticity coefficient.

33. If we take the most conservative estimates for Iraqi civilian and armed force casualties, 126,000 and 13,500 respectively, and assume $3.8 million in 2011 US$ as the VSL for Iraqis, the most conservative estimate for the macroeconomic cost of the loss of life to Iraq would be as high as $530 billion. The estimate for total social-economic cost of the war to Iraq would simply exceed $1 trillion if we just take into account the economic costs inflicted on Iraq due to the internal displacement of 3.5 million Iraqis, the emigration of more than 1 million Iraqis, and of the hundreds of thousands injured.

34. We assume a multiplier of 0.5 for reconstruction aid and 1.5 for domestic non-defense sectors, similar to our assumptions for the 1991 Persian Gulf War.

35. Almost all the budgetary costs of the war were financed through federal debt (Stiglitz and Bilmes, 2008; Edwards, 2011).

36. Values in both tables are the average value for the 1990s and 2000s.

37. According to an analysis by the Center for Strategic and International Studies, October 2010 (http://csis.org/blog/saudi-arms-deal-links-nonproliferation).

38. According to Arms Control Association, May 1998 (http://www.armscontrol.org/print/360).

39. According to the *Financial Times*, September 2010 (http://www.ft.com/cms/s/0/ffd73210-c4ef-11df-9134–00144feab49a.html#axzz1TzGdV6rG).

40. "Washington considers selling bunker-busting bombs to UAE," *The Telegraph*, November 14, 2011.

41. According to the Global Military Index (GMI) as reported by Bonn International Center for Conversion (BICC).

42. Although we have calculated the cost, or the price, of three recent wars in the Persian Gulf, we should restate and emphasize that our calculations are not complete. A number of cost items have been omitted because of data limitations. In practice, each and every cost must be estimated and included to bring the price of aggression to its full level if we are to end conflicts and wars.

6   How Conflicts and Wars Can Be Ended

1. This is not to say that leaders in advanced countries don't also inflict pain on their citizens. *The Economist* on its cover of June 9, 2011 carried the title, "The

Man Who Screwed an Entire Country," in reference to Silvio Berlusconi of Italy. Throughout history, the welfare of nations and of hundreds of millions of people can be frequently connected to the quality of their rulers.

2. Although Saudi Arabia used Tactica armored vehicles, manufactured by UK's BAE Systems, for its incursion into Bahrain to suppress pro-democracy movements in the first half of 2011, both Saudi Arabia and Bahrain were invited to the UK's premier biannual arms fair in the fall of 2011. While the government in Downing Street condemns the crackdown in Bahrain, the UK's Foreign and Commonwealth Office decides to invite Saudi Arabia and Bahrain to London to acquire more lethal weaponry!

3. The International Criminal Court (ICC) should not be confused with the International Court of Justice (ICJ). The ICC came into being in 2002 and is located at The Hague, as is the ICJ, but can hold its proceedings anywhere. The ICC can prosecute individuals for crimes against humanity, genocide, and war crimes (prosecution for aggression is not yet operational) that were committed after the court came into being in 2002. Not all countries have accepted the treaty's jurisdiction; a number of countries have signed the treaty but have not ratified it; many countries have not signed; and the United States, Israel, and Sudan have unsigned and at this time have no intention of becoming member states. Only two of the five permanent UNSC members, namely, France and the UK, belong to it. No one from the permanent five has been targeted by the court. Most Middle East countries do not belong to it either. Its activities have been largely focused on Africa. For example, it has indicted Omar Hassan al-Bashir of Sudan but he is still in office. The court has no enforcement mechanism. The UNSC could help in such cases by at least adopting sanctions against countries that do not cooperate with the ICC, but it has not done so. In its 10-year history, the court has issued 20 arrest warrants but only 10 arrests have been made. Most recently in March 2012, the ICC handed down its *first* guilty verdict against Thomas Lubanga Dyilo, a warlord in Congo; a narrow verdict on child abduction and forced military service that did not even include thousands of cases of rape and murder. The court's meagre resources have limited its reach to high profile leaders in developing countries while the men involved in rape and doing the killing are untouched. Members of the United Nations, as opposed to individuals, can bring cases to the court's attention. The court can prosecute if the accused is a national of a member country; if the crime took place on the territory of a member state; or if the UNSC refers a case.

The ICJ, on the other hand, is the primary legal organ of the United Nations. It adjudicates legal disputes between member states that are referred to it and gives legal advice to the United Nations.

4. Mathangi Subramanian. "Are NGOs Overrated? Ten Year Anniversary Double Issue." *Current Issues in Comparative Education* vol. 10, no 1 and 2 (Double issue) (Fall 2007/Spring 2008).

5. We should acknowledge that at a more mundane level some NGOs are questioned on their day-to-day governance. How transparent are their operations? Do they have a board of directors? Do board members have conflicts of interest (personal board's representative of global civic interests)? Are staff salaries

and benefits excessive? What percent of their resources is spent on salaries and benefits? As we are aware of these and other shortcomings of some NGOs, we would try to avoid them and we can learn from the success of environmental advocacy NGOs, which have undoubtedly received the most favorable recognition (Jasanoff): "The place of non-governmental organisations (NGOs) in international governance seems nowhere more securely established than in the field of environmental action. Within the United Nations system, NGOs have been recognised as essential contributors to environmental protection for well over a decade."

6. http://www.youtube.com/watch?v=Y4MnpzG5Sqc.
7. A world without war must surely appeal to Christians, Jews, and Muslims alike. Peace is God's work while war belongs to the devil.

Bibliography

Abrams, E. et al. "An open letter to President Clinton: Remove Saddam from power." In *The Iraq War Reader: History, Documents, Opinions,* edited by M. L. Sifry and C. Cerf, 199–201. New York: Simon and Schuster, 2003.

Abu-Badr, S. and A. S. Abu-Qarn. "Government Expenditures, Military Spending and Economic Growth: Causality Evidence from Egypt, Israel, and Syria." *Journal of Policy Modeling* vol. 25 (2003): 567–583.

Alnasrawi, A. "Economic Consequences of the Iran-Iraq War." *Third World Quarterly* vol. 8, no. 3 (1986): 869–895.

Amirahmadi, H. "Economic Reconstruction of Iran: Costing the War Damage." *Third World Quarterly* vol. 12, no. 1 (1990): 26–47.

Apostolakis, B. E. "Warfare-Welfare Expenditure Substitutions in Latin America." *Journal of Peace Research* vol. 29, no. 1 (1992): 85–98.

Arms Control Association. "UAE to Purchase 80 F-16C/Ds, Arms in Deal Worth $7 Billion." (1998). Retrieved from http://www.armscontrol.org/print/360.

Arunatilake, N., S. Jayasuriya, and S. Kelegama. "The Economic Cost of the War in Sri Lanka." *World Development* vol. 29, no. 9 (2001): 1483–1500.

Bahgat, G. *American Oil Diplomacy in the Persian Gulf and the Caspian Sea.* Florida: University Press of Florida, 2003.

Baker, J. A. and L. H. Hamilton. *The Iraq Study Group Report: The Way Forward—A New Approach.* New York: Vintage Books, a Division of Random House Inc, 2006.

Bigombe, B., P. Collier, and N. Sambanis. "Policies for Building Post Conflict Peace." *Journal of African Economies* vol. 9, no. 3 (2000): 323–348.

Bill, J. A. "The Geometry of Instability in the Gulf: The Rectangle of Tension." In *Iran and the Gulf: A Search for Stability,* edited by J. Al-Suwaidi, 99–117. United Arab Emirates: The Emirates Center for Strategic Studies and Research, 1996.

Bill, J. A. "US-Iran Relations: Forty Years of Observations." (2004). Retrieved from http://www.mideasti.org/transcript/us-iran-relations-forty-years-observation.

Bilmes, L. J. "Current and Projected Future Costs of Caring for Veterans of the Iraq and Afghanistan Wars." Watson Institute for International Studies, Brown University, 2011.

Brasoveanu, L. O. "The Impact of Defense Expenditure on Economic Growth." *Romanian Journal of Economic Forecasting* vol. 13, no. 4 (2010): 148–168.

Brauer, J. and J. T. Marlin. "Defining Peace Industries and Calculating the Potential Size of a Peace Gross World Product by Country and by Economic Sector." Confidential Report for Economists for Peace and Security, Annandale-upon-Hudson, New York, USA, and Vision of Humanity/Institute for Economics and Peace, Sydney, Australia, 2009a.

Brauer, J. and J. T. Marlin. "Nonkilling Economics: Calculating the Size of a Peace Gross World Product." In *Toward a Nonkilling Paradigm*, edited by Joám Evans Pim, 125–148. Honolulu: Center for Global Nonkilling, 2009b.

Brezezinski, Z., B. Scowcroft, and R. Murphy. "Differentiated Containment." *Foreign Affairs*, May/June (1997): 20–29.

Bronson, R. *Thicker than Oil: America's Uneasy Partnership with Saudi Arabia.* New York: Oxford University Press, 2006.

Brown, L. David, Mark H. Moore, and James Honan. "Strategic Accountability for International NGOs." Hauser Center for Nonprofit Organizations, Harvard University, 2003.

Brown, P. "Gulf Troops Face Tests for Cancer." *The Guardian*, April 25, 2003. http://www.guardian.co.uk/uk/2003/apr/25/internationaleducationnews.armstrade.

Buhaug, H., S. Gates, H. Hegre, and H. Strand. "Global Trends in Armed Conflict." Report delivered to the Norwegian Ministry of Foreign Affairs, October 5, 2007.

Campagna, A. S. *Economic Consequences of the Vietnam War.* New York: Praeger, 1991.

Caputo, D. A. "New Perspectives on the Public Policy Implications of Defense and Welfare Expenditures in Four Modern Democracies: 1950 1970." *Policy Sciences* vol. 6 (1975): 423–446.

Cavill, Sue, and M. Sohail. "Increasing Strategic Accountability: A Framework for International NGOs." *Development in Practice* vol.17, no. 2 (2007).

Center for Strategic and International Studies. "Saudi Arms Deal—Links with Nonproliferation?" (2010). Retrieved from http://csis.org/blog/saudi-arms-deal-links-nonproliferation.

Charnovitz, Steve. "Accountability of Nongovernmental Organizations (NGOs) in Global Governance." Working Paper, The George Washington University Law School: Public Law And Legal Theory no. 145, 2005. http://ssrn.com/abstract=716381.

Chowdhury, A. R. "A Causal Analysis of Defense Spending and Economic Growth." *Journal of Policy Modeling* vol. 35, no. 1 (1991): 80–97.

Clark, J. M. *The Costs of the World Wars to the American People.* New York: Augustus M. Kelley Publishers, 1931.

Clayton, J. L. *The Economic Impact of the Cold War.* New York: Harcourt, Brace and Company, Inc., 1970.

Cockburn, A. and P. Cockburn. *Saddam Hussein an American Obsession.* London: Verso, 2002.

Cockburn, A. and P. Cockburn. "We have Saddam Hussein Still Here." In *The Iraq War Reader: History, Documents, Opinions*, edited by M. L. Sifry and C. Cerf, 91–100. New York: Simon & Schuster, 2003.

Collier, P. "War and Military Expenditure in Developing Countries and Their Consequences for Development." *The Economics of Peace and Security Journal* vol. 1, no. 1 (2006): 10–13.

Collier, P., A. Hoeffler, and M. Söderbom. "On the Duration of Civil War." Working Paper, University of California, Irvine: Center for Global Peace and Conflict Studies, 2001.

Conetta, Carl. "The Wages of War: Iraqi Combatant and Noncombatant Fatalities in the 2003 Conflict." Research Monograph, no. 8, Cambridge, MA: Project on Defense Alternatives, 2003.

Cook, P. and J. Ludwig. *Gun Violence: The Real Costs*. New York: Oxford University Press, 2000.

Cordesman, A. *Saudi Arabia: Guarding the Desert Kingdom*. Colorado ; Oxford, United Kingdom: Westview Press, 1997.

Cordesman, A. "Defense Cooperation." (2008a). Retrieved from http://ncusar.org/programs/08-transcripts/1031-DEFENSE-COOPERATION.pdf.

Cordesman, A. "Military Cooperation in the Gulf: Action Rather than Words and Intentions." Center for Strategic and International Studies (2008b). Retrieved from www.csis.org/burke/reports.

Cottam, R. "The United States and Iran's Revolution: Goodbye to America's Shah." *Foreign Policy* vol. 34 (1979): 3–14.

Crain, M. W. and N. V. Crain. "Terrorized Economies," *Public Choice* vol. 128, no. 1–2 (2006): 317–349.

Cranna, M. ed. *The True Cost of Conflict*. New York: The New Press, 1994.

Crawford, N. C. "Civilian Death and Injury in Iraq, 2003–2011." Watson Institute for International Studies, Brown University, 2011.

Dabelko, D. and J. M. McCormick. "Opportunity Costs of Defense: Some Cross-National Evidence." *Journal of Peace Research* vol. 14, no. 2 (1977): 145–154.

Daggett, S. "Costs of Major U.S. Wars." Congressional Research Service, 2010.

Daggett, S. and N. M. Serafino. "Costs of Major U.S. Wars and Recent U.S. Overseas Military Operations." Congressional Research Service, 2001.

Dakurah, A. H., S. P. Davies, and R. K. Sampath. "Defense Spending and Economic Growth in Developing Countries, a Causality Analysis." *Journal of Policy Modeling* vol. 23 (2001): 651–658.

Dansc, A. "International Assistance Spending Due to War on Terror." Watson Institute for International Studies, Brown University, 2011.

Daponte, B. O. "A Case Study in Estimating Casualties from War and Its Aftermath: The 1991 Persian Gulf War." *Physicians for Social Responsibility Quarterly* vol. 3. no. 2 (1993): 57.

Deger, S. and S. Sen. "Military Expenditures, Spin-off and Economic Development." *Journal of Development Economics* vol. 13 (1983): 67–83.

DiAddario, S. "Estimating the Economic Costs of Conflict: An Examination of the Two-Gap Estimation Model for the Case of Nicaragua," *Oxford Development Studies* vol. 25, no. 1 (1997): 123–141.

Dickinson, F. G. "An After Cost of the World War to the United States." *American Economic Review* vol. 30 (1940): 326.

Dunne, J. P. "The Economic Effects of Military Expenditure in Developing Countries." Working Paper (2000). Retrieved from http://carecon.org.uk /Chula/MILLDCSnew.pdf.

Dunne, J. P. "The Military Spending and Economic Growth in Sub-Saharan Africa." Working Paper (2010). Retrieved from http://www.csae.ox.ac.uk /conferences/2010-EDiA/papers/110-Dunne.pdf.

Economist. "Privatizing Peace." *The Economist*, July 2, 2011, 50–51.

Edwards, M. "Does the Doormat Influence the Boot? Critical Thoughts on the UK NGOs and International Advocacy." *Development in Practice* vol 3, no 3, October (1993).

Edwards, R. D. "Post-9/11 War Spending, Debt, and the Macroeconomy." Watson Institute for International Studies, Brown University, 2011.

Edwards, M. and D. Hulme. "NGO Performance and Accountability: Introduction and Overview." In *Non-Governmental Organisations: Performance and Accountability*, edited by M. Edwards and D. Hulme, 3–16. London: Save the Children, 1995.

Edwards, M. and D. Hulme. "Too Close for Comfort? The Impact of Official Aid on Nongovernmental Organizations." *Current Issues in Comparative Education* vol. 1, no. 1 (1998): 6–28.

Energy Information Administration. "Persian Gulf Oil and Gas Fact Sheet." Retrieved from http://www.eia.doe.gov/cabs/pgulf2.html.

Espinoza, R. and A. Senhadji. "How Strong are Fiscal Multipliers in the GCC? An Empirical Investigation." Working Paper, International Monetary Fund, WP/11/16, 2011.

Fiorito, L. "John Maurice Clark's Contribution to the Genesis of the Multiplier Analysis." Working Paper no. 322, SSRN e-Library, 2001.

Fisk, R. *The Great War for Civilization: The Conquest of the Middle East, First Edition*. New York: Alfred A. Knopf, 2005.

Ganiyu, O. "Preventing Interstate Armed Conflict: Whose Responsibility?" Jönköping University, Sweden, 2010.

GD—Geneva Declaration on Armed Violence and Development. "Global Burden of Armed Violence." Geneva: Geneva Declaration Secretariat (2008). Retrieved from http://www.geneva declaration.org/resources-armed-violence -report.html.

Gettleman, M. and S. Schaar. *The Middle East and Islamic World Reader, First Edition*. New York: Grove Press, 2003.

Glaser, M. "Trends in Conflicts in the Last 10 Years. Humanitarian Assistance in Conflict Workshop." Soesterberg, The Netherlands, 2001.

Glaspie, A. "Saddam Meets the US Ambassador." In *The Iraq War Reader: History, Documents, Opinions*, edited by M. L. Sifry and C. Cerf, 61–71. New York: Simon & Schuster, 2003.

Goldin, C. and F. D. Lewis. "The Economic Cost of the American Civil War: Estimates and Implications." *The Journal of Economic History* vol. 35, no. 2 (1975): 299–326.

Graham-Brown, S. and C. Toensing. "A Background on Inspections and Sanctions." In *The Iraq War Reader: History, Documents, Opinions*, edited by M. L. Sifry and C. Cerf, 165–173. New York: Simon & Schuster, 2003.

Grebe, Jan. "The Global Militarization Index (GMI)." Occasional Paper, Bonn International Center for Conversion, 2011.

Harbom, L. and P. Wallensteen. "Armed Conflicts, 1946–2009." *Journal of Peace Research* vol. 47, no. 4 (2010): 501–509.

Hartung, W. "The Cost of the Iraq War." Taxpayers for Common Sense, Washington, DC, 2004.

Hegre, H. and N. Sambanis. "Sensitivity Analysis of Empirical Results on Civil War Onset." *The Journal of Conflict Resolution* vol. 50, no. 4 (2006): 508–535.

Heinemann, A. and D. Verner. "Crime and Violence in Development: A Literature Review of Latin America and the Caribbean." Working Paper, *World Bank Policy Research Working Paper 404* (2006). Retrieved from http://www-wds .worldbank.org/servlet/WDSContentServer/WDSP/IB/2006/10/18/0000164 06_20061018162733/Rendered/PDF/wps4041.pdf.

Herrmann, R. K. and R. W. Ayres. "The New Geo-politics of the Gulf: Forces for Change and Stability." *The Persian Gulf at the Millennium: Essays in Politics, Economy, Security, and Religion, First Edition*, edited by G. G. Sick and L. G. Potter, 356. New York: St. Martin's Press, 1997.

Hess, G. D. "The Economic Welfare Cost of Conflict: An Empirical Assessment." *CESifo Working Paper Series* no. 852 (2003).

Hewitt, J. J., J. Wilkenfeld, and T. R. Gurr. "Peace and Conflict 2010." University of Maryland, Center for International Development and Conflict Management, 2010.

Hiltermann, J. R. "The Men Who Helped the Man Who Gassed His Own People." In *The Iraq War Reader: History, Documents, Opinions*, edited by M. L. Sifry and C. Cerf, 41–44. New York: Simon & Schuster, 2003.

Hirnissa, M., M. S. Habibullah, and A. Baharom. "The Relationship between Defense, Education and Health Expenditures in Selected Asian Countries." *International Journal of Economics and Finance* vol. 1, no. 2 (2009): 149–155.

Hitchens, C. "Realpolitik in the Gulf: A Game Gone Tilt." In *The Iraq War Reader: History, Documents, Opinions*, edited by M. L. Sifry and C. Cerf, 47–57. New York: Simon & Schuster, 2003.

Ichino, A. and R. Winter-Ebmer. "The Long-run Educational Cost of World War II." *Journal of Labor Economics* vol. 22, no. 1 (2004): 57–86.

International Court of Justice, Annex III, IV, V. "Activities in and Against Nicaragua: Memorial on Compensation." Retrieved from http://www.icj-cij .org/docket/files/70/9621.pdf.

International Court of Justice. "Case Concerning Military and Paramilitary Iraq Survey Study Group Final Report (2004)." (1988). Retrieved from http://www .globalsecurity.org/wmd/library/report/2004/isg-final-report/.

International Monetary Fund. *World Economic Outlook*. Washington, DC, 2010.

International Reconstruction Fund Facility for Iraq. "UN/World Bank Joint Iraq Needs Assessment." (2003). Retrieved from http://siteresources.worldbank. org/IRFFI/Resources/Joint+Needs+Assessment.pdf.

Isseroff, A. "The Algiers Accord between Iraq and Iran" (2002). Retrieved from http://www.mideastweb.org/algiersaccord.htm.

Jasanoff, Sheila, "NGOs and the Environment: From Knowledge to Action." *Third World Quarterly* vol. 18, no. 3 (1997): 579–594.

Khalaf, R. and J. Drummond. "Gulf States in $123bn US Arms Spree." *Financial Times*, September 20 2010. http://www.ft.com/cms/s/0/ffd73210-c4ef-11df -9134-00144feab49a.html#axzz1TzGdV6rG.

Kinzer, S. *All the Shah's Men: An American Coup and the Roots of Middle East Terror*. Hoboken, NJ: John Wiley & Sons, Inc., 2003.

Knight, M., N. Loayaza, and D. Villanueava. "Military Spending Cuts and Economic Growth." Staff Papers, *International Monetary Fund* vol. 43, no. 1 (1996): 1–37.

Krug, E. G., L. L. Dahlberg, J. A. Mercy, A. B. Zwi, and R. Lozano. "World Report on Violence and Health." Geneva: World Health Organization (2002). Retrieved from http://whqlibdoc.who.int/publications/2002/9241545615_eng.pdf.

Kusi, N. K. "Growth and Defense Spending in Developing Countries: A Causal Analysis." *Journal of Conflict Resolution* vol. 38, no. 1 (1994): 152–159.

Kuziemko, I. and E. Werker. "How Much Is a Seat on the Security Council Worth? Foreign Aid and Bribery at the United Nations." *Journal of Political Economy* vol. 114, no. 5 (2006): 6–29.

Lacina, B., N. P. Gleditsch, and B. Russett. "The Declining Risk of Death in Battle." *International Studies Quarterly* vol. 50 (2006): 673–680.

Laipson, E. *America and the Emerging Iraqi Reality: New Goals, No Illusions*. Washington, DC: The Century Foundation, 2008.

Lehman, Glen, "The Accountability of NGOs in Civil Society and Its Public Spheres." *Critical Perspectives on Accounting* vol. 18, no. 6 (2007).

Lemann, N. "The War on What? The White House and the Debate about Whom to Fight Next." In *The Iraq War Reader: History, Documents, Opinions*, edited by M. L. Sifry and C. Cerf, 283–294. New York: Simon & Schuster, 2003.

Lindsey, L. "The Deficit Is Worse than We Think." *The Wall Street Journal*, June 27, 2011.

Lutz, C. "US Coalition Casualties in Iraq and Afghanistan." Watson Institute for International Studies, Brown University, 2011.

Mearsheimer, J. J. and S. Walt. "An Unnecessary War." In *The Iraq War Reader: History, Documents, Opinions*, edited by M. L. Sifry and C. Cerf, 414–424. New York: Simon & Schuster, 2003.

Mearsheimer, J. J. and S. Walt. "The Israel Lobby and U.S. Foreign Policy." KSG Faculty Research Working Paper Series, Harvard University, 2007a.

Mearsheimer, J. J. and S. Walt. *The Israeli Lobby and US Foreign Policy, First Edition*. New York: Farrar, Straus and Giroux, 2007b.

Miller, J. and L. Mylroie. "The Rise of Saddam Hussein." In *The Iraq War Reader: History, Documents, Opinions*, edited by M. L. Sifry and C. Cerf, 18–29. New York: Simon & Schuster, 2003.

Mofid, K. "Economic Reconstruction of Iraq: Financing the Peace." *Third World Quarterly* vol. 12, no. 1 (1990): 48–61.

Molavi, A. *The Soul of Iran: A Nation's Journey to Freedom*. New York: W. W. Norton, Co Inc., 2005.

Mundy, K. and L. Murphy. "Transnational Advocacy, Global Civil Society? Emerging Evidence from the Field of Education." *Comparative Education Review* vol. 45, no. 1 (2001): 85–126.

Murdoch, J. and T. Sandler. "Economic Growth, Civil Wars, and Spatial Spillovers." *Journal of Conflict Resolution* vol. 46, no. 1 (2002): 91–110.

Mussa, M. "The Impact of Higher Oil Prices on the Global Economy." Research Department, International Monetary Fund, 2000.

Ohanian, L. E. "The Macroeconomic Effects of War Finance in the United States: World War II and the Korean War." *The American Economic Review* vol. 87, no. 1 (1997): 23–40.

Phillipson, Nicholas, *Adam Smith: An Elightened Life*. New Haven: Yale University Press, 2010.

Pieroni, L., G. D'Agostino, and M. Lorusso. "Can We Declare Military Keynesianism Dead?" *Journal of Policy Modeling* vol. 30 (2008): 675–691.

Poast, Paul, *The Economics of War*. New York: McGraw-Hill Irwin, 2006.

Pollack, J. "Saudi Arabia and the United States, 1931–2002." *Middle East Review of International Affairs* vol. 6, no. 3 (2002): 77–102.

Pollack, K. "How Saddam Misread the United States." In *The Iraq War Reader: History, Documents, Opinions*, edited by M. L. Sifry and C. Cerf, 76–85. New York: Simon & Schuster, 2003.

Pyakuryal, B. and K. Uprety. "Economic & Legal Impact of Conflict on States & People in South Asia with Specific Reference to Nepal." *Journal of Social, Political & Economic Studies* vol. 30, no. 4 (2005): 459–495.

Reinhart, Carmen, and Rogoff Kenneth. *This Time Is Different: Eight Centuries of Financial Folly*. New Jersey: Princeton University Press, 2011.

Rotman, David. "Nicholas Stern." *Technology Review*, July/August (2011).

Scheetz, T. "The Evolution of Public Sector Expenditures: Changing Political Priorities in Argentina, Chile, Paraguay and Peru." *Journal of Peace Research* vol. 29, no. 2 (1992): 175–190.

Schofield, R. N. "Border Disputes in the Gulf: Past, Present, and Future." In *The Persian Gulf at the Millennium, First Edition*, edited by G. G. Sick and L. G. Potter, 127–166. New York: St. Martin's Press, 1997.

Seligman, E. R. A. "The Cost of the War and How It Was Met." *American Economic Review* vol. 9, no. 4 (1919): 739.

Shah, Anup. "Global Issues—The Arms Trade Is Big Business." *Global Issues* (2010). Retrieved from http://www.globalissues.org/article/74/the-arms-trade-is-big-business.

Sharma, K. "Economic Policy and Civil War in Nepal." Working Paper, *WIDER conference* (2004). Retrieved from http://website1.wider.unu.edu/conference/conference-2004-1/conference%202004-1-papers/Sharma-1905.pdf.

Sick, G. G. "The Ghost at the Table." *The World Today* vol. 55, no. 2 (1999): 15–17.

Special report: Persian Gulf War. No. Catn89–0000013576. Washington, DC: CQ Press, 2003.

Steiner-Khamsi, G. "Too Far from Home? 'Modulitis' and NGOs' Role in Transferring Pre-Packaged Reform." *Current Issues in Comparative Education* vol. 1, no. 1 (1998): 35–41.

Stern, N. "Stern Review on the Economics of Climate Change." London: Executive Summary, HM Treasury, 2006.

Stevens, R. W. *Vain Hopes, Grim Realities: The Economic Consequences of the Vietnam War.* New York: New Viewpoints, 1976.

Stiglitz, J. E. and L. J. Bilmes. *The Three Trillion Dollar War: The True Cost of the Iraq Conflict, First Edition.* New York: W.W. Norton & Company, Inc., 2008.

Stockholm International Peace Research Institute. "SIPRI Yearbook 2010." 2010.

Stork, J. "The Iran-Iraq war." In *The Oxford Companion to Politics of the World, Second Edition*, edited by J. Krieger, 432–433. New York: Oxford University Press, 2001.

Stromquist, N. "NGOs in a New Paradigm of Civil Society." *Current Issues in Comparative Education* vol. 1, no. 1 (1998): 62–67.

Subramanian, M. "Are NGOs Overrated? Ten Year Anniversary Double Issue." *Current Issues in Comparative Education* vol. 10, no 1 and 2 (Double issue) (Fall 2007/Spring 2008).

Telegraph. "Afghanistan and Iraq Have Cost Taxpayers £20bn." *The Telegraph*, June 20, 2010. http://www.telegraph.co.uk/news/worldnews/asia/afghani stan/7841631/Afghanistan-and-Iraq-have-cost-taxpayers-20bn.html.

Telegraph. "Washington Considers Selling Bunker-Busting Bombs to the UAE," November 14, 2011. http://www.telegraph.co.uk/news/worldnews/middleeast /unitedarabemirates/8883615/PIC-AND-PUB-Washington-considers-selling -bunker-busting-bombs-to-UAE.html.

Telhami, S. "The Persian Gulf: Understanding the American Oil Strategy." (2002a). Retrieved from http://www.brookings.edu/articles/2002/spring _globalenvironment_telhami.aspxT.

Telhami, S. "The Stakes: America and the Middle East: The Consequences of Power and the Choice for Peace." Boulder, CO: Westview Press, 2002b.

Telhami, S. and F. Hill. "Does Saudi Arabia Still Matter? Differing Perspectives on the Kingdom and Its Oil." *Foreign Affairs* vol. 81, no. 6 (2002): 167–178.

UNDP—United Nations Development Programme. "Crisis Prevention and Recovery Report 2008. Post-Conflict Economic Recovery: Enabling Local Ingenuity," New York: UNDP Bureau for Crisis Prevention and Recovery, 2008.

United Nations Environment Programme. "Updated Scientific Report on the Environmental Effects of the Conflict between Iraq and Kuwait." (1993). Retrieved from http://www.unep.org/dewa/westasia/data/Knowledge_Bases /Iraq/Reports/UNEPGCIraq1993.pdf.

Uppsala University. "UCDP Database." (2011). Retrieved from www.ucdp.uu.se /database.

Van Raemdonck, D. C. and P. F. Diehl. "After the Shooting Stops: Insights on Postwar Economic Growth." *Journal of Peace Research* vol. 26, no. 3 (1989): 249–264.

Waas, M. "What Washington Gave Saddam for Christmas." In *The Iraq War Reader: History, Documents, Opinions*, edited by M. L. Sifry and C. Cerf, 30–40. New York: Simon & Schuster, 2003.

Wallsten, S. and K. Kosec. "The Economic Costs of War in Iraq." Working Paper (2005). Retrieved from http://www.bepress.com/ev/vol3/iss2/art1.

Walsh, Eoghan and Helena Lenihan. "Accountability and Effectiveness of NGOs: Adapting Business Tools Successfully." *Development in Practice* vol. 16, no. 5 (2006).

Wapner, Paul. "Introductory Essay: Paradise Lost? NGOs and Global Accountability." *Chicago Journal of International Law* vol. 3, no. 1 Spring (2002).

Waslekar, S. and I. Futehally. "Cost of Conflict in the Middle East." Mumbai, India: Strategic Foresight Group, 2009.

Waters, H., A. Hyder, Y. Rajkotia, S. Basu, J. A. Rehwinkel, and A. Butchart. "World Health Organization, the Economic Dimensions of Interpersonal Violence." Geneva: World Health Organization (2004). Retrieved from http://whqlibdoc.who.int/publications/2004/ 9241591609.pdf.

Wheeler, W. T. "Uncountable: Pentagon Spending on the Post-9/11 Wars." Watson Institute for International Studies, Brown University, 2011.

Wilkins, N. "Defence Expenditure and Economic Growth: Evidence from a Panel of 85 Countries." Working Paper (2004). Retrieved from http://cama.anu.edu.au/macroworkshop/Nigel%20Wilkins.pdf.

Wils, F. "Scaling-up, Mainstreaming, and Accountability: The Challenge for NGOs." In *Non-governmental Organisations: Performance and Accountability*, edited by M. Edwards and D. Hulme, 53–62. London: Save the Children, 1995.

World dataBank "World Development Indicators (WDI)." (2011). Retrieved from http://databank.worldbank.org/ddp/home.do.

Yildirim, J. and S. Sezgin. "Defence, Education and Health Expenditures in Turkey, 1924–96." *Journal of Peace Research* vol. 39, no. 5 (2002): 569–580.

Zahrani, M. T. "The Coup That Changed the Middle East Mossadeq v. the CIA in Retrospect." *World Policy Journal* vol. 19, no. 2 (2002): 93–99.

Zapotoczny, W. S. "The Impact of the Industrial Revolution on Warfare." (2006). Retrieved from http://www.wzaponline.com/InductrialRevolution.pdf.

Index

Printed by Printforce, the Netherlands